COCO

THROUGH THE

LOOKING GLASS

Marie-Claire Patron

BALBOA.
PRESS

A DIVISION OF HAY HOUSE

Balboa Press books may be ordered through booksellers or by contacting:

Balboa Press
A Division of Hay House
1663 Liberty Drive
Bloomington, IN 47403
www.balboapress.com.au
1 (877) 407-4847

Because of the dynamic nature of the Internet, any web addresses or links contained in this book may have changed since publication and may no longer be valid. The views expressed in this work are solely those of the author and do not necessarily reflect the views of the publisher, and the publisher hereby disclaims any responsibility for them.

The author of this book does not dispense medical advice or prescribe the use of any technique as a form of treatment for physical, emotional, or medical problems without the advice of a physician, either directly or indirectly. The intent of the author is only to offer information of a general nature to help you in your quest for emotional and spiritual well-being. In the event you use any of the information in this book for yourself, which is your constitutional right, the author and the publisher assume no responsibility for your actions.

Any people depicted in stock imagery provided by Getty Images are models, and such images are being used for illustrative purposes only. Certain stock imagery © Getty Images.

Print information available on the last page.

ISBN: 978-1-5043-1284-4 (sc)
ISBN: 978-1-5043-1285-1 (e)

Balboa Press rev. date: 04/13/2018

AUTHOR'S NOTE

This narrative is built from the personal experiences of Coco, a 50+ naturalised Australian of French background who grew up in Melbourne, Australia, after her arrival in the sixties. For the sake of expediency and confidentiality, pseudonyms have been created in this chronicle and specific details have been adapted to protect the identity of all characters. This facilitates the thematic analysis of relevant issues. This is the messy nature of ethnographic writing.

CONTENTS

SWAMPS, QUAGMIRES & OTHER CHALLENGES

ENDINGS

ACKNOWLEDGEMENTS

It is no easy task to find adequate words of praise and gratitude for the dearest people in my life who have assisted and supported me on this journey, especially my BFFs, Female and Male. My Confidants have encouraged and counselled me and their feedback has kept me on the straight and narrow throughout this project. Their guidance, enthusiasm and perceptive comments were heartfelt and deeply appreciated. They provided invaluable insights into the precarious world of internet dating for Boomers – in their fifties and above, whilst the contributions and sound advice of my beautiful daughters and friends of both sexes from the 30+ demographic provided balance and contrast. I also owe a huge debt of gratitude to my 83-year-old Mother for her reiterative readings of the manuscript. Her sharp eyes can spot a typographical error at a distance and her counsel keeps me grounded. I now hope to have all bases covered.

PREAMBLE

Have you ever wanted to discover the intricacies of internet dating? Live vicariously through the trials and tribulations, the laughter and the tears of your BFFs[1] who have courageously thrown themselves head first into this murky unconventional mode of dating? Understand the machinations of the minds of depraved individuals whose predilection is to prey on unsuspecting souls too naïve and gullible to defend themselves? Or perhaps, rejoice in a fascinating journey of self-discovery, self-acceptance and fulfilment of the lucky ones who find themselves and their Soulmates? This is not a fairy tale with a guaranteed happy ending. There are indeed happy tales where love conquers all online, albeit impossible to verify or quantify. The trick is to achieve acceptance of the challenges that life deals out.

Well, if you are sufficiently intrigued, you can hop on board this roller-coaster ride with Coco and you will learn a thing or two about the psyche of individuals involved in online dating, especially the males, because Coco is on a mission to find her Prince. You will witness the dynamic process of identity transformation that she takes you on. A word of caution, though; you will need to wear sunglasses or other protection. If you are going to make hay whilst the sun shines, protect yourself!

Happy or unhappy Divorcée?

"Help, my heart is broken!"

---

[1] There are those who remain implacably opposed to the notion that we can have more than *One Best Friend* – and of course, nothing is *Forever*. This narrative aims to set the record straight. Some of us are blessed to count several male and female friends as our best friends. Though some may live across the globe, the visceral bonds we share are undeniable.

"At long last" comes the chorus reply.

"Seriously? Call that support? After all this time, you Ladies were just waiting for me to admit to this. The truth is, I am over the self-flagellation and the recriminations; the conjecture, the loneliness, the "what ifs?" Who needs that? Embrace change? I feel cornered. No way out…"

"Coco, you know our *Happy Divorcées' Club* is ready to welcome you with open arms…"

"The invitation to your exclusive club sounds enticing. Thanks, but I think I will sit this one out. Not for this Princess! I am an unhappy divorcée. I want to find my Prince Charming and live happily ever after. Stop laughing… I am allowed to believe in forever, am I not?

Are you ready? You will need to sit down. I am about to rock your boat. If I cannot beat them, I might as well join them."

"What the…? Who are you joining?" came the response.

The Sisterhood

Buckle up in your comfy armchairs Ladies! You can keep your flannelette PJs on. Fill your glasses with some Bubbly and join me on my roller-coaster of dating for 50s. Brace yourself for the hills and thrills, plunging into valleys; feel the despair, over the top, nausea and negative Gs; and a whole load of laughs as you watch me navigate my way safely to the end. Promise you progress reports. If you do not want to join me, I will save you the trouble; take a leaf out of my book. Just do not judge me, Okay?

Ladies, we are not old, we are gold. I know what you are thinking. This is the domain of the Millennials, the young, and we are no Spring Chickens, but I, unlike you, need to engage in this brave new world. The youngsters will be my mentors, my guides – and from time to time, even my suitors. Just watch and laugh with me, not at me. I have always been a bit of a Cougar. Might as well own it. I would rather be hit on by guys closer to my age, or, as you have already witnessed, younger. That is just me, Coco!

You all know the French maxim I live by, *Mieux vaut seul(e) que mal accompagné(e)*, "Better to be alone than in bad company." Or, "Better to be alone than fake it." I know that you, my more worldly BFFs might relate better to this version. Or perhaps, we could refer to my male friend's motto, "If you can't be with the one you love, love the one you're with." Take your pick!

"Coco, you know you're stepping into a *mind* field, right?"

"Ready, aim, fire…"

Katarina shook her head, "Careful Honey! Are you really ready for this?"

The Happy Divorcées' Club

I realised I had to either get with the program, stop being so damned discerning, or resign myself to a life of loneliness, unless of course, I subscribed to *The Happy Divorcées' Club*. I took nearly four years to ponder over this. Sorry, not for me. I had become a confirmed workaholic. But not for long.

The adherents of this club, including many of my BFFs, shun the dating scene because they refuse to hop on the band wagon of Turbo Dating with its ensuing dramas. This Club is exclusive because the male counterparts have their own *Male Yacht Club*. Women have their own Gyms, so why not their own club? Make no mistake. This Ladies only club is not the *Hollywood First Wives' Club* searching for justice and vengeance, but this club is elitist. These gorgeous women are not bent on revenge, male-bashing or gratuitous vilification of the opposite sex. There is no need. They are above that. They may well include the guilty feminists who cannot quite position themselves along the continuum but wherever they stand, this select cohort of women refuses to succumb to the pressures and vulnerabilities that becoming ensnared in another allegedly doomed relationship represents.

Multimedia sources, the world of Hollywood and anecdotal evidence give credence to such claims, suggesting that the contented souls of this club, fulfilled, serene, self-assured and independent, wear their badge of *Singles* with pride; they no longer care what anyone else thinks; they do not mind the lack-lustre title of Ms that I detest; they refuse to embark on yet another journey to discover love, that they are convinced will ultimately end in a litany of broken hearts, stressful arguments, diminished bank accounts, depression and a shattered self-esteem.

The challenges

The horrors of internet dating are not a figment of anyone's imagination but friends who are teetering on the brink of loneliness, and some courageous souls like me, are ready to take the plunge, to embark on a love boat so doomed, it could be called the *Titanic*. Nothing ventured, nothing gained...

How do we compete with youth, navigate our way through the turbulent waters of online dating when we are not of the Millennial mindset? This playground is governed by a new era of Millennial mechanisms and expectations where sexual gratification rules. It has never been so easy for daters to get what they want, particularly as the demographics have merged, become fluid; barriers no longer exist in this world. If we do not abide by the rules set by the youngsters, how will we fare in the challenging context of this brave new world?

The promise of uninhibited pleasures, part and parcel of the Smorgasbord of profiles that awaits adherents, fills the air as I begin to surf the waves of internet dating. The allure of this new medium draws me in as I start to search through the "Zoo," a favourite term adopted by many guys.

I, at least, am willing to test the theory that internet dating, though daunting and potentially demoralising at times, is still a preferable platform to meet guys, because, currently, it seems that greater dangers await us, the women especially, who endorse the old-fashioned ways of conventional dating.

Those of us willing to brave the bars and clubs need to be prepared for the embarrassing and very awkward moments perched on a bar stool, cocktail in hand and engrossed in a mobile phone to remain inconspicuous, as smoking pensively and nonchalantly is a thing of the past. I have never smoked, so that makes it harder for me. Awkward! Thank God for mobile phones! It is not easy to induce a BFF to be my Wing Lady just to go out for a drink. We are acutely aware that waiting for a date, hoping, just praying that a drop dead gorgeous male will approach us and begin a conversation, is the stuff of fiction. Yet, this does not deter me. Soldier on! It could, just could happen.

Alternatively, we may have to fend off those who cramp our style, continue to hit on us and will not take "NO" for an answer.

Age, but also era, and ageism are significant issues for my cohort of 50+ daters, but is it the same for both sexes? I would soon find out. I confess, I refuse to reveal my veritable age. I stand by my convictions that fibbing about one's age cannot be compared to lying about identity issues that are at the core of one's being. I have my reasons. Like many of my male suitors, my objectives are to avoid complete and immediate identification online by identity fraudsters. There is already too much information out there and too much at stake. Just as importantly, some of us, Guys and Gals prefer to date people closer to our age, or younger. This logical outcome brings me some peace at least. Self-justification is common, yes, but I need to stick to my guns here.

The problem is, if the stigma of internet dating for our age group is perceived as insurmountable, are we cutting our nose off to spite our face? It is not easy for us Ladies to compete in the dating game in bars and night clubs. How do we reveal home truths in a bar? How many of us go to night clubs? Society has changed dramatically.

On the other hand, I realise it is not always easy for nice guys in bars and clubs either, who finish last because they feel intimidated by the solidarity of women out on the prowl. Guys are finding it increasingly hard to decipher what can be construed as harmless flirting and what constitutes sexual harassment. They can attempt to break into the pack, and if they get lucky, they now have to think twice about how to proceed. What are the potential ramifications? We are about to witness a whole new era of dating challenges as a result of the Harvey Weinstein scandal and others that have exploded globally.

Increasingly, individuals of all ages are becoming aware of the dangers of playing games, as the blurred lines of sexual encounters increase in clarity. The scandals have brought in their wake a raft of sexual harassment and assault charges, rape allegations and other disgraces that are provoking waves of fear and distrust. We are entering an era where the rules of sexual engagement need to be established clearly, in all contexts before we move from square one. Work Christmas parties are now in the limelight and are becoming fertile ground for allegations of this kind, not to mention encounters in bars and clubs. Perilous pursuit these days if one does not come from an abstemious culture. Sobriety is the answer to this issue, but it is hard for many individuals to restrain themselves during festive occasions. Old habits die hard.

Given these challenging scenarios, the talents of many subscribers to the *Happy Divorcées' Club* are in big demand. They prefer to don their new hat (metaphorically speaking), as Rescuer, and in this role, the Confidantes Extraordinaire are ready to empathise, watch, listen, laugh and cry with a friend who has stoically dived into the foggy waters of Internet Dating. They witness the trials and tribulations of their BFFs; girlfriends like me, whose susceptibility is heightened, whose roller-coaster ride increasingly culminates in soul destroying adventures. Each and every one of my episodes reinforces the firm resolve of the Divorcées, that the temptation to search for love, romance and passion will never again plague them, most especially online…

They reiterate, "Who needs it?" They are not prepared to relinquish their hard-fought autonomy, the luxury of answering to no one and their healthy bank balances, if, and when their offspring finally fly the nest. Increasing numbers of 20-35-year old offspring are returning home to save money for their mortgages or their travels, especially if the parents are single. Those on social media who castigate these women for being selfish need to realise that it is this group of Ladies who can best serve those around them because they refuse to bow down to the pressures of a relationship.

The Divorcées can eat, pray, love, laugh and sing without sacrificing endless sleepless nights stressing and crying over problematic relationships; guilt feelings after breaking up with a 'nice guy'; surrendering to self-doubt because 'he' has not called or texted; putting up with a snoring or wheezing partner and morning breath (except in Hollywood, of course); or a partner whose sonorous flatulence is enough to drive away even the most tolerant. At the risk of sounding pretentious, why is it that many women of a certain age will go to excruciating contortions à la *The Great Houdini*, to avoid blowing a gasket in bed when they suffer from intestinal pain and gassiness, as opposed to guys?

The embarrassment it can cause when they share a bed, especially with a new partner, is unthinkable! Well, at least for some of us anyway! I really admire some Millennials today though, who simply giggle their way through these natural human eruptions, diffusing the situation by turning it into a cacophonous competition. Not the Y Generation I am told, in no uncertain terms. Interesting! Truly remarkable! Some of us Ladies, I dare say, and not just the aristocratic set who live by the rules of etiquette that articulates, "Horses sweat, men perspire and Ladies glow", would be mortified if they were to inadvertently let off any kind of gas in front of a man. Let alone use the loo within earshot of a new guy.

As I write this, I cannot believe that *Airwick*, air freshener manufacturers, have just aired a bizarre advertisement on Australian television, aimed at shocking people into submission. With terms such as "punish the porcelain" and "poopulate" anywhere with confidence, *Airwick's* handbag-sized bottle of "*V.I.Poo* forms a protective layer trapping the icky smell of devil's doughnuts."[2] Seriously? News.com's article reveals this cringe-worthy advertisement originated in the US and has provoked a backlash amongst viewers in the UK and Australia, not only for its ridiculous use of idiomatic terms but because "we, who have watched this, can never unsee it." The commercial caused outrage but is this fake news when you consider that "Men aren't so fussed but women have poo paranoia and will blame any escaping odours on their partner or dog before confessing to the unforgivable crime of having a functional bowel."[3]

Well, up to individuals to make their own mind about this, or better still, check the ad on the internet and have a giggle. The advertisement has increased its television profile, so, the ad is bound to get increased airtime.

If this little piece of trivia does not convince the sceptics that living alone avoids such embarrassing moments, think about the number of couples these days that increasingly choose to sleep in separate bedrooms. A lot to be said about this new trend, the *règle du jour* (rule of the day), currently being established in the 50+ homes, on the grounds that couples need their beauty sleep. I know of many couples who credit their long unions to this. Fantastic, if it works. Besides, if British Royalty admits to separate bedrooms, what is stopping the rest of us?

The privileged tranche of women in the 50+ and 60+ age groups, in

---

[2] The launch of V.I.Poo pre-poo toilet spray is baffling people. (News Limited Copyright © 2017.) **www.news.com.au**/finance/business/retail/the-launch-of-vi**poo**-pre**poo**...)

[3] Ibid.

lieu of complex relationships with a partner, find themselves in a state of perceived relative bliss; and it is this group of contented women of the *Happy Divorcées' Club* who are increasingly required to step in, embodying their remodelled identity of Rescuer or Confidante. Their identity undergoes a transformational process as these confidantes, consciously or subconsciously, assume a new identity as unwitting counsellor. In this new role, they find themselves rather ill-equipped to proffer advice as they lack the requisite credentials. Irrespective of this, they instinctively know that the anguished BFF simply needs to vent. Let off steam through both ears.

Consequently, the confidantes abide by the unwritten code of the BFF; they lend a sympathetic ear, console their friend with a box of tissues and chocolates, a bottle of wine and a tub of ice cream with two spoons, interjecting when necessary with a cautionary tale and propitious soothing words of advice for future forays onto new dating sites. Katarina, especially, has assumed this role one too many times. Must say I enjoyed the decadent ice cream with two spoons. Had never done that before.

The uplifting effects of their total devotion as they reinforce the visceral bonds of friendship of the Sisterhood have been portrayed in film for decades. The American romantic comedy series *Sex and the City* that made its debut in 1998 is the epitome of this Sisterhood and the episodes are still a popular rerun for single women globally, or at least for those who can cope with the crass language; and who can ignore the falling out of the female stars in real life, (if you believe media outlets about the cancelling of their latest movie?)

The glamour involved with going out on the town, in stockings and stilettos and fancy clothes, on dates or to meet friends, has lost its appeal to many women, and surprisingly, not exclusively for women of this age group. Popular culture suggests just as many young women now apparently search for excuses to avoid going out.

Many women over 50 now have disposable income to travel, indulge in writing clubs and other educational and social pursuits; they are empowered and can enrol in further education, join the University of the Third Age, Probus Clubs and other intellectual societies, enrol in self-improvement courses in the arts and crafts, self-defence and yoga classes and increasingly, take up the challenge of ballroom dancing. It is addictive, trust me! If, and when menopause is relegated to the back burner, (I have girlfriends who cannot seem to escape this change of life cycle) they can nurture their true friendships and regale in the joys of their clan of the Sisterhood, at home. They can happily watch their Netflix or reruns of their favourite soaps at 4:00 AM in their cute Peter Alexander flannelette pyjamas or their fetching department store *jim jams* and enjoy their guilt-free Australian *Bubbles*, hot chocolate or ice cream.

This group of Divorcées no longer panders to the whims of the significant 'Other' and they have no need to fear the debilitating effects of menopause from a partner who shows no empathy, is unresponsive and exigent. Men witness extraordinary physical and emotional changes in their wives and partners during menopause as they battle the escalating symptoms, including quasi psychotic mood swings caused by their hormones.

Well, there we have it!

I have done my due diligence on this scary online dating game and I have weighed up my options.

I am satisfied, ready to dive in, but perhaps, I need to learn how to hold my breath under water. Should have taken formal swimming lessons as a child!

LOVE AT FIRST SITE
/ BABY STEPS

A lure or allure?

Before I started internet dating, I had a deep, well-developed and abiding bias against the idea of online dating. Internet dating is for those who are unable or unwilling to date the old-fashioned way. Why would anyone choose to expose their evident inadequacies of failing to find a date to the public? It smacks of desperation by the hopeless. Not for me, no way. And, I remained unrelentingly opposed to the idea for nearly four years.

But what of me? I am not desperate, I am filled with hope. But here I was searching for my Soulmate in a vast sea. I am not drowning, I am waving. Of course, I was not drowning. I was splashing around in the shallows. The reality is that the males had migrated to the deep pools, the world of online. If I am waving (in the shallows) and none of the males out at sea sees me wave, how am I going to find anyone?

For all that might be wrong about online dating, it had a lengthy heritage. Before the internet, people placed ads in personal columns. Yes, I considered that a little sad although I had to admit that it seemed to work for some – like those who like *Piña Colada*, getting caught in the rain… a generation thing.

My daughters persuaded me to some degree. Alessandra had used various apps, she had swiped left and right. I did not understand - and I was not sure I really wanted to understand.

But a few more months of going out with friends, a couple of blind dates, some well-intended but disastrous introductions, a deep disappointment descended. He was out there somewhere. So how was I to find him – and he to find me?

"Try it Mum" my daughters encouraged me. "Give it a go" said one BFF. "What do you have to lose?" suggested some of my male friends.

I was not sure whether to believe them. But perhaps the perceived stigma was simply a product of my own mind. I had the distinct impression that a couple of my friends wanted to live vicariously through my experiences of online dating. They were certainly not willing to enter the fray.

I tested the idea cautiously with Angelina and Alessandra, my daughters. They could not hide their pleasure and proceeded to inveigle me into online. I asked their advice and they obliged. A turnaround for me – to be taken under the wings of my daughters. The reversal of roles was extraordinary, and their genuine concern for me increased in intensity as the journey progressed.

At first, I felt awkward about asking them about how to date online. Later, I realised that they were schooling me in the art of dating. Married at a young age, I had never really dated - or at least not as my daughters had dated. After my divorce, things were no different. I still did not date in the real sense of the word.

I felt foolish, awkward, naughty and even a little impulsive. I felt like I was an internet virgin. I blush at the thought that I was. The pragmatics of internet dating are quite a challenge. I thought this would be easy, until I started crafting my profile. What to say in a perfect profile, using class, wit and humour, and just enough mystery; how to make contact, how to respond, follow up... more importantly, what exactly I wished to manifest through this exercise.

I spent a couple of hours shaping my profile, in consultation with my girls and their partners of course, and I posted it after due consideration. I am a perfectionist.

And I sat looking at the screen waiting for a response. As if it should be instant. So, I walked away to do something else.

Jason – a big fish on the first bite

The first response in my IN Box was from Jason... Unbelievable. Only two hours after having posted my profile! Wow! This was going to be one hell of a ride. I could not contain my excitement. I was bubbling with energy, having dismissed my usual walk for the day. Exercise could wait. The thought of cooking dinner was the furthest thing from my mind. Who needed to eat anyway? There was no stemming this tidal wave of expectancy, and trepidation. Could I, should I reveal all in the online messages? Was it safe? What were the repercussions of disclosing too much information? Could I trust this guy?

Jason was the epitome of the suave, sophisticated, educated, well-to-do man of the world, the perfect package. I felt flushed with pleasure. I felt like a little girl. Someone wanted to talk with me, someone was attracted to me. I was a teenager again with a massive crush on the most popular boy in the playground. The biggest difference was that this time, he was actually into me too. Wow! My head was buzzing with questions for the sexiest, most attractive guy from Brisbane who had approached me so soon after having joined. My self-esteem was on an upward curve, instantaneously transformed. This augured well for my journey into cyber space and I was excited. And delighted to have found someone quickly so I might avoid this mode of dating which was still uncomfortable for me.

The frisson of pleasure I felt as I engaged in this new world of online dating, the anticipation, the enthusiasm, were palpable – checking emails, match-boxes, the joy of communicating with someone, that someone showed an interest.

The thrill stayed with me. I would spend hours chatting with interesting men.

Jason sent me his first message, "Hi Coco. Wow! You are an accomplished, gorgeous Lady. My lucky night. How long have you been single? Have you had any luck on this site?" He told me that he found my profile intriguing and wondered what I was doing online. He asked if I wanted to chat... That was weird because I was thinking the same thing. Why the devil would he need to go online to find anyone?

I told Jason about my job, my girls, my hopes, my dreams. His messages were witty, clever, light. My responses were instant, uninhibited. We jested verbally, to and fro, laughs and joy.

I then chatted with Jason from 7:00 PM until 2:00 AM. In between snippets of television shows that held little interest compared to the excitement of my exchanges with Jason, we delved deeper into personal issues. We discussed the challenges of dating at our age, reasons for our relationship breakups, personal preferences… How refreshing that there was no disparagement for ex-partners, no bitter recriminations, no regrets. Just two people ready to move forward, searching for love. We were compatible. My God, was that possible so quickly? I wondered about the uncanny nature of this new way of dating, how we ended up revealing so much information to a complete stranger…

So, this is online dating! I had deprived myself of this pleasure.

But I checked myself. I did recognise my enormous beginner's luck. The first bite had been a big fish. I had hooked a charming, attractive, educated man. Of course, I did not tell him, but I had all but chosen the colour scheme for the wedding. I was smitten.

Aryan in appearance, and of course, tall, blue-eyed, blond hair just curling over his ears, Jason's one cheeky photograph showed him to look much younger than his 51 years. The photo was taken in the lounge of an exotic five-star hotel in Paris, Rome, or Dubai. He was well-travelled and was depicted sitting nonchalantly with a glass of white wine in hand (our favourite variety).

We chatted into the night until we both needed to get some sleep. It was by then 1:00 AM. We both had to work the next day and I began to worry that these nocturnal activities may deplete my energies. His final words, "Sweet dreams Gorgeous! Look forward to a chat tomorrow. Let's meet soon."

At 2:00 AM we reluctantly ended our chat. I wake at 4:00 AM sometimes, so it was time for me to go to bed. Nonetheless, I felt like Cinderella, being rushed away from the Ball. But I left my glass slipper with Prince Jason – or rather, had him promise to send me a message first thing that morning.

I awoke at 6:00 AM. The first thing I did was open my laptop and visited the site to see the message from Jason. Nothing was there.

Perhaps he had slept in. Or perhaps he had not had time before racing off to work. I had to do the same and vowed to check in again in an hour. I did so, and still nothing.

What was the etiquette here? He had said he would contact me this morning. Would I appear pushy if I contacted him? Needy? Would it be rude? My daughters were not around to help me. I wrote him a brief note, hoping he was well and telling him I was looking forward to hearing from him. And I took myself to work.

It was a busy day – most of my days are – but on my breaks, I sneaked into the site on my mobile phone to see if Jason had responded. Nothing! Not at 10:00 AM, not at 12:00 PM, not at 7:00 PM.

The shiny bright bubbles in me began to pop. I tasted soap in my mouth. Had something happened to him? Had I said something to offend him? Had he lost my contact details? Why had he not responded?

I scrolled through his profile online. He was as gorgeous as ever. The lines of his profile made my heart sing and reminded me of our conversation. Two strangers who had found a connection so intimate, in so short a period of time.

I checked one last time before going to bed; I needed a good night's sleep. I would check on the morrow. My insomnia made sure I had very little rest.

The next morning, I awoke at 4:00 AM. I checked. No message. And so, it went for a week until I discovered not only no message, but no more Jason. His profile had disappeared.

I felt like the Crow in *Jean de la Fontaine's* fable, *Le Corbeau et le Renard* (The Crow and the Fox). The Crow was so busy accepting the sycophantic flattery of the wily Fox that he dropped the morsel of cheese he had firmly held in his beak.

In hindsight, I do recall in the general excitement of our conversations, that Jason mentioned that he was not keen for anything serious to begin with. Funny how I missed that! Overwhelmed and infatuated by my first "real suitor", I wondered if I had come on too strongly. Or if he was still dealing with some drama as he said, "I've recently come out of a three-month relationship. I'm not looking for anything serious right now, but down the track, for sure."

Ignoring the warning, I focused only on what I wished to manifest, and I conveniently dismissed the comment. I was effectively engaging in confirmation bias, my choice to focus on and recall the information that confirmed my pre-existing beliefs. Must make a note to avoid falling into this habit of selective recall.

Gerry – whoa there, Cowboy!

Gerry was a fit, active 69-year-old from Western Australia, ready to fly across Australia in his own plane to the Gold Coast to spend the day with me, on a whim and a prayer, so to speak. Honesty and integrity were high on his list of personal attributes that he provided, unsolicited, with a CV and an extensive portfolio of businesses and properties; add to this, an array of expensive toys, his plane in pride of place. Keen, I must say. No one could possibly reject a guy with such an incredible profile, could they? He was quite a catch. The plan was to pick him up from the airport and we would get to know each other, no expectations. No pressure.

"Hold your horses Gerry! Before you jump on your plane, we need to have a little chat. I will call you." Gerry was too old; despite being in excellent shape. And our tastes were diametrically opposed. He wanted to spend the day starting with lunch and then a theme park riding roller-coasters. I loathe roller-coasters; quite scared of them. Besides, I had just hopped onto one to begin this journey.

Nonetheless, I was blown away that a guy was willing to fly such a distance to meet me. I will never forget his words, "Distance is only a small hurdle to be with the one you want." That felt great but did not make it great. Fun, I had to admit. I was on a high. I could feel the Serotonin levels in my brain working their way up.

Matteo

I quickly discovered that there were also guys who despite being well-intentioned, could not quite follow through in their attempts to meet and befriend a Lady and hopefully engage in a meaningful relationship. Quite early in the piece, I met Matteo, of European cultural background like myself, a little younger and most eligible because we had an instant connection online. The only issue of significance, not hard to guess, involved the distance that separated us. Queensland is a massive State.

Unbeknownst to him, Matteo made undertakings that were going to prove disappointing, leaving a trail of exciting and alluring promises. He chose to meet me, not for coffee as per the norm, but booked a classy restaurant on the Gold Coast in peak holiday season. Quite incidentally, this venue was to prove a very popular, if ill-fated rendezvous favourite for my dates and me; three times in fact. Perhaps that restaurant became jinxed. The locals knew only too well the nightmare of attempting to park in the vicinity of these favourite precincts in peak season. I warned Matteo of this issue and he had already calculated a suitable alternative. He knew the place well despite living 250 kilometres away, knowing where to park.

The banter in the text and phone messages between us was intoxicating, and I could not believe my luck that I had met, online at least, a man who fulfilled my exacting criterial selection and we were culturally most compatible. Okay, he was not as tall as I would like, but he made up for it in other ways. Matteo's integrity and core values were exemplified in his open and frank conversations; his willingness to surrender substantial information that verified his career accomplishments and current successful business. His family values, being Southern European were unquestionable, supported by photos and videos and most importantly, daily communication that underscored our mutual interests. That was indeed promising! I also shared personal information in verification of my profile and interest in Matteo. This was ostensibly a developing long-distance relationship that held much promise, until the dreaded day when we were to meet for the first time, after a month of communication.

Matteo had driven interstate to spend time with his family and was eager to drive back through the Gold Coast to meet me. I was excited and eager for this date, just like a teenager… On that day, Matteo was caught in traffic interstate, moving ten kilometres in two hours. Perennial traffic jams, roadworks and intense heat and humidity are enough to test the mettle of any honourable and self-respecting Gentleman and when I received the dreaded phone call, I knew that the long-awaited meeting was never to materialise. When Matteo announced, "it's all just too hard" because there was an emergency at his home that required his immediate attention, I read between the lines that the excuse had seemed plausible but unlikely.

The tyranny of distance, the bane of my existence, reared its ugly head for the first time, thwarting a potentially compatible and enduring relationship. Matteo abandoned the desire to meet me because it was realistically and logistically too challenging. We chatted on the phone and online for a little while but that was that. I sincerely believe that Matteo was trying to save face and I had not intentionally been played. I had, at that stage, not yet discovered the article that alerted me to the varied and common tactics used in online dating. Bruised and battered, I vowed to lower my expectations. Hmm… Was that feasible?

Strategising

Time is of the essence! I realised after a short time online that this venture was going to be more challenging than first anticipated. I had to beware of the traps. So easy to fall for profiles that ended up being fictitious. It was time to devise strategies that would avoid continual disappointments, deliberate or not. I would have to restructure my profile to avoid attracting guys who had the potential to play me. I had to reflect on the images I included. I needed to remain circumspect, read between the lines and really pay attention to the tenor of the messages I was receiving from some guys. I was not going to be fooled. I am not naïve and not desperate, but I am not online dating savvy, yet… I have no intention of relinquishing my power, not to any man, but this is a real challenge. So, how do I attract a gorgeous guy who is genuinely into me? How do I decipher what is really behind the mesmerising blue eyes that I find so attractive? I remain on my guard. I am learning fast…

On a happier note, my youngest daughter, Alessandra found her Soulmate, Marcelo on a dating site and they are building their lives together with her gorgeous puppy. She did not use, "Must love dogs" in her profile either, yet, Marcelo is besotted by her puppy. It took them one year to find each other; my youngest is definitely more patient than me. So, who the hell was I to think that I can find my Soulmate so quickly? Do I have tickets on myself? No, just too discerning… I was at least encouraged by this success story. I forged ahead.

Some guys were evidently a breath of fresh air; not into games and not expert at breaking a Lady's heart. Some were online for the same reasons as me.

A little ditty by Mr B.

It's a funny feeling
This thing they call love
So said stupid Cupid
Or was it the dopey dove?

What's this internet dating?
It's clearly all the rage
Even my mum does it
Who cares about your age!

Some seek them far
Others seek them close
Some men are tall and handsome
Others are short and gross

Shall I keep it a secret?
Or should I beat my drum?
But if my sister finds out
She's sure to tell mum

Do I send a short message?
Or maybe a really big kiss?
But without a recent photo
I'm sure to miss

Who should make first contact?
The lady or the gent?
But what if there's no stamps left?
Because they've all been spent

Some ladies sound too fussy
Others couldn't give a toss
But when they take a photo
They don't forget their lip gloss

Hopefully I amused you
Or just made you smile
I'm here to find true love
Even if it takes a while

Alchemy and algorithms, chemistry and chimeras

A nagging thought continued to plague me. How does an algorithm account for indescribably raw chemistry and pheromones? Are there really people out there who consistently ignore immediate attraction and the combustion that it brings because it might be considered shallow? We have enough friends to satisfy all other desires, so why bother to search for love if it is not for an authentic, electric and captivating union? Whilst many settle for lust, I was on a mission to experience love at first sight. Can one compromise on chemistry? I, for one was not willing to try. I believed that the first kiss usually revealed if there was a real connection or not. However, sometimes, just as love is not always enough, neither is chemistry! A little cryptic, but whichever way I look at this, it is very subjective.

I am faced with a genuine conundrum. I am on a mission to find love, convinced I will know it on the first kiss. However, as I am already 50+ and looking for a life partner, I find myself constantly re-examining "what is this thing called "true love"? I believe that I have found it before but why did it prove ephemeral? Where did it go? I would never have married had I not been in love; or bothered to engage in a subsequent long-term relationship. This begs the question; "if they went, were they "true love"? In which case "true love" is not necessarily forever. This is not a comforting thought and really offers me more questions than resolution to the paradox. Is this ultimately because I have not yet found my true "Soulmate"? Where can he be?

The issue is to work out if chemistry is the same as "true love." I suspect that the connection is much easier to dismiss. In fact, chemistry comes closer to lust or perhaps infatuation. It is real, but it is not enduring for a range of reasons. Clearly, people find true love without chemistry. Mahatma Gandhi did not get to choose his wife (like many in the world even today), but he claimed he loved her. Not that hard to believe. Many of us do not get to choose our relatives, but we do love them... I cannot speak for everyone.

Little did I know that romantic chemistry was predicated on science. Just look at the animal kingdom; so much can be explained by observing various species in their natural habitats. Carl G. Jung's quotation on the subject needs no elaboration, "The meeting of two personalities is like the contact of two chemical substances: if there is any reaction, both are transformed." Makes sense to me.

Delving into studies on chemistry and pheromones, I discovered that the first kiss is said to offer many clues into the soul of a person. It appears the powerful first kiss designates an individual's sexuality, intentions, patience and health, with 66% of women apparently ending a relationship after a first bad kiss.[4] The biological response of "love at first sight" is explained by Anthropologist, Helen Fisher Ph.D. This may appear farfetched, but the science behind kissing is based on smells, on pheromones, the chemicals credited for creating attractions released through the olfactory senses to the brain. This chemical substance is produced and released into the environment by an animal, especially mammals or insects, and it affects the physiology or behaviour of others of its species. Pheromones are sometimes called behaviour-altering agents. This helps to explain why sometimes people react so dramatically when first introduced. I only need to think of the films I have seen... Smells are hugely significant as we kiss

---

[4] Heyen, Gina D. The chemistry of romance. LCMFT; Monday, February 07, 2011. http://wichitacounseling.blogspot.com.au/2011/02/

because the brain unconsciously responds to the immune system of the other. If we find the kiss unsatisfactory, it probably means that our immune systems do not match.[5] I found this fascinating and pertinent to my online dating experience.

One of my BFFs, Jessica, has confessed to an involuntary non-verbal behaviour when she kisses a guy for the first time; her nostrils flair imperceptibly as she gently inhales the masculine scent that emanates from her date. It may be mixed with his aftershave lotion, or even his body odour. The ultimate test is that if his "scent" matches hers, it's a win-win situation. The famous Hollywood movie *Scent of a Woman* is a classic case, where Al Pacino's award-winning role as cantankerous retired blind Lieutenant Coronel teaches his young carer, Chris O'Donnell a thing or two about life. The mesmerising scene of the Tango performance between Pacino and Gabrielle Anwar is indelibly marked in my memory.

This captivating theory seems intricately tied to one's eyes as well. It might shed light on the popular maxims, "The eyes are the windows to the soul" and "Beauty is in the eye of the beholder." If we believe what expert, Beverley Palmer, Ph. D suggests, "the most important sign of attraction is mutual eye contact."[6] What an amazing revelation. Everything is falling into place now. I have always, unreservedly looked at a person straight in the eyes, a Southern European trait that has landed me in hot water in the past if the object of my gaze was a male. We are comfortable in our sexuality and have no fear of looking straight into a man's eyes. Quite inconsistent actually, when I profess to be reserved and suffer from low self-esteem. Paradoxical, more aptly. However, I must admit that I have, to a certain degree, succeeded in integrating the image of the confident Lady as part of my identity thanks to my simulated role of actress that protects the shy little girl inside.

Making eye contact is a cultural issue that needs to be understood to avoid cultural dissonance or worse, altercations and abuse, if the intent is misconstrued. I therefore now try to amend my behaviour in certain contexts. The language of the eyes is certainly lost in translation a little more often these days because we live in a global village. The chance

---

[5] Ibid.
[6] Ibid. p.1

of offending someone has increased exponentially, especially in contact situations with Middle-Eastern and some Asian nationals.

My dating experiences convinced me that Palmer's research was sound, that my attraction to guys with amazing blue eyes was based on science. This is no longer a mystery. It is not simply a case of opposites attracting, although, that evidently plays a part in the equation. Eight out of ten dates with men who have magnetic blue eyes constitute sufficient proof for me; another had green eyes and the last hazel. I am powerless to change this. Reading on, I reflected on my first dates and could not hide my amusement as Dr. Beverley Palmer's assertions were confirmed. I immediately blushed at the memory of my first "chemically-induced" encounter.

> *After the initial attraction [Palmer] states that you will then witness preening from the interested male or female who will begin to mirror your behaviors of touching hair, lips, or crossing legs. This is a signal that states, "I'm interested in you."*

Palmer might have been watching Michael and me.

Michael

Michael, a Brisbane Beau, was another incredibly attractive male who responded to my expressions of interest; 6', blond, blue-eyed, sportive, intellectual, witty, communicative... My girlfriends agreed. I noticed his profile in my MATCHES box and could not believe my eyes. Was this profile real? He was younger than me, reassuringly, not an issue for Michael (one more tick), as the statutory disclosure of my real age was swift, to avoid disappointment. What a relief!

Unbelievably, Michael had the same star sign as mine (irrelevant to most people who dismiss Astrology as nonsensical, but certainly significant to us). We were already on the same wave length both through the stars and about the importance of the stars, even if perceived as quirky and dismissed by out-groups. Not surprising that this Gentleman was the most romantic guy I had ever met.

Pure and unadulterated chemistry was in the air. Michael's ethical conduct, empathy, caring and affectionate nature was exactly what I was looking for. It only took one hour for my BFF, Louise in Melbourne to verify Michael's credentials. Louise was insistent on doing this, naturally worried that I was setting myself up for a very big fall. Someone had to act responsibly. I did not sleep for two days. I had to pinch myself that this online attraction had been reciprocated instantaneously. Self-doubt clouded my judgment and I psyched myself into a go-slow mode, ignoring my inner voice warning me that this could be a ruse. I was by then aware of the online tactics and was determined to remain cautious, but not cynical.

I was about to surrender to my fears as the communication had slowed over the 48-hour period, when Michael called me and said that he was coming to the Coast for the weekend, staying with a mate, and wanted to meet me for coffee. He had been inundated with messages from others and was attempting to respond curtly, cutting and pasting, as I did, telling them he had found someone, on the day he had posted his profile. He asked to meet me in my district because he was considerate and generous to a fault.

Whilst attempting to keep my expectations low, after the quick transition from messages online to phone calls, the anticipated meeting was to take place only three days from the initial contact. Little had I known that Friday night was reserved for the football. Let's weigh that up... Dates? Football? Like the other suitors I had met, Michael was also from Mars! On the other hand, could he have been on another date?

I was on Cloud Nine, singing the praises of this wonderfully clever site with algorithms that worked for once. I would need to re-evaluate my assessment of online dating.

Synchronicity described our first encounter perfectly. A scene from my own Romantic-Comedy I was hoping to write. We recognised each other instantly, our photos authentic, even if Michael, like the other guys, also attested that I looked better in real life. An instant of doubt crept in but was quickly dismissed.

Cutting to the chase, the coffee date lasted exactly forty-five minutes and neither of us was going home. Michael booked a restaurant on the ocean, unknowingly picking my favourite, on a glorious day that we hoped would never end. As I headed to the bathroom, he asked me to re-enact, on my way back, our first moment of recognition and peremptory kiss on the cheek. Clichéd? You think? This time, however, as I walked back towards him, Michael had the most incredible smile on his face. I found this hilarious but played along, just a little surprised when he planted a kiss on my lips. Fireworks. Wow! I could not contain my excitement. Except that the lessons the Nuns had schooled me in kept coming back to haunt me.

The meal was inconsequential because the image we irradiated was of a couple madly 'in love.' I was not hungry. The chemistry was incendiary. Chimera in motion. I was flying high on my roller-coaster, the attraction between Michael and me so intense that what transpired could have been mistaken for a scene from a *Chick Flick*.

On the terrace of the restaurant, where the ocean was the same colour as Michael's eyes, a party of three guests, an elderly couple and their daughter had been observing us. They could not contain their curiosity and asked us if we were on our honeymoon. Michael did not disappoint, highly conscious of the effects this inquiry had on me. "We are in love" he responded. I could not believe my ears! He had instinctively understood that, had he confessed this was our 'first date', it would have been highly embarrassing. And, the strangest part was that we were not misbehaving!

It gets better! As he accompanied me back to my car, still located where we had had coffee seven hours earlier, he kissed me goodbye, both of us oblivious to the inquisitive stares from a couple passing by. Michael assured me of his best intentions, promising that the second date on the Sunday would surpass this first romantic encounter. He retraced his steps and came back to whisper in my ear, "I love you." I dropped my keys... "We have just met!" Michael was unapologetic. We met the next afternoon and I broke all the rules of dating after an estimation of the risks involved, given his eminent professional status and allowed him to pick me up from my home. A classic case of "Do as I say, not as I do," but predicated on verification of the profile.

What ensued was the continuation of a daydream; *apéritifs* at sunset at a trendy surf club; romantic walk on the beach acting like teenagers and then dinner in an exclusive French restaurant on the coast. This was only the second date so, as to be expected from two people who were convinced there to be a lifetime of memories, we said goodnight, brimming with anticipation at the prospect of the following weekend.

Then the roller-coaster tipped into its downward trajectory. The projected weekend did not eventuate. I sat in a disenchanted sulk in the hairdresser's chair, saying very little until the appointment had finished.

Reflection

So, what of the chemistry and pheromones? Michael cited reality checks concerning distance, the pull of a career, and three adult children. Cold feet that comes from standing on Cloud Nine. Neither of us could relocate to turn this dream into reality. We would remain friends, of course. We never really intended to, of course.

Out of the blue, months later, Michael did however, contact me and suggested we catch up, if I was unattached. I was dating Francis, the Captain at the time, (Chapter 18), and he immediately accepted the fact and moved on.

When a whirlwind romance with combustible passion and promise is extinguished in an instant, could this be my fault? Do I need to be more patient? Do Michael and I have trust issues? Are we both scared of the ability to sustain the intense emotions that engulfed us? So many questions flood my brain. The crux of the matter is that I need to be true to myself, realising full well that complete answers are unfathomable! Am I actually willing to relinquish my independence? Hmm … this question was to haunt me for my entire journey…

Looking at my brief interlude with Michael, it is now clear that perhaps in time we may have had to deal with some worrying issues, but we had been so caught up in the romance. Yet, I refuse to envisage a world where relationships of convenience are the order of the day for our age group, or even the unthinkable alternative that so many singles are now opting for – joining other individuals in the playground of sexual fantasies. Magazine articles always feature stories of this nature. Not my scene, I am afraid. I prefer to imagine a world where there is still a Soulmate for each of us on this planet. The eternal romantic is not ready to give up on her search.

The chemical can feel so solid and is yet so ephemeral. Perhaps it was infatuation.

The episode left my soul singed, the embers still glowing, but luckily not incinerated. I almost gave up on the search for love. I was at my lowest ebb on the ride that was taking convoluted routes on the way to happiness. For the first time in my life, I had admired the Coco mirrored in Michael's magnetic blue eyes.[7] Oh, those blue eyes kept getting me into trouble! Yet,

---

[7] Jacques Lacan, The Mirror Stage as Formative of the Function of the I as revealed in *Psychoanalytic Experience in Écrits: A selection*

16

I was powerless to change my preferences. When I was with Michael, I felt attractive and self-assured and was at last ready to accept myself for the way my mirror saw me. I had regained my self-respect, largely decimated during my previous relationships. The mirror of Michael's eyes enabled me to see the woman I aspired to be. One week, all I had seen in a mirror was smoke.

Mirror, Mirror, on the wall ... You have a lot to answer for!

Jean Cocteau's famous quotation serves as sombre admonishment to those of us who gaze into our mirrors and forget that we are no longer young and nubile, *"Les miroirs feraient bien de refléchir un peu plus avant de nous renvoyer notre image"* (Mirrors ought to reflect (think) more before reflecting (sending) our image.)[8] The pun around "reflect" is very apt.

Michael had pulled the pin and was devastated, though not enough to rethink his actions. Our subsequent lengthy phone conversations revealed he feared the intense emotions we had experienced. He instantly validated that what we had experienced was real but confessed he did not want to hurt me down the track. He was honourable, at least. He said that he had pulled the pin because he felt unworthy of me. He believed he was batting above his average. Where did he get that impression from? I was devastated. Come to think of it, he had been surprised that I had been interested in him? Go figure. He was a gorgeous individual, inside and out. Michael was also going through some personal challenges at the time and I acknowledge that I did not know him at all. How could I after a week? Was it love at first sight? Or pure, unadulterated obsession? What is the difference? The truth was that, chemistry or not, the timing was all wrong.

I came to the realisation that my mirror could just as easily shatter the illusory positive self-image I had construed for the first time in my life. Was I achieving a stage of self-actualisation and self-awareness, ready to accept myself, to like myself only to see it evaporate in an instant? Why do I rely so heavily on others for the process of identity validation? Why do I need constant reinforcement of my looks, qualities, character, personality, intelligence from 'another'? I am a Virgo; and in my opinion, this has a lot to do with the way I think and act.

---

[8] Jean Cocteau Quotes. https://www.goodreads.com/quotes/147172-mirrors-should-think-longer-before-they-reflect

3

Looking for love - just love a checklist

My online journey so far has led me to understand an important factor. I must re-examine exactly what I am looking for. There is no denying this. The angst of writing profiles cannot be underestimated. Remaining inflexible even when first attempts prove disheartening is asking for trouble. There is no point in sticking to a prescriptive checklist of physical attributes and values in the individual I hope to find online, only to be disappointed when the prospective suitor does not meet my expectations in various ways. If we are not compatible, try as we may, it just does not work. I did not want to change the guys I met; I respected them too much for that, and I had to be careful not to force the issue, kidding myself that it would work because I had the best of intentions, even if this was tantamount to pushing a boulder uphill; much like *Sisyphus*, from Greek mythology, who taunted me whenever I realised that I was actually trying to do just that – change the long-term habits of the guy I fell for.

At this age, especially, are we so set in our ways that the task of changing for someone we really like is so challenging that we eventually give up? We may have the best of intentions but forcing the issue is likely to result in heartache. I would like it all, but I now realise that I might be able to get some, but not all. Compromise is paramount if a new relationship in the fifties and sixties age groups, and beyond is to succeed; but to what extent was I ready to compromise? On what bases? It is tough enough for young adults who are relatively malleable and willing to adjust to a new partner. From my perspective, the 50+ contingent is destined for the crate of immovable objects.

I know exactly what I do not want, and I am adamant that somewhere, there is someone for me. That is a good place to start, right? I am not seeking perfection; I only wish to tick most of the boxes and then decide which ones are really the most important, discarding the rest. There are no rubrics offering the essential qualities of friendship, emotional intelligence and employment stability, but I can check these characteristics quite quickly during the first phone chat. My online description needs to include a desire for good morals, unquestionable values and compassion. If we are incompatible on that score, it will not augur well for a solid foundation of the relationship. As for the physical side, I might as well focus on what I want and compromise afterwards! This was not going to be easy.

When I reflect on my long-term relationships as benchmarks for obtaining what I am looking for, I realise that I only ticked approximately 80 % – 90% of my boxes, physically, intellectually, spiritually and emotionally, in my two main relationships. When I was married, the percentage was high. I was very young, and I believed the union would last forever. Times were so different; familial and social obligations, pressures and expectations were punitive and highly repressive, and I did not envisage separation or divorce as a viable option should the situation go pear-shaped. I thought my husband was the "One" and therefore I believed that he ticked 90% of my boxes. With the laws of diminishing returns, so to speak, age and perceived wisdom taught me that it was well-nigh on impossible to expect anyone to meet my expectations in a partner.

In the subsequent long-term union, I was willing to accept a much lower percentage, and that had less chance of lasting the distance. Was I now attempting to achieve what I was unable to do as a young adult, by going online to prescribe what I was hoping to find in a male of my age? Was there anyone for me who could actually tick more than 80% or 90% of my boxes?

When two individuals are so set in their ways, what are the chances? Our established patterns of behaviour, our emotional attachment to the familiar way we do things, our adherence to maintaining the status quo? Change is difficult, and it becomes increasingly harder as we age. Might as well throw my hat into the ring, expect the best and then accept the mediocre if negotiation is an option... Was I truthfully prepared to compromise on my criteria, or would I simply despair of ever finding my Soulmate?

Time to re-examine my checklist...

- ❑ *Tall*
- ❑ *Caucasian*
- ❑ *5'11 – 6'3 (1.80m – 1.91m)* (I did not factor in shrinkage – evidently, for the 50 to 60-year-old bracket, this is a serious consideration)
- ❑ *Blue, green, hazel or grey eyes*
- ❑ *head of hair* (no category available to eliminate hirsute men)
- ❑ *athletic build*
- ❑ *family oriented*
- ❑ *intellectual*
- ❑ *cultured*
- ❑ *professional*
- ❑ *sophisticated dresser*
- ❑ *sociable*
- ❑ *divorced/single* (married is also on the menu for some, of course! Not for me thanks!)
- ❑ *Non-smoker*
- ❑ *European heritage*
- ❑ *ambitious...*
- ❑ ...and the list goes on. Am I asking too much?

And then, there is the list of what I do not want...

- ❑ *not hirsute* - I am not fond of hairy men and unfortunately many Europeans tend to be hirsute – too ticklish. Now, it cannot be denied that many men occasionally shave or wax their ENTIRE bodies; but, just in case we, the Ladies thought otherwise, it is not really to please us, but more to avoid sweating and chafing in their chosen sport, cycling, running, rock climbing and swimming come to mind. God's honour! This is what I have been told.

The problem is, these guys generally find a way of shaving their unwanted hair as best they can (just imagine the contortions as they attempt to shave their backs), and when the hair grows back, it is tantamount to spooning a prickly pear, or worse, a porcupine, even if the growth is close enough to a five o'clock shadow. More often than not, their backs are sporting a four-day growth. Each to his own, but not all women like prickly pears or beards and certainly do not appreciate the resultant rash.

Now, I, on the other hand plan my regular visits to waxing salons prior to a promising date. The beauty routines I put up with are culturally based; the adage, *il faut souffrir pour être belle* (Beauty is pain) is not every woman's cup of tea. Good little Girl Scout, always on the ready, just in case I have the courage to discard the draconian lessons on the dos and don'ts of courtship the Nuns imposed on us at school. They certainly did a number on us.

I feel sorry for the poor guys though, as these salons tend to have far fewer female beauty therapists who work on the males. I have never seen a guy in the salon I frequent. I suspect the guys might yelp in pain just as I do. Even more embarrassing for the guys I would think, depending on which parts of the body they want waxed... My threshold is extraordinarily low. Women can only hope that the excruciatingly painful stripping of their unwanted hair is appreciated by the males. Should any of them show anything less than complete approval and gratitude for the expensive and painful effort, it may hex any chance of longevity for the relationship. Some brave souls, dare I say, foolish men, have apparently proclaimed that they prefer their women to adopt the hirsute days of old, whilst others request specific areas to be waxed. Not hard to imagine the indignation and frustration of these women upon hearing that. How strange that the Americans, Australians and Europeans, all western nations, are said to have vastly different cultural preferences concerning the amount of hair they are prepared to have waxed? Each to her own. Let's not even consider the alternative cultural habits!

I wonder if I will ever become *au fait* with Australian vernacular. In anticipation of a promising third date with a Gentleman I hoped may be the "One", I was enjoying a drink with my friends. Quite excited for me, my BFF, Zara wished me luck, saying, "Go Girl! You need to clear those cobwebs." to which I innocently responded, "Waxing all under control thanks but I want to take things really slowly." I had not realised that I had it all wrong. Hmm.... Zara was encouraging me to hop into bed with the guy to clear the cob webs of the past few years.

Okay, back to focus on the reconstruction of the perfect male specimen. How exciting to program everything I desire in a man? That is a definite plus! Designer babies are illegal in this country but designing the perfect partner is something I can indulge in. Of course, I trusted some of the experts, most notably my daughters, who had patiently done the hard yards (quizzing me at every stage to verify the information) to fill in the tedious pages that would guarantee a 'MATCH'. I was no longer so trusting to believe that the dating site's algorithms could accurately match me with the perfect partner, but I had to try. I had always hated Maths and did not trust the calculations to conjure up the man of my dreams.

Does he exist? Well, perhaps there is a better chance online than heading to the bars and clubs on the Gold Coast, an increasingly hazardous pursuit these days. I am convinced we are going through a man drought.

Joining a new site was the perfect opportunity to reconfigure my profile by injecting new ideas. Adapting my entry in response to feedback, it appears a little mystery is, in fact, enticing and will hopefully generate some interest. Ever the optimist, I was on a roll. How about more concrete and desirable qualities that I am seeking in a man, just to weed out unsolicited attention? It goes a little like this,

> *Integrity, romantic, loyal, affectionate, empathetic, sophisticated and accepting, a healthy sense of humour...*
> *A little too discerning? At this stage of my life, it pays to be!*

Was I trying to be too clever? Let's see! Well! I asked for it. What did I think would really happen? It did not take long to stem the flow of interest. At least there were fewer messages to attend to; but seriously? It would be nice to get SOME response. That exercise weeded out just about everyone on this site. Not happy!

This remodelled profile represented the perfect counterpoint to my inexperience when I first put my heart on my sleeve and told everyone I was searching for my Soulmate.

I was mocked, and I retreated. Now, I know what I want. And, as one would expect, I now have to deal with new consequences, which is far fewer responses. This correlates perfectly with the allure of internet dating, the superficial pleasure of being engaged by ephemeral others.

Be careful what you wish for, Coco!

Whilst I progressively made changes to my profile entries, I refused point blank to diminish my capabilities in order to impress or attract a guy. When a close male friend, Joseph suggested that I not mention my tertiary education until I knew a guy better, I fiercely rejected the idea, defending my stance on this issue. I still find it disconcerting that some guys are so intimidated by the female intellect, but I will never gratify their swollen ego by minimising my professional status just to catch the prize. Yes, I am willing to forgo the "One" – or perhaps, if my intellect blocks him from contacting me, then he is not the one. Either the partner in my life and I find a good fit, or "On your bike Squire!"

Joining a third site whose scope offered interesting national profiles proved to be a definite improvement on the first two. So why did it hurt when the guys I approached turned me down, without so much as an explanation?

Still hurts! Some sent curt messages, just as I did with the guys I dated in Queensland. At least the polite ones were kind. The over sixties cohort restored my self-esteem slightly as they apparently found me "exotic, stunningly beautiful, mysterious, Mediterranean…," some adding, "Yes, you do look mysterious, Coco; others volunteered, "Definitely fit your criteria for a partner. Happy to share more if your interested"; yet others commented, "Nicely done. Good luck." Okay! Balance nearly re-established.

Happy dragon, happy castle

Considering the quirky online profile entries from this first foray into internet dating, I assessed my exacting list of requirements in a partner.

The exigencies commonly reported in the list of attributes and values of many female online daters searching for their perfect partner, (including mine, of course) are brilliantly portrayed in the sassy, tongue-in-cheek lyrics of Meghan Trainor's hit song, below. It is a good thing I can laugh at myself!

Firstly, a little gem reflecting male humour admirably; but there is also some truth about what some older men might be looking for.

> *I want someone who I can share my entire life with, and who will leave me alone most of the time. Happy dragon, happy castle.*

And just so it is clear this is showing just one planet's view, here is the other planet's view, *Dear Future Husband*. I am sure many will have heard this song. It is a classic and this brief excerpt is hardly subtle.

> *... 'Cause if you'll treat me right*
> *I'll be the perfect wife...*
>
> *...You gotta know how to treat me like a lady*
> *Even when I'm acting crazy...*
>
> *...If you wanna get that special lovin'*
> *Tell me I'm beautiful each and every night...*
>
> *...After every fight*
> *Just apologize...*[9]

The slightly exaggerated lyrics clearly defy the hookup culture that defines internet dating today, even if not all women subscribe to idea that the attributes and values are attainable. There is so much truth in the words and it is hilarious - "funny but true." If some of us, Ladies of the new Millennium are honest, are we really going to deny this? No comment from Feminists please!

It may appear that an increasing number of guys and gals nudging 60+ may not have realised it yet, but they might just be happy to settle for companionship instead of the dramas that fully-fledged relationships

---

[9] Kadish, K. & Trainor, M. Dear Future Husband. 2015. http://www.metrolyrics. com/dear-future-husband-lyrics-meghan-trainor.html

entail. This is particularly if they have been through acrimonious and costly separations and divorce.

Searching for the ideal mate was ostensibly a click away and an individual who mirrored my values, embodying the physical attributes of Prince Charming, or James Bond, financially independent etc. would magically appear as I responded to my messages. Where could he possibly be, at 50 kilometres from my district, 100km? Or perhaps I needed to cast the net more widely in other States of Australia? And why not? If one finds the right partner, everything becomes possible.

Or maybe not, because distance can do dastardly things. Television programs such as *Farmer wants a wife, Married at first site, the Bachelor* franchise and others of the genre bring together men and women from around Australia. But what happens to the fairy tale ending when the experiment is over? Surely geography plays a colossal role in fulfilling the couple's dreams of a future together. This issue is certainly explored in these series, and ostensibly resolved by the end, but is it really?

I now have a clearer understanding of this process. It is easy for me to cast aspersions on individuals I admire on the screen in these contrived situations. I am quick to criticise the way they respond to issues that arise when it comes to the crunch. I deplore their actions if they do not match my ideals, when they act in ways I find reprehensible, injudicious, thoughtless, sabotaging the chances to secure the "One" they have found.

However, having been caught in these scenarios, I have learned to think twice about abandoning my career, my family and my friends. And I have decided that I am not ready to relocate to the other side of the country to be with my newfound love. Okay, at least not yet... The internet diminishes distance and that works for the start, for the superficial front end of an incipient relationship. But distance is potentially a dam break that can quench true love, or so I believe.

Reverse Psychology

My favourite line in the first message to a suitor I find attractive from Brisbane or interstate, is, "The tyranny of distance may be an issue. I live on the Gold Coast... but I hope to hear from you." I realise this sounds paradoxical because I have just acknowledged the tyranny of distance is very real, but I like to leave things to the universe. Never say never! Too many absolutes are not helpful at all.

I feel a little sassy and brazen, but if the guys I am attracted to are in my MATCH box, I can throw my hat into the ring. This is an effective strategy to discover if the intentions of the prospective partner are honourable, if he is a Gentleman, if he is willing to really get to know me. When they only respond with quasi monosyllabic answers, "Hi" or "Hey there" the gist of the conversation turns into a game. Are they just as weary of false profiles as I am? Are they playing games, or are they intimidated by my profile, possibly not articulate enough to hold a conversation?

The calibre of men I was searching for was not always an exact match, evidently, but I persevered with my search even as I conceded that I may never find the "One" on or offline.

Refusing to relinquish my quest to find my Soulmate, I focused on my checklist and considered if I needed to compromise on any aspect before persevering with this venture. The qualities I admired in a partner had to include respect, ethical conduct, compassion, family values and emotional intelligence. Impossible for me to make concessions on core values. The physical attributes, I knew would be a tough ask to achieve, but I was not giving up on securing my cyber Prince totally because, after all, I had strategically outlined my preferences on the dating sites. As I continued to reflect on the complex and quixotic nature of relationships, I pondered the following questions. Why was there such urgency to race to the altar, so to speak? From my experience, this paradigm was emerging for many guys from the 50+ groups; and the crux of the issue was clearly age. The question became instantly rhetorical as I recalled the dates I had been on. The guys were ready to terminate all other contacts online, elated to finally have a reason to shut down their profiles.

Daniel – a match or an illusion

I contacted Daniel because his profile requirements matched mine. And I met his, as I immediately discovered. I related to his quirky introductory spiel.

> *Friendly and sociable. Low mileage, high performance. Very low maintenance. Bumped a few times however has never*

been involved in a major accident. Proven ability to hug the
road, not wander off course and maintains perfect control in
any conditions.

Daniel had a sardonic and witty sense of humour that made for scintillating banter over five dinner dates. I congratulated myself for actually "getting it!"

His image was gorgeous... However, it was just a postage stamp picture.

Daniel declared we had a great deal in common. He was interested and attracted to my values and outlook, attributes he also shared. What a great start! We chatted briefly online, both wary of disclosing too much information. He said the dating site was, "a trophy hunters and cougars site from my experience. They say if you want sincerity, affection and love, get a dog!" Hearing this, I wasted no time in disclosing my age, being older than him; and Daniel's response brought a big smile to my face,

Thank you for your honesty and please don't be concerned as
age does not bother me. It's more than that in what I value
in a person. You look youthful in your pictures and that
represents you I'm sure.

But then, 24 hours after I contacted him, his profile disappeared. Daniel had swiftly removed it because the image had almost caused his hard drive to crash. Fascinating! How fortunate for me to be one of the lucky Ladies with whom Daniel had chosen to correspond! My profile had touched a nerve and we declared we were on the same page. I could not eliminate the image of the sun-bleached blond Adonis with a five o'clock shadow from my mind, yes, another one; I have a type; even when I discovered that the photograph with the curly locks just covering his ears was five years old, taken while heli-skiing abroad. A picture is worth a thousand words. Daniel had promised more photos at my request, as I had none to refer to, but they never came. He had lost his phone with all photos and he hated Selfies... as did I...

Yes, I wondered about that, but hey, he was gorgeous – clearly visible even in a postage stamp photo. And so, we maintained contact afterwards anyway. Then we had made phone contact... He was the perfect guy.

I couldn't wait to meet him. In my mind's eye, he met most of my requirements, physically, emotionally, intellectually. I remained a little nervous though and hoped we could meet sooner rather than later. He was taking a while to come down to the Coast to meet me.

After one month, Daniel came to the Gold Coast. When I first met him, there was a complete discrepancy between the impeccably dressed business man with a crew cut facing me and calling me by name, and the postage stamp. Add to this, my imagination, the construed romantic picture I had concocted in my brain.

Nonetheless, 6'2 Daniel in his tailored suit, the eminent, jet setting business man… was a great guy. The reality was at least equal to my imagination constructed through our phone conversations. The individual standing before me did not quite match the guy with the physical features I recalled even if the quirky personality traits were unmistakably accurate.

Daniel was not as he presented himself and he was not the man I came to imagine him to be. He checked many boxes (witty, cheeky, intellectual, generous) – and he unchecked some others I thought he checked (gregarious, social, available). He was still a workaholic, like me and travelled a great deal. He was very reserved and more comfortable on the phone than face-to-face. He relaxed significantly, however after the first couple of dates. And, I daresay that it was the same for him – that I was not quite as he imagined.

Reflection

I really liked Daniel, but if the spark was not there, how could I contemplate moving forward? Family was high on his agenda, as it was on mine and he spent a lot of time with his children, in different States. The last time I went out with Daniel was four months after meeting him and we have only exchanged cursory emails since then. He went on extended overseas trips, where his potential dates proved lacklustre. We planned to reconnect soon, having missed the banter, but life has a habit of getting in the way.

I hope that we can maintain our friendship even if I feel that Daniel would like considerably more from me. A bit of a dilemma. We cannot have our cake and eat it too. We are adults and we need to make choices in our lives and some of them are painful. When I think of the incredible guys with whom I could form lasting friendships based on compatibility, it breaks my heart to think that most of them cannot envisage any less than a full commitment.

I am so glad to have Daniel as a friend who has at least not turned down my friendship because of an inflated ego. He is someone I can spar with on an intellectual, social and political level. I respect him and he is fun to be with.

I must admit, I felt like a naughty school girl when Daniel scolded me a couple of months later for having contemplated a long-distance relationship in Melbourne.

> *I thought I'd had a discussion with you about distance relationships and pursuing them was not ideal and always ends badly. Why is it that the Gold Coast is so devoid of a suitable male for you? Lucky I'm in Brisbane, so, out of that demographic!... So miss our catch ups and banter my dear. Let's see if we can align the stars and make it happen soon. Daniel.*

Daniel ended his message with these words before our 6th date, that was unfortunately cancelled due to his work commitments.

> *Don't pursue distance relationships; if they are that good they would have been taken locally! Believe me please, you're too nice to be wasted on the heap of failed long-distance relationships/flings or whatever!*

Ouch! That hurt! That was not exactly my intention but what did I really expect would happen when both parties are unable to relocate? The jury was still out however, as I was not prepared to cut all ties with my suitors from interstate. The thought played on my mind though, that another suitor from Melbourne also, could be playing games... So easy to do...

Okay! Daniel may hold hopes of more than I can offer right now but I do miss his company and look forward to seeing him when he is ready.

Does this make the process, the journey, worthwhile? Who can say?

If I leave a trail of broken hearts, how can I possibly rejoice in the journey of self-discovery? It is certainly not my intention to collect broken hearts in my treasure chest.

So, my thirst remains unquenchable; the quest for my Soulmate remains fervent. Self-protection is paramount, so I try to convince myself that long-distance relationships are exactly what I am looking for. Would I give up my freedom, my established lifestyle to share my life with the man of my dreams? In an instant. Evidently, I have not yet found the "One."

Going fishing... hooked on

Jason's bite was very exciting and very painful as he wriggled away. Gerry's nibble was adorable, but I was happy to throw him back.

Despite this, I realised that I was now hooked. Where are you, tall Fish, smart Fish, hunky Fish? Oh no! You do not want to lose this Beauty. Now there's a catch!

And getting hooked means most of the time you need to pay. Upgrade your membership to see if he has read your messages. Quick! He will swim away. You need to get in quick. Special offer, just for today. Most popular deal, don't miss out! It's a bargain. But wait, if you use your credit card, you will get two for the price of one. Come on now! What are you waiting for?

I was hooked on these instantaneous connections that made me forget my addiction to my soap operas on television. I could always record those. Anyhow, my own soaps were more exciting. Fluctuating levels of Dopamine have me constantly hooked on one activity or another.

Made sense; and so, I persevered. To be brutally honest with myself, internet dating, despite its nefarious side, was beginning to fill the void of loneliness in my life. This is perfectly in line with the allure of the chase and desire for connection that online dating provokes. When my highly charged days were over, my sporting activities effective in energising me, my evenings now had purpose, other than working and indulging in news broadcasts followed by my favourite shows. I could chat online with new suitors for as long as my eyes would stay opened. This internet venture was, in fact, tantamount to going out to meet people and chatting each evening, except that I could do this in the comfort of my home. I realised then and there, that life was pretty good. I was beginning to accept that the tactics used by so many users online simply needed to be negotiated and I was determined to survive the journey and eventual battles, come what may.

Reflection

And the wheel turns. My early escapades on internet dating sites might have dissuaded me from venturing further into this unconventional way of finding love, but it also revealed something I liked. I realised that I might have to do the hard yards to get what I wanted. But is that not what life is about? I need to understand that with the pain, there are rewards at the end of the journey. Was it possible to have the glorious pleasures of love without the gory pains? I found myself unprepared for my journey, as unprepared when I first dated and partnered, an internet virgin. But I spied the promise, the potential – and yes, I had felt the buzz of hunting online for love.

Too good to be true? Harry, Harry, are you real?

YOU [who I am looking for]: smart, sassy, sexy - with a heart of gold! … Emotionally mature, kind and loving… knows how to carry a conversation, and who loves kissing and cuddling (preferably me, and not the milkman!) Rest assured you do not need to look like a model for me to be interested in you, (because I certainly don't), and we both know that beauty is only skin deep anyway.

ME: happy, kind, patient, optimistic, pleasant, fun, funny, cheeky, polite, virile, naughty, uninhibited, energetic, successful, financially solvent, loving and considerate - even if I do say so myself ;-) I like good conversation and I'm hoping to find a good-natured and intelligent woman with whom I can chat and laugh easily, preferably over a glass or two of wine. I like to be a gentleman, so I prefer women who appreciate the difference between a gentleman and a 'bloke'.

I also rescue fluffy kittens from trees, work tirelessly (yet anonymously) for charity and help little old ladies across the

*road - whether they want to cross it or not! When I grow up
I want to establish a centre for kids what can't read good.*

*'Salt and pepper' hair, and the usual wrinkles/laughter lines
for someone my age, so please don't expect perfection. To
paraphrase George Clooney, I'm not trying to compete with
twenty-something year old boys... No emotional baggage,
debts, or a beer belly. What I do have is a desire to meet
someone who intrigues and stimulates me; someone that will
respond to a little bit of romance and is open to possibilities.
Above all, I'm looking for someone who is emotionally
mature, kind and loving. P.s. I floss, and I smell great too! Xx*

Six photos depicted 48-year-old Harry, 5'10, one thoroughly gorgeous
man, of course, from interstate! Where else would he be hiding? Yet
another fetching candidate aged in his late forties, who was none too subtle
in boasting about his wealth online. He was strategically positioned in
front of an array of expensive toys to underscore that he was "financially
solvent." Money was clearly no object. Given this scenario, contemplating
an encounter with a Lady from another State posed few challenges but the
tenor of his conversations alerted me to a scam.

I make no apologies for aiming high.

Harry, in a tailored suit was the epitome of the dignified London
businessman, and the strategically selected shots depicted the suave and
sophisticated Gentleman in all contexts. By all accounts, he was well-
educated, equipped with emotional intelligence, and had a quirky sense
of humour. My weakness for British guys in smart business suits was not
new! His profile entry offered an insight into the meticulous approach, if
a little too contrived, that some guys employed to lure the right woman.
Harry appeared to know exactly what he wanted also. Refreshing change,
I thought.

Telling myself that Harry's profile was too perfect to be authentic did
not exactly appease my disenchantment, but it had to do. I simply chose
to believe he was not real. How could I pass that one up just in case I was
wrong?

I was willing to make an exception that he was not six-foot-tall and did not have blue eyes. Hazel were beautiful too. I was attracted to guys who spoke the Queen's English. I could already hear his classy accent melting my mobile phone. His profile was among the most attractive I had come across and he largely satisfied my criteria for a match. Okay! He was also a few years younger than me.

Did I smell a rat? The burning question was, of course, what the hell was he doing on a dating site? Did he not simply need to look at a woman for her to fall under his spell? At first glance, there was nothing suspicious in his description that would immediately alert a discerning woman. Feminists please do not beat up on me. Lighten up! Life is so serious. I am a romantic and I cannot help what I like. I know he is not real.

His first words, "Why am I on this dating site? Well, I'm English and I arrived in Australia recently... I'm never going to find the girl of my dreams unless I take the plunge and put myself out there." If Ladies buy that line, they are more gullible than me! But I was willing to be trusting this time, for just a little while longer.

Harry ended up taking the prize in this narrative for the most tenacious suitor I came across on a dating site. Located hundreds of kilometres away overlooking a beautiful harbour in NSW, Australia, the British Gentleman was clearly unaccustomed to being rejected by women. He belonged on a *Millionaires* site, not the ones we, mere mortals consulted? Why did he need to dip his toes into this pool?

Harry went out of his way to lure the educated woman for this prize catch, promising interesting rewards for the ones who could detect the incongruous error in his partial profile? I did, and pointed it out to him, thinking he was never going to get around to me anyhow!

The bottom line was, there was no accounting for individual taste. Human beings are just like the popular pack of sweets - *Liquorice All Sorts*.

He responded! Perhaps I was on the wrong track. Could Harry be real? I had become circumspect and I was learning to trust my intuition. I was starting to heed Daniel's advice.

If I selected the hottest guys, with all of the desired attributes, these guys were automatically spoilt for choice in their own State with the array of young, nubile, intelligent and well-presented women who projected the very best images of themselves and were local. No accounting for laziness also. Who wanted to commute when there was eye candy right on their doorstep? Under the circumstances, why would any guy choose me? There was stiff competition out there, although, many guys had told me that many women could not hold an intelligent conversation. I hoped I had the advantage there at least.

However, my age put me behind the eight ball. Has it become more obvious why some of us tell at least this one little fib? We can only hope that we can move past that barrier after the first contact. Ageism is so rampant in our western societies.

Harry's initial invitation to chat further proved difficult to resist, "Hi there Sexy! Want to chat? You are just the kind of Lady that I have my heart set on. Want to play?"

Hmm… Alarm bells… "Want to play?" What began as an exciting and witty exchange where we sparred and laughed for several days turned into a scene of ridiculous sycophantic pleas to meet me. His persistence in getting to know me had me on my guard from the second day when he professed his love for me. I had no intention of falling prey to his games. Five months later, Harry was still contacting me, the following words echoing earlier attempts to get me to change my mind,

> *I'm available and still in love* 😍 *with you xxx [the same message is repeated the next day]*
>
> *Would you care to chat live to see if we connect … lovely profile btw. Told you that the first time… just what I am looking for. here's my phone number again… please call me…*
>
> *Money is no object. I will sail to the Gold Coast to meet you. Please give me the chance to get to know you. Sail away into the sunset with me. You won't regret it, I promise. I will treat you like a Princess, Coco. You deserve it!*

What could I do if deleting profiles was an absolute joke? Ignoring his advances seemed to work temporarily but reporting him seemed a little dramatic, unless of course the tenor of his messages became abusive or obscene.

I kept ignoring Harry, whose succinct, yet eloquent profile entry revealed an educated background and high-powered, entrepreneurial career that positioned him amongst the most privileged on these dating sites. If they were real, of course! There was chemistry. Only, it was in cyberspace! It also begged the question; in case he were real, just how smart was he to keep on pursuing a woman who had absolutely no interest in him? The thrill of the chase still motivated many guys to *Catch,* and sometimes *Release* that intangible love interest, another well-known tactic I had discovered by that stage (Chapter 12). I tried not to judge a book by its cover, but it went against the grain for me to lure him here just to verify my suspicions.

Profile no-nos

For those who are on dating sites for "nothing serious", this is the perfect playground to satisfy all of their desires. For those of us in search of the real deal, not so good!

Still, I was in too deep to give up.

Geoff was a 59-year-old Queenslander, a self-confessed fashionista who wanted nothing serious, whose message arrived in my IN Box, replete with photos displaying his wares.

> *Hi. Im looking for fun food music and fitness. These r wt im interested in. Wking fr an airline i travel regularly. The world is yr oyster. Wd lv to meet a lady who likes these activities and **some mischevious fun.***

> *honest, trustworthy, loyal & affectionate & would expect the same from you. I am after a companion to have a really good time sharing things with.....Hold my hand & come along for a ride with me...Together. I will treat you with respect & caring. I will give you a shoulder to cry on if you need it. I will make mad passionate love to you. We will do everything together and have some of our own space when needed. Life is short lets get our party started today... I am a genuine man...*

I nearly lost my breakfast. At least he was being honest and not attempting to find his Soulmate. But how then, did the site's algorithm send me this match? Especially irksome as I cannot unsee what I saw.

I can still dream... a message for Coco

Learning to listen to my intuition is an ongoing challenge for me but I realise that if I hone this aspect of my personality, with a little perseverance, through trial and error I can achieve my goals... I give myself a high five when trusting my instincts produces the desired results. I am, nonetheless, only human and when trusting my gut leads me astray, I am ropable. What ensues is not pretty. Am I not, after all, still a work in progress? Insomnia kicks in and an unhealthy dose of recriminations and mortification takes root, and this is not easy to shake off. If my behaviour induces this pathetic scenario, I have learned to brush it off before it begins to fester and ruin my life. This is an infinitely worthy addition to my new identity of liberated woman. Let's face it, there is really no point in tormenting myself with doubt and uncertainty; undermining myself, underestimating my own capabilities to snap out of a bad situation and move on. Luckily, there are plenty more fish where the dubious ones came from. The best way of changing this negative mindset is to hop back on my horse.

My neurotransmitters, Dopamine and Serotonin levels will hopefully assist in making me successful this time, bringing me the rewards I am hoping for. As I reignite the fires that brought me to internet dating in the first place, I witness a sudden surge of hope as an attractive individual shows interest. It is sometimes enough to pull me out of the doldrums after a prospective relationship vaporises into thin air. All I need is a little patience. It would also help to find a balance between my high expectations and reality. Always a challenge!

Why not enjoy the journey, stop to enjoy the romance, simultaneously getting to know one or two guys before deciding with whom to move to the next stage? If I am sincere and am genuinely looking for love, that could pose a massive problem if sexual relationships become part of the equation, as emotional attachments are likely to exacerbate the situation. It is bound to affect me psychologically; much more than it does a male, or am I making assumptions? I need to read into the messages, or lack thereof from my suitor. Is there any perceptible emotion, affection, sincere interest conveyed through the text messages? Are they rather a little too egocentric? Has he bothered to call me, to reminisce about the first dates? I cannot afford to ignore my intuition, despite how much I wish to be loved.

I can make myself believe what I wish, ignoring my gut feeling and I will always resort to self-justification to make myself feel better. Is this not human nature? The bottom line is the dating game is ruthless. I have discovered that if I respond too quickly to the Spartan messages, if I appear too needy, too keen, the guy I have fallen for will not rush back to me. He knows I will be there waiting for him. I do not want to play games at this age; if he is into mind games, I let him go. I do not want this trait to define my narrative.

At this stage, I need to look into my personal mirror and discover who I really am, intent on not allowing anyone to hurt me or destroy my self-esteem again. Try as I may, I may never surrender to ageing, but I intend to look after myself. I continue to allow honesty and integrity to guide my moral compass. I am in total control of my thoughts. I cannot control the world, but I can control how I react to it. I will no longer permit anyone to impose their will on me. I have learned to be wary of those who appear to be everything I am looking for early in the wooing stage. I now watch out for little signs that display the propensity for a male to be dictatorial. At this stage of my life, I seriously do not need to have a partner tell me what to do, ever again.

I am now aware that I can so easily set myself up for disappointment. This is one of the toughest lessons online dating has taught me, because I may have given the impression on my profiles that I have delusions of grandeur – an inflated image of my own importance. I am empowered, my personal mirrors reflect the best image of myself that I wish to portray to online users. It was daft for me to make spurious assumptions that I could attract exactly the type of person I was looking for simply because I had never had this Smorgasbord to choose from. He must be out there, right? In a bar or club, the chances of locking eyes or lips with an attractive guy are dramatically limited.

I seriously need to come down a peg or two to avoid ending up a basket case. Jumping back onto the roller-coaster will bring hope for brighter prospects and should assist in extricating myself from the despair that sets in when the sought-after relationship turns out to be lacklustre or at worst, ends up in disaster.

At this point, I am wondering whether I am engaging in self-sabotage... I am not being negative, but my *Happy Divorcées' Club* is beckoning right about now, where my BFFs and others of the Elite Club are engrossed in joyous and frank conversations, waxing lyrical on topics that are taboo in other circles, without being judged; feasting and indulging in champagne and merriment; and not a guy in sight. Even if there is an intrepid heterosexual male within their midst, he is likely to be welcomed; alternatively, he will be put through the wringer and may not venture their way again. Who likes to tread on broken glass? Ouch! That large Pizza Margherita, the Sauvignon Blanc, the tub of Gelato with two spoons and the box of guilt-free chocolates are looking rather appetising right now.

Never fear! All is not all lost. I am entitled to make my own choices and my own mistakes; that is what makes me liberated without having to endorse everything the *Women's Libbers* stand for. I am Coco! Sassy, mighty, independent and I have a voice. Knowledge is power!

Sam the A-checklister

Of course, this is all about my checklist, but the guy's checklist is just as important. I knew I would ignore this at my own peril. I'm guessing that those who contacted me, I ticked their boxes. But, when I contacted a few guys, it really annoyed me that they rejected me.

Do guys have checklists? You had better believe it. And it is deeper than just good looks. Here is one of my favourites,

> *I love my boatin, my campin, my fishin. If you aint into motocross. Then your four out of four – and your outta here.*

Well! That was inviting! Not! It dawned on me that we were not that different after all. Perhaps, the sensitive guys were too scared to lay their feelings on the line; for the same reasons I avoided making myself too vulnerable. No one likes to be bullied, abused emotionally or disparaged. Online dating was a steep learning curve for all of us. The confident and arrogant ones did not give a damn what a woman wanted, really, still convinced they could catch their prize, by hook or by crook.

4

Present your best face forward, but I have so many facets

There appears to be an obvious discrepancy in ratings of 'adequate profiles' when the sexes are juxtaposed with each other. An assessment of various sites illustrates that archetypal middle-aged male profiles are notoriously poorly constructed. This causes frequent derision for their lack of effort and imagination; instead of a self-portrait, profiles often feature distorted Selfies and/or images of their favourite animals, tiger, gorilla or snake; not just their pets. This trend suggests low self-esteem and insecurity are not the preserve of females only, a perception reinforced in discussions with my male friends. Irrespective of this, these profiles are not necessarily an impediment to instant sexual 'hookups'.

Testimonies of some of the male participants have judged the female profiles to be largely well-presented, the majority of women posting the best possible images based on their self-perceived attributes, physical, social and emotional. In sharp contrast to this positive evaluation, some women's profiles are allegedly classed as offensive and insulting and any self-respecting male would simply move on to the next one, or report them; or, let's face it, indulge in gratuitous sex. Why do they not simply join the sites that are expressly engineered for 'frisky hookups'? The erroneous assumption that if these women are found on ostensibly "legitimate" sites, there is some measure of respectability is quite a worry for me. It really pays to heed the advice I was given before I began this journey, "Due diligence is mandatory prior to joining a dating site."

New Day, New Dawn, Full Moon…

Here we go! Long day at work. I decided to try a new free dating site. So much hype about it but I do not need to stay on it for long. I just need to do some research. How weird that I keep doing this around the full moon. My attention span on these sites is short-lived, fortunately, because I am so busy with work.

Glass of wine, nibbles. Who needs dinner anyway? Cooking? No way!

Swipe right, swipe right. Cute, Hmm… Not bad at all. Wonder if he is going to respond… Exactly what I am looking for.

> *White Caucasian, blue eyes, well-educated professional, handsome, 1,85cm, principled with old fashioned values, well-travelled, sportive and only adult children visiting!*

Sounds like another fairy tale! Coco was about to journey through the looking glass once again.

Hope it is not too good to be true, except that he lives in Brisbane. Damn! I am sick of this broken record.

I will send him a quick message; nothing to lose. No one knows who I am, even if some clever ones have used a dictionary to decipher my cryptic online names. Interesting sensation of freedom. No tangible censure…

Yet, I still react vehemently to criticism… I am finally satisfied with my profile. "Average" build was the first thing that I needed to change on my existing profile; "athletic" more accurately depicting my stature according to Michael who insisted I was anything but average. Comforting to know. I quickly adjusted my page but hoped to get off this "Zoo."

I am now more aware of my thoughts and insecurity about how guys respond to the information I post online. Work in progress! I will amend my profile only if I deem it justified. I was getting pretty good at the subtle remodelling of my cyber identity. This site was a welcome change after having been duped into paying a lot of money for a site that was clearly fraudulent. Everyone knew of it, so I thought that I could get lucky.

Swipe left! Left. Left. Left. No, no, no! Seriously, you have got to be kidding! One swipe right after all this time. Useless. Move on!

Profile creation – learning to read between the lines

I realised finally during this journey, that people do not use a magnifying mirror when they look at me. I need to relax…

So, here I am at the coal face trying to conjure original ways of remodeling my identity, a perennial exercise, whilst focusing on ethical conduct. Now, being mysterious is not a bad thing if I want to find someone who is really interested in delving beneath the mask I present to the world for self-preservation. However, being too enigmatic could cause a problem. It is really hard to know exactly what to divulge on these sites where scammers are ready to pounce. I did not want to scare away the fish in this pool of men on the Gold Coast; although our mutual lack of interest was patently obvious. Whilst the parameters set in place efficiently screened the profiles on one site at least, allowing only a select few to pass through the cracks, I had to admit that the diminished interest continued to play on my mind.

I had effectively maintained the potential for Matched candidates at almost zero! Not a comforting thought… I could not feign my annoyance and it disturbed me. If I did the Maths, by the time I had eliminated those I believed to be ineligible, based on age, level of education, marital status and dissimilar interests as the preliminary criteria, the remaining eligible fish on the Gold Coast were few and far between.

I had to face reality. I was examining the theory that that the biggest impediment to my finding a partner on the Gold Coast was that I was a fish out of water. Pure and simple! I hate the heat and the humidity, and my favourite pursuits do not revolve around the sun, the surf, and the sand. If I prefer more sophisticated and cultural activities, I guess I had to pay the price somehow. This town has huge advantages. It is a friendly place and family oriented and logistically, there is no better place to be. The new suburbs on man-made canals and lakes are beautiful and new, and the winters are gorgeous. What winter? I need more!

The nasty comment from one of the very first contacts I had on one site had a lot to do with my decision to keep a wide berth for a while, hiding my profile from public view; counterproductive but safer. Unfortunately, those I rejected could still reach me to try their luck again or to proffer caustic remarks if they so wished. I could denounce them or leave them alone in the hope they would desist.

Adrian was one of the annoying intellectuals I met when I thought that being ultra-polite was the done thing, but I stopped chatting with him online after two weeks, ignoring his repeated attempts to reinitiate the conversation. He had taken umbrage at being ignored and waited for three months before sending me a biting comment that took me aback, "Take a break, Honey!" I found this ironic as Adrian was clearly a persistent subscriber on the site; I wondered how many women he had met. I was learning fast… The internet savvy appear to know exactly who is on that site and when; and some have even worked out how many times you are on it as they keep tabs. Are they stalkers?

I was irate by that stage; still smarting from the criticism as if Adrian had said it to my face. What a bizarre effect! A lesson for me when I have heated arguments or feel the need to use invectives to decimate the character of those who abuse me. I had to invent ways of shutting the conversation down with Adrian, but I remained dignified, always. It was rather sad really. I felt quite guilty as I wondered how many lonely guys had posted inadequate Selfies and poorly constructed profiles that generated little or no interest. Were online interactions all they had to brighten their day? The women could well be in the same boat. I really had little to complain about under the circumstances. Always a little wisdom to be gained from perspective.

This incident led me to deeper self-reflection. It suddenly dawned on me that I too, could end up like Adrian and a few other guys whose registered names are visible each time I log on. On second thoughts, no way! Not for me! Some individuals appear to be trawling continuously for a desirable companion. If they have been internet dating for years, are they likely to stop? Is their search for whatever it is they hope to find tantamount to an addiction? This game seems impossible to reverse, but perhaps they could be *voyeurs* instead of actively searching for someone? Who knows? Whatever the motivations of such daters, this is not my story.

This episode, in fact, reinforced my bad habit of immediately integrating other people's negative opinions of me. Why did I react so vehemently to a comment from a guy who did not even know me? Why was I so over-dependent on the opinions of others to accept myself the way I was? I still could not resolve this question. Rejection or negative comments in all contexts, not just online, always induced me to effect changes to my personality, looks and behaviour. Why did I give "others" such supremacy over me? The revelation was disquieting.

I was powerless to change this dependency on others because of my vacillating levels of self-esteem. It always led back to this. I suddenly realised that my efforts, since my separation, to rebuild my self-worth had not produced the desired effects. I had attempted to restore self-love, to believe that self-ness, a laudable trait according to self-help books, was in fact not narcissistic; I convinced myself that I did not need the opinions of others to make me feel good or bad, reiterating to myself like a broken record, "You have to stop caring what others think!" By this stage my kids were probably ready to sign the paperwork to have me institutionalised.

Burrowing more deeply within myself, I wondered if I appeared desperate to the males who spent so much time on these sites? Whilst this was a new journey for me, some had been on the sites intermittently over ten years or more. I was astounded to learn this from some guys and wondered at their instrumental motivation, hooking up, looking for love or friendship? I was being judged and I objected to this. I had tried to make it clear that I was not hopping onto the Millennial bandwagon of sexual pursuits. Online dating and sex were so intricately entwined. Heaven help those of us who do not subscribe to this behaviour.

My efforts to explain this stance produced a spirited exchange with a gorgeous Italian guy with whom I communicated in Italian, to begin with. The conversation was light-hearted and fun initially...

Sandro - the charm of southern Europe

Sandro, short for Alessandro, represented a potentially suitable Beau for me, even if he was in Melbourne; where else? The 6', 51-year-old was the tallest Italian male I had ever come across; and this time I did not consider him out of my reach. I wanted to investigate just how compatible we were. Sandro's views on internet dating were enlightening.

> *I'm not in to dating games. I'm sick of the fake photos on dating sites. I'm not looking to meet or date as many women*

as possible. I came out of a relationship and I don't think a relationship is for me, not at this time in my life. Also I'm not planning to live the rest of my life in Australia, hoping I can go back to Italy one day... there is no spontaneity and curiosity in people down here... I'm not promiscuous, I don't like that. I am very careful about who I'm having sex with. Great sex is only great when I can feel safe about the woman I'm enjoying it with.

When I told Sandro that I found his honesty refreshing, telling him I was not into hookups either, he misconstrued my reply and became quite cheeky, "You must enjoy great sex then... Nice sensual and curvy body. Too bad you are far away! Would you like me to come up to see you??" Lost in translation!

What ensued then surprised me. "Do you want to talk on the phone? Here is my phone number." Sandro promptly changed his profile heading into Italian suggesting he was heading off... to Italy I imagined, where his adult son had returned. I also noticed he had posted four other recent photos.

Okay! We had only just met online, communicating on and off on a Saturday. Those Italian boys sure moved fast! What I had not counted on that evening was an impassioned debate on Italian politics that lasted into the night. Sandro was polyglot; proficient in four languages, and his command of the English language was excellent after years in the US. However, his heavily accented pronunciation and mix of Italian, American and Australian vernacular made for an interesting conversation.

Sandro and I talked for a while on the usual topics and then the conversation turned abruptly to politics. Thoughts of romance can easily turn to politics for the Italians I have met. I watch Italian news each morning, so I was *au fait* with political developments in Italy as well as other European countries. The Italians I know are passionate in their views on the perceived malaise currently troubling their beloved country (and Europe) – from high youth unemployment and a stagnating economy, to immigration, corruption and organised crime. I decided at midnight that

I needed to get some sleep. Wow! That was intense, but energising. I ended up dreaming of Italy that night…

The spirited discussions continued for a few more days but did not lead to an encounter between Sandro and me. Shame! Life, and distance just got in the way. Would have been nice to meet him…

Tactical plans

It seems that my strategies to find Mr Right call for far more sophisticated measures to complement the linguistic and physical reconstruction of my online profiles, all subtly different, covering all bases. My immediate strategy is retail therapy. Easy and ever so satisfying! I have acquired some excellent pieces for my new wardrobe and hope to maintain my desired weight. Retail therapy is an effective adjunct in lifting my self-esteem and whilst it makes a dint on my Credit Card bank balance it is more satisfying than consuming chocolates and sweets. Chocoholics might disagree with me. Next, reflecting on my physiological traits, I have decided that it is time to change several aspects of my physique, a tough ask without plastic surgery - not part of my agenda. This is a very foolish move I realise because I seem to be the only one viewing my imperfections with magnifying glasses.

I am my own harshest critic.

Whilst it is human nature for individuals to be dissatisfied with some aspect of their physiological features, such as a big nose, skin conditions, freckles, short stature, frizzy hair or baldness, most people manage to find a balance between their looks and their personalities and other redeemable qualities. Having said that, men in general are, I suspect, less inclined than women to be too self-critical about their physical appearance. Empirical evidence supports this fact. Some individuals at least succeed in reconciling the differences, dismissing the perceived "flaws" when they acknowledge that there is no solution other than self-acceptance.

That some people literally do not care what they look like still amazes me! I tend to focus on the negative aspects, amplifying them until I rectify the problems. Because I had allowed it in the past, people preyed on those weaknesses. Fortunately, those who have my best interests at heart or those who meet me for the first time focus immediately on the holistic image, the whole package. This is human nature, so why do some of us tear ourselves to shreds, attempting to fix every imperfection; making a mountain out of a mole hill? Like the proverbial pimple on one's nose that is magnified in our imaginations. When my friends fail to see what is troubling me when I gaze into my mirror, I am completely baffled that they cannot detect the imperfections, the blemishes that I have been trying to erase or hide, coming at a cost, of course.

Beauty therapy is expensive, and I have taken care of every aspect that does not require surgical intervention. I ask myself if I am self-indulgent? And my judge declares 'Guilty!' I am on a mission to become the best version of "me." I have gone to great lengths to try to be the healthiest version of myself using herbal medicines. I acknowledge fully that the vitamins and minerals that I consume are often considered to have a placebo effect but my answer to the sceptics is always the same, "I realise this constitutes expensive urine, but if I feel fabulous with boundless energy and vitamins help me defy my age, I think that I am doing something right."

When those closest to me happen to pinpoint one little tell-tale spot on my face that escaped my magic mirror, all hell can break loose! "Really? Where? [the compact mirror is always at the ready] I really did not need more complexes...

Debates on self-esteem issues on social media are common, often endorsing a view that it is the women themselves who are their own worst enemies when it comes to self-sabotage. Some women are effectively too harsh on themselves, even if the blame is invalidly attributed to males. It is difficult to undo decades of emotional abuse in the form of judgments that individuals make on their self-image, some more vulnerable than others. This certainly reveals the fragility of the human psyche. Even if a woman is slightly overweight, it is highly likely that her personal mirror will project an enormous image of her body. That is all she can see. If she sees a woman with beautiful legs, she will automatically wish her legs were just as slim and long, like the allegorical stairway to heaven. There does not appear to be a solution to the exponential threats to our self-worth to which we are exposed because multimedia is so aesthetically-focused. We simply need to educate ourselves and become more aware of coping strategies that can assist in mitigating the adverse effects.

These deliberations triggered a horrid thought. Could I potentially be diagnosed as suffering from *BDD (Body Dismorphic Disorder)?* Further investigation on this issue in conjunction with an appraisal of my own behaviour during this dating process reassured me that this was just me catastrophising.

At this juncture, it is important to note that, in the era I grew up, dating for women was not encouraged in many Southern European cultures and my family endorsed this tradition as my siblings and I progressed from puberty to adulthood. Therefore, the dating game is somewhat confronting to many of us from such religiously draconian backgrounds that had vastly different rules for the males and females. Arranged marriages are fortunately not part of my family tradition but it is not easy to engage in the dating game in the same way as those from liberal backgrounds have always done. I find it hard to discard the strict Christian moral codes that were inculcated during my formative years; irrespective of age. For me, this dating game is the first I have experienced in the true meaning of the term, something that is proving puzzling for some of the guys I am dating. Thankfully, most of my Beaux respect and appreciate me for who I am, rather than challenge this traditional behavioural trait; some even welcome the lack of pressure; refreshing for me to hear.

Still, not an easy question to negotiate. This is an emotionally charged issue for me as my mother is concerned that people might get the impression that I am capricious; a *Butterfly* perhaps? I was mortified by this. My mother needs to understand that online dating does not imply loose morals. This form of dating is here to stay, and semantics play a significant role in what the term entails. We must adapt but not necessarily discard our values. Hard for that generation to accept so many new trends.

Whilst past relationships have contributed to a negative impact on my self-concept and consequent lack of self-acceptance, I believe that I am on the way to recovery, still very much a work in progress but, nonetheless, making inroads into redefining my identity. I aim to find synchrony, in the way that I wish to be perceived and the way others perceive me. Mirrors are incredibly significant in establishing the happy medium but ultimately, I believe I know what I need to do.

The poignant lyrics of the beautiful song of my idol, Whitney Houston echo in my ears,

> *...Learning to love yourself*
> *It is the greatest love of all...*
> *...Show [the children] all the beauty they possess inside,*
> *Give them a sense of pride...*
> *...Find [our] strength in love.”[10]*

I do not need to depend on others to achieve this state of well-being. Or do I? I can learn to like myself first and this will be a stepping stone to loving myself. The powerful lyrics are life changing for me and I draw strength and courage from this amazing artist who passed away at the age of 48.

---

[10] *Houston. W.* (1985) Greatest Love of All. Songwriters: LINDA CREED, MICHAEL MASSER© Sony/ATV Music Publishing LLC, Universal Music Publishing Group. https://www.azlyrics.com/lyrics/whitneyhouston/greatestloveofall.html

PRINCES OR TOADS?

5

Quirky, weird and not so wonderful

Anecdotal evidence suggests that in protest of the largely derogatory perceptions of masculine profiles on dating sites, honourable men are rising in defence of the contingent of males who distinguish themselves from the masses. A small army of good guys are lining up to catch the prize... In some of the profiles, many guys in their fifties and sixties are challenging the trends by becoming more obdurate in the face of gender-based discrimination. Go Guys! You are exactly what we, Ladies are looking for.

It did not take long for me to reach a stage of my journey where a period of contentment and decompression replaced the stresses and challenges that defined my dating experience from the beginning.

The boys in their fifties sure gave me a run for my money. I have certainly enjoyed my exchanges with many of them online, a few graduating to exciting dates along this journey. That they did not work out is no one's fault. These are guys I appreciate and like a lot. Unfortunately, with no spark, only friendship remains, and this, only in some cases. The following vignettes depict the panoply of odd or quirky dating behaviours that created a lot of mirth and provoked further reflection on my progress in finding the one I seek.

Gerard, The Mad Professor

When I met 51-year-old Gerard, 5'11, from Brisbane, he looked dramatically shorter and effectively personified the Mad Professor with grey hair, in contrast with the attractive figure he posted online in a suit and sporting a *short back and sides* haircut. Old habits die hard. To my consternation, this penchant for draconian haircuts was a behaviour that was entrenched in many guys from the 50+ cohort. Do they imagine that we all prefer a number one haircut? Ultimately the grey hair always becomes much more prominent and sticks out. This changes their image totally in some cases, especially when their photos are dated.

I could not contain my surprise when Gerard turned up; his British sense of humour left me even more wide-eyed as he joked that he had run a kilometre from where he had parked – plausible but not smart! His first comment was, "Wow! You're brown!" Considering Gerard had asked me on the phone, "Has anyone ever called you *Chocolate Éclair?*" I looked baffled. I had paid that one. It was hilarious. I had been called *"Café au lait"* before, being olive-skinned, and had not taken offence. But, my photos were genuine, not airbrushed. I am of European heritage, I have olive skin. His ex-wife and ex-girlfriends were Italian. Why was he so surprised? He quickly explained this was a compliment. Go figure! Gerard was not as tall as I had visualised from his posts, possibly because I had recently spent time with Daniel, who was 6'2. He was proud of his strategically torn designer jeans that is the rage with the youngsters but did not quite work on a man in his 50s, at least in my eyes. He donned his favourite jacket, confirming that it had turned 30 the day before. I could not agree more, for vastly different reasons.

In our phone exchanges, Gerard had suggested he bring his two dogs to our first date; whilst I love *Fluff Balls,* I began to worry. He reconsidered, and I was relieved. He was caught in traffic as the early winter weather was spectacular and everyone was heading to the Gold Coast. Gerard pre-empted my reaction by apologising on the phone for his wild, unruly hair that had resulted from the bad haircut the day before. It could not be tamed, and he warned me that he looked like a Mad Professor. Being a little overdressed for our brunch date, he assured me that whilst he was smart casual in a T-shirt, jeans and jacket, very debonair, this was not an issue. The guys I had met from Brisbane had looked good in shorts and

T-shirts on past dates, quite refreshing, because they largely missed the mark on the Gold Coast, complete with thong sandals! Some high-class establishments on the coast apparently now accepted diverse standards in the male dress codes. The women were dressed to the hilt in contrast; this made for a largely incongruous image.

I felt silly because I did not do "casual" well, but I had no intention of changing this part of my personality. We had a stimulating afternoon over coffee and lunch, covering wide and intellectually dynamic discussions on many issues. On this level, we were most compatible. When we returned to the Surf Club for lunch, the place was teeming with people. Gerard handed me a $20 note and said, "I'll race out on the balcony to find us a table. A Schooner or fifty lashes!" I stood there like a stunned Mullet and said, "Qué?" I said I was buying and asked him what he wished to drink. He repeated, "A Schooner or fifty lashes and a Sav Blanc for you" pointing at the beers on tap! My ignorance on all things beer-related became evident, as I hated the amber liquid. I had not heard "...of *Fifty Lashes* (a type of beer)." Who knew? He added sardonically that he did not visualise himself a Buccaneer who was going to give me 50 lashes unless I bought him a beer. Goes to show, how many things get lost in translation.

Poor Gerard was not happy when I did not take him up on a second date, but I had vowed to no longer prolong an encounter if it did not hold promise. I thanked him profusely, admitting that I liked him but could promise no more. I did not "get" his sense of humour but he was a very nice guy. Future meetings were totally up to him. His response had surprised me, "I can deduce from your text that we didn't click and that's ok. You/I need to know these things. No point one person liking the other's company and not reciprocated. That's obvious!"

Further miscommunication occurred in our text messages that left me mystified but we luckily clarified these. I believed I had made a friend and I was pleased, but I have not heard from him since.

I suspect this face-saving measure is fast becoming popular for both sexes when one does not wish to continue dating someone.

It might seem ruthless but the *Band-Aid Strategy* that the Millennials employ is starting to make a lot of sense to me. Hurting the nice guys I meet is anathema to me! I do not want to discombobulate them. Confusing messages are not good for anyone and friendship is rarely an option for many guys. Perhaps they have too many friends and cannot contemplate adding any more to their busy lives? "All or nothing? Take your pick!" is fast becoming the recurring slogan of online dating. Quite sad in my opinion, because I love to make new friends. There is no harm in this as I wait for Prince Charming to turn up.

Bill - Compulsive dater

Bill's profile looked most promising - good looking, blond and blue eyed, of course. I was amazed that he had contacted me and met me so quickly. This was the antithesis of the online dating tactic - *Breadcrumbing,* (Chapter 12) employed by gamesters, that I was soon to discover. An interesting phone conversation confirmed that we had common interests. His photos included attractive images in various locations, just as other attractive profiles had done. They portrayed a well-to-do, debonair, educated Australian. This was indeed interesting and looking good for my future meetings. I was delighted to have attracted a man who was not an armchair sportsman; most auspicious for me. I was very keen to meet this intellectual, well-travelled and interesting guy.

Whilst Bill was a tad shorter than the 6' Hunk I had expected to find, the posted image dating back five years was no issue and he was casually but impeccably dressed. He recognised me instantly, telling me that I was curiously in the minority of online daters who presented current or recent photos. Yet, the guys persisted in providing dated pictures. As it was 3:00 PM, a little late for coffee, the gentleman suggested a drink and a bite to eat. I opted for a glass of wine whilst Bill ordered a beer and an intricately composed, fancy burger. I wanted to avoid tackling a messy burger on a first date. Bill's lunch arrived, and he gazed hesitantly at his crisp, white linen shirt and trendy pastel coloured shorts and back at the "fancy burger" once again, but he was starving!

Bill was from south of the border and I met him quite early in online dating. I nicknamed him the Compulsive Dater. Confessing he was averaging an excessive number of dates per month, mostly coffee, I also thought of adding "Coffee Snob" to his profile. I marvelled at his addiction to online dating and his inexhaustible stamina and imagined he was quite wealthy to be able to afford this lifestyle because he insisted on paying! He was hooked on this game. How did he manage to work? Perhaps he was a self-made millionaire.

I had already started to wonder about this date when, without so much as an apology, Bill began to undo the laces of his Loafers (masculine footwear) and promptly took off his shoes. It was a hot day, but the restaurant was air-conditioned. Perhaps it was the anticipation and excitement of our date that had him a little flushed? Next, Bill attacked his meal, literally, strategically trying to catch most of it in his mouth; a tad cleverer than the restaurateur who had devised this burger, garnished far too generously with beetroot. Not, I would imagine, strongly conducive to encouraging return custom.

I could not hide my sardonic grin when he narrowly missed his shirt as the beetroot and mayonnaise covered the sides of his mouth and careered back onto the plate. The incredibly farcical episode took a turn for the worse. I had found the encounter amusing, even promising until he had removed his shoes. I let him out of his misery and wiped his mouth for him. He was a nice guy, after all.

What happened next floored me! We have all, at one time or another suffered undue embarrassment because of wilted spinach leaves or other offending morsels of food that latch onto our teeth. How does one delicately extricate oneself from such situations? Not advisable, but forgivable, if you cannot make a quick exit to the bathroom, you may politely excuse yourself, turn around and cover your mouth and use a toothpick to dislodge the offending titbit.

Quite unperturbed, the complete reverse image of the "cultured" Gentleman that he had portrayed, Bill began to pick his teeth with his nails (no idea whether toothpicks were available or not), prodding in several places before succeeding in dislodging the food that he promptly swallowed. I watched in amazement, trying to hide my indignation that Bill had such little respect for me. I was most embarrassed. Whilst he continued to pose questions that I was no longer inclined to answer, I deflected them and brought the encounter to an abrupt end, feigning another engagement in 30 minutes.

Bill had spent the whole 90 minutes posing leading questions that allowed me little time to reciprocate, making me feel uncomfortable. I felt under pressure to reply honestly and openly, with my heart on my sleeve as per usual. Under the gaze of the Spanish Inquisition, (there was a definite pattern emerging) I gauged his reaction before disclosing information about my family, my career and more tentatively about my former relationships and the type of guy I was hoping to find. He seemed honest enough but was far too inquisitive for my liking.

When I quizzed him about his life he did not reveal a great deal. He talked a little about former relationships and more about the "interesting" dates he had been on. One-sided conversations are no fun! He had driven a long way and he had another date in the evening. Thank God, this awkward date was over!

To make matters worse, I was standing at his side when he paid the bill and the lady asked how everything had gone. Bill laughed and said this was our first date. I wanted to sink into the floor. As the girl had witnessed the eating fiasco, she tried hard to hide her amusement. I was a local. He was not.

Bill left knowing a lot about me and I had discovered little more than his first phone call had revealed. Except of course that he had poor etiquette. The body language was priceless that day and would have provided a brilliant skit for those who love to post their dining experiences on social media.

At the car, Bill hugged me like a long-time friend and left, promising that we would see each other again. The image of his behavioural *faux pas* came back to haunt me. Neither of us intended to arrange a second meeting as could be expected. Very practical indeed.

This date left me wondering what Bill hoped to achieve by dating women whom he interrogated without disclosing his own personal information. Was this a power play, revealing autocratic tendencies? It could just be his *MO (Modus Operandi)*, and I suspect that the moment he understood I was not beholden to him, there was not much point in pursuing the lead. The incident with the Loafers was a definite deal breaker; strike one! The teeth picking was strike two, and he was out! Not waiting for strike three in this game. The dating experience was making me quite intransigent, feeling the pressure of finding someone. No point in pussyfooting through the tulips. Plenty more fish in the sea!

So much for the good looking tall, blond, blue-eyed guys! When I viewed the photo gallery of the males I had contacted, there was an ocean of the deepest blue eyes staring back at me. I am blushing! Is this bordering on insanity?

If I have been a little unfair to Bill, rest assured that Karma would bring me down a peg or two! On the 4th date with a charming guy named Steve, who was happy to accept friendship, prior to a movie, we headed to my favourite Burger restaurant. This was four months after meeting Bill. I have rarely eaten other than homemade burgers to avoid embarrassment, but it was more expedient than dining late after a movie. My vain attempts at trying to bite into the burger in a ladylike manner triggered my experience with Bill. Say no more... Must be an art to this! Best to leave the farcical image to the imagination - five large paper serviettes later, all crumpled into a mess says it all. Steve was the perfect Gentleman and reassured me that I had not disgraced myself. In truth, I had not dropped anything on my clothes, but I felt it was payback. It was hilarious because Steve really liked me. It was Karma! Of course, Steve somehow managed not to drop any of the sauce on his plate!

Jeremy and Cas

Now, best not to jump to conclusions. I have not dated two guys at once. *Mon Dieu!* Even French Ladies would not do that. Or would they? I just happened to have a third date with a 52-year-old Gold Coast Gentleman who had his 14-year-old son, Cas for the week. Who the hell takes his son on a date? Only teasing. I had no objections in having dinner with both. What an amazing evening. Who has so much fun with a teenager around? We giggled the whole night speaking in two languages and learned a thing or two from each other. So entertaining to see the exchange between father and son. They had a language all their own and the connection was a joy to observe. When I posed a question about the behaviour of a guy I had dated, wondering how I should interpret it from a male's perspective, the ensuing "look" between the two boys was priceless. "Please explain!" I requested, but really needed no explanation.

By the time we left, Cas agreed with me that we really were from different planets. He found this so cool. One thing left a massive grin on my face, anyhow. When Cas queried my age, I asked him to guess. Jeremy warned his son not to fall into the trap of "Does my *derrière* look big in this?" but Cas came straight out with, "Late thirties!" Woohoo! Friends for life! Whereupon, we ended up with our own version of the secret handshake/high five, standing up in the restaurant, no less! Almost made up for the innocent question Cas posed when I was speaking about the manipulative antics of some women online who were chasing a rich man. "Are **YOU** a Gold Digger?" That, I must say, left me floored.

When I told Cas how old my daughters were, he stopped in his tracks and started to recalculate how old I should be. Memorable night. So much fun. Cannot blame me for allowing such a compliment go to my head! Kids are brutally honest. No need to doubt the veracity of their words.

A post-script to this story describes eloquently what the look between Cas and his father signified, and why words were superfluous. Cas' mother had arranged for her son to go to a function without asking whether he was interested in attending or not. That look between father and son was evidently par for the course where interactions between the ex and the teenage son were concerned.

Jeremy and I have become close friends and we decided to treasure our friendship instead of searching for more.

Other behaviours

As the dating journey progressed, I was surprised that a significant percentage of the males readily confessed they were their own worst enemies when it came to structuring their profiles. Just as many criticised their cohort of daters as emotionally inept, telling me they had no idea how to express themselves to attract the type of woman they were seeking. In admitting this, they hoped to attract women who appreciated their vulnerabilities. I was evidently no expert but for those candidates who approached me, finding the task challenging, I offered a few pointers to help them along their way, but only when solicited. I did not have the answers, but I wanted to encourage them along their way.

I, for one, firmly subscribe to Dr John Gray's theory that *Men are from Mars and Women are from Venus.*[11] It is not rocket science to comprehend that if some guys engineer their profiles to suit the tastes of other men, they are highly unlikely to secure the woman of their dreams. I do not know how many women are enthralled by all manner of adventure sports

---

[11] Gray, J. (1992). Men are from Mars, Women are from Venus. Harper Collins. US

that are traditionally the sanctuary of males, but that cohort can feel free to pack their bags and move to the Gold Coast, like so many "Mexicans" have done for decades, my family included; the term, in no way derogatory, refers to those of us relocating from Victoria and New South Wales. They are sure to find what they are looking for. I could assist in finding them if they wish because I am now savvy in this internet dating game. I would never have moved to the Coast if my parents had not migrated up north in the eighties. Give me the cooler climates any day! Constant rain... not so much!

My dates volunteered more information to help me understand why the archetypal male profiles were not the least bit complimentary. These guys voiced their opinions on other men's headlines and the content pages because they recognised the negative effects gleaned from the perspectives of the women they dated. They confirmed that these profiles incurred derision and disparaging comments from the female members who simply skipped over the less imaginative entries.

Those who are self-assured, educated and privileged are clearly not part of the general population and they go to great lengths to distance themselves from the tribe. The majority of males who do not belong to the *Male Yacht Club* rate their personal efforts in constructing a profile as 'a challenge, ineffective, inarticulate, inadequate, inappropriate...' Their reliance on dreadful Selfies, coupled with their lack of expertise generates distorted and pixelated images with only a modicum of lexical support, and no effort at correct spelling. Bizarre how some sites refused numerous clear photos I posted, because of excessive or insufficient degrees of pixels. Frustrating, considering the lengths I had to go to, to view some belonging to males! Did not appreciate the double standards.

The consensus from the male and female daters who provided anecdotes about their journeys online does not paint a pretty picture, especially about those from the Gold Coast. They are largely pejorative. It appears, little attempt is made by the guys to do better because they are clearly "stumped for words", to employ a familiar term I recorded. Every imaginable outdoor activity depicts them to a tee... disclaimer attached, "Woman who dont, dont bother applying!"

I was not the only one with a draconian criterial selection! Each to his own, but really? Was the predominant stereotypical image posted in order to attract only certain types of women? Or, to dissuade the Ladies from searching for the "One"? The Australian vernacular is colourful. There was a plethora of beer-swilling middle-aged men, *Bogans* (unsophisticated and proud of it) with beer gut protruding from their singlets and their *Stubbies* (workwear shorts), their prized catch in prominent position - a large Groper, no less; their 4x4 or their Ute (Utility Truck), their motorbike, their *Tinnies* (open boats), their pets, bizarre pets in some cases or their favourite – patting a tiger; some posted their pet instead of their face; try a Gorilla! I swear. And who could forget the epitome of Australian mateship - their best friends in tow with a *Stubby* in hand (small beer in this context)? Which one was it? Who was the candidate? Perhaps two birds with one stone? Cheeky! Deciding which male was on offer to the women clearly involved a game.

The most depressing thing was that many men tended to be judged by their proverbial covers. I admit fully that I turned down an attractive male responding to my criteria selection when, with one click, I was assaulted by the image of the guy and his snake! If you have a snake phobia as acute as mine, yes, I realise it is irrational, there is no way I can contemplate being anywhere near a man who loves snakes. It is probably his pet. Neuro Linguistic Programming and Hypnotherapy have failed. I have tried, to no avail to rid myself of this debilitating fear.

The most appalling comment I recorded from a 54-year-old male in reference to the images of the 60+ age groups, was quite confronting; he was deploring the older guys who hit on the younger women, "All overweight and don't care how they look... Nasal hermit crabs hanging out..." Ouch! Where did that come from? I was aghast to hear this. The complex issue of self-portrayal, honesty and integrity was evidently contingent on the instrumental motivation of both sexes when they embarked on this dating game. I certainly gained fascinating insights into the male psyche, and anecdotally into the female. My aim was not to maraud as a male to examine the female profiles. That is tantamount to Catfishing (Chapter 11) - a complex ruse where individuals with nefarious objectives post multiple fictional personas in order to lure unsuspecting online daters into a relationship that most likely will never materialise.

Most of the guys I met in their sixties living on the Gold Coast were largely Australians who had not exactly looked after themselves; perhaps because of a hedonistic lifestyle. They gave the impression they were invincible and would not die of skin cancer. They were not *SNAGS, Sensitive New Age Guys* who displayed their emotions, who moisturised, and were acutely aware of their health; let alone conscious that at least 30+ sunscreen as part of their daily ritual would preserve their youthful complexion!

The contingent of well-preserved 60+ males I had contact with, similarly to their counterparts in their fifties, were the ones who lied about their age online to avoid being pursued by older women on a mission to secure a younger man. If their group fell into the wrong age bracket, it was not unusual to hear the following comment, "I am tired of 78-year-old women hitting on me. And they are relentless. Let's face it, there are not too many women out there who look like Jane Fonda at 79." Well, for some women, plastic surgery is fine if you are so inclined and you have the means; and if you are prepared to endure the painful recovery.

Reflection

Why do some guys think they are the only ones who can snare a youngster? With the ostensible over-proliferation of eligible females engaged in online dating, I doubt there are too many younger men who have succumbed to the temptation of spending the rest of their lives with older women. Recent reports indicate a large number of 60+ guys suffer from skin cancers and ongoing complications from prostate issues, knee and hip complaints, that are becoming more prevalent in our society, yet many live in denial and refuse to see a doctor! Let alone give natural therapies a go. In addition to this, they continue to search for a younger woman, settling for one in her fifties if they must. The poor old Dears will just have to do!

Make no mistake! It seems we share something after all, the practice of telling a little white lie about our veritable age.

David

When an apparently suitable candidate in the medical field contacted me, my interest was piqued. Eligible? Hell, yes!

David was a professor with tenure in a Brisbane university and a specialist with his own practice. He was very busy but ready to find love again. Anticipation filled the air as I prepared for a date after just a brief phone conversation.

The self-professed millionaire did not meet my prescriptive list of desirable values, attributes, and physiological features, but to avoid being shallow, I wanted to meet him because I had perceived a witty and cheeky personality. He was not tall and athletic, but I did not want to judge. He had a unique sense of humour and his text message intrigued me, "I had better meet my future wife. Suggest time and place! Will be there!" We met in a popular bar on the Coast where he took three calls without so much as an apology as I waited at the bar. At dinner, within the first half-hour, David admitted to still being in love with his ex-wife. He was boastful and self-absorbed as he recalled his recent travels with her. He reiterated several times that he was brilliant at what he did, exhibiting the classic traits of guys who were on my exclusion list.

David's professional prowess was admirable but if his exploits as extreme sportsman were meant to convince me to go on a second date, he was sadly mistaken. I refused to contemplate any kind of association with conceited males and left it at that. Yet, David was a philanthropist; how incongruous an image with his bravado! I was puzzled by this and suggested he try to woo his wife back to him. He agreed that it might be a good move. David left our dinner date knowing very little about me; I had learned not to divulge too much information with such guys, had he inquired, that is. What occurred as we went to our cars left me dumbfounded.

Reality TV attempts to fool us into believing that *Marriage at First Sight* and other similar programs work, but most of them are largely contrived situations. Blind dates can be a nightmare. This date could have been a blind date because neither of us had provided much information, yet we had both been willing to jump in feet first, compatible on the professional level and seemingly on a variety of fronts.

All the guys with whom I had coffee, lunch or dinner offered to walk me back to my car, in broad daylight or in the evening, except for David, who, having been given a vague indication of the whereabouts of my car in a massive multistorey carpark at 11:00 PM, took off in the opposite direction to hop into his fancy sports car. He had to show it to me I believe, as if I had never been in one before.

I ended up just in front of him at the exit where my credit card became stuck in the machine, at which point I was frantically arguing with the woman through the intercom to release my card. Growing progressively impatient behind me, my wealthy date reversed his car and headed to a different lane where his card was accepted, and he took off with a wave of the hand. Some Gentleman! Well! Not impressed! David had not had the decency to step out of his car to help retrieve my card. When a week later, he called to invite me out once more, I hesitated but a moment, before making an excuse that I was busy.

This is tricky. How do I say "No"? Am I doing a guy a favour when I say, "Not now" when I mean, "Not ever"? But, "Yes" sounds so final. And it is! To make matters worse, when I explained after the meal that I did not want to insult him by offering to pay, he categorically replied, "Oh no! I will accept your credit card. You can pay if you want to!" This had left me bewildered. Hard to figure out these guys. How did I get it so wrong? I had already been insulted for offering my card, by another millionaire who had taken me to lunch. What was the correct protocol? The challenges kept coming.

Chivalry can be interpreted in different ways. I appreciate being walked to my car, especially at night, but I am not so naïve to think that some of these guys are not checking out my wheels. I had the distinct impression that ego was at the forefront of this behaviour, gauging by some of the comments I received after a date. I am not so shallow that I would refuse to ride in a man's car because it does not have a badge on it. Okay! Guilty! Once only! I was going to a ball and the Ute was not quite the choice mode of transport for Cinderella. Then again, what about the pumpkin coach?

Look in the mirror, become aware of what you see.

I have discussions with my mirror, insulting the glass, hating my reflection. I am prepared to remodel my identity, though still unsure of the changes that I need to integrate into my psyche; which lessons to reinforce.

When I discussed the issue of satisfaction with my mirror image with family, friends and colleagues, most appeared to be totally satisfied with their self-image and could not care less what anyone thought of them. However, my BFF, Katarina did admit to having spent considerable time on self-reflection before arriving at a life-changing conclusion, 30 years ago. This revelation gave me increased hope. My self-respect was increasing steadily; I had a better understanding of aspects of my physiology, personality and behaviour that my self-reflection was producing.

Yet I continue to feel challenged as confronted by the impacts of the intense encounters on my well-being during this dating process. But, I remain confident that I can move forward on this journey of self-discovery.

Katarina considers the Mirror the most wonderful invention man has ever invented. She described the phenomenon in the following words,

> *A mirror reflects "everything" in every thinkable and possible way! No question or answer is too stupid or difficult because the person looking back at you is your inner "soulful" true self. Everything is allowed – talk, ask, reply, respond with defiant multiple responses… The epitome of insanity! Am I an idiot for doing this? Why did I say that? Why do I do that to myself? Why? Why? Why?*

Like Katarina, I find myself surprised by how the mirror reflects "everything." I ask a question, and I see it as stupid or difficult. I am antagonised by what I see – both the questioner and the responder. I talk. I ask questions. I receive replies aplenty, multiple responses. Some defiant, some defensive, some revealing, and uncertainty remains. Why did I say what I said? Why do I beat myself up? Why? Am I insane?

Even digesting Katarina's profound words, herself of European background, I see more about myself. Her story is a traumatic trajectory that defines her childhood, adolescent and young adult life. But her reflections and deliberations have, in my view, helped her to accept herself.

Is chemistry a sufficiently solid foundation on which to base a lasting relationship? Was this an example of shallowness? Were my standards too exacting; my morals and code of conduct too Edwardian? Was I too impatient? I did not need to seek an answer to that question. I know that impatience is a great issue for me and I am making a concerted effort to reflect before jumping into situations that can potentially end badly.

From the masculine mirrors during the dating process, I discovered that I was perceived by some to be "too high maintenance and a perfectionist."

I should simply have shrugged off these negative interpretations of my character, but I could not. I kept wondering if my past issues had not been completely resolved. Whilst trying hard not to live in the past, references to past events occasionally had to be revisited for their cathartic effect, to examine them and release them and then move on.

6

The Intellectual Aspirants - Sort through the good ones to find the right one

I have had the honour of meeting some interesting males in their fifties and sixties who showed genuine interest in me on this journey even if their stories did not constitute a happy ending. A Silver Fox is quite attractive if he has looked after himself.

Perhaps I need to re-examine my motives! I have classed the following group of guys under the banner of the Sexagenarian Set, for their clichéd, idiosyncratic characteristics. I must be attracted to quirky personalities as this trait keeps resurfacing in this chronicle. It is uncanny how generalisations tend to mirror real personalities.

It should come as no surprise that this is the cohort of men who admit from the outset that they are the most eligible, wealthy bachelors on the dating sites, many of them retiring on the Gold Coast. The issue is to persevere long enough into the dating game to work out if they are indeed men of integrity and good repute. I could end up with so much more than I bargained for. Unfortunately, even if they are the epitome of the cultured, gallant and successful Australian male, there are underlying issues that can mar the experience if I have too little in common with them. When two people are on entirely opposing paths, the relationship could well be too rocky; the twain is not likely to meet any time soon. My swift learning curve is a perfect example of how to navigate these intrepid waters.

Marcus – the Suave Sailor. "Sail away with me into the sunset..."

Marcus, a wealthy 65-year-old retired businessman from Perth who owns property on the Gold Coast was quite the Prince Charming. I had responded without hesitation to his ingeniously-crafted, witty invitation (one page long) that had only one typographical error. That was a first! At least on an intellectual level, I found his profile intriguing but was not immediately attracted to the 6'4 athletic man portrayed in various contexts on his profile. Was he too old for me? Given his professed sporting prowess, I thought not...

Vigorous prompting from the kids, who perceived Marcus to be sincere, with old-fashioned values, inspired me to continue the quick banter we had begun. He was a local for part of the year and that was a definite plus! Marcus had not only volunteered impressive credentials (CV, websites, company details) to prove he was real; but he had invited me to do a background check on him, knowing that his friends in high places would vouch for him. This is characteristic of the suitors in this age group who go to great pains to distinguish themselves from the masses, the excellent tactic guaranteeing the love interest does not follow through.

This intriguing Gentleman did not mess around; skipping coffee, we went straight to a classy river side seafood restaurant for this special first rendezvous. The two-day repartee quickly progressed to the next stage as Marcus ticked each of my boxes a little too perfectly.

The date of the decade almost did not materialise as the wind chill factor caused a slight misunderstanding at the meeting point. This Gentleman never carried his phone when he was meeting a Lady. Come on! Just not done. The problem was that I had texted him to say I was waiting inside the establishment, a little cold in my carefully selected outfit. After ten minutes, trying hard to avert the stares and grins I was attracting, I became uncomfortable.

Feeling dejected that Marcus may have stood me up, I started to head back to my car to call him one last time, giving him the benefit of the doubt. He had not answered my previous two messages, so, my surprise was evident when, lo and behold, 15 minutes after the designated hour, Marcus was still outside by the escalators coming from the carpark, looking very dapper, his strategic pose conjuring up images of *Rodin's* Sculpture, *Le Penseur - The Thinker,* in deep thought. I smiled and walked toward him and discovered that he too thought he had been stood up. That set the scene for the hilarity and wit that permeated our teasing over an exquisite lunch.

I had to devise a way of avoiding such quizzical and embarrassing stares when out on a date because no one would misconstrue the situation for other than two people meeting on a first date. The tell-tale signs were not lost on anyone. Conscious of the stigma of internet dating for the Boomers, I felt uneasy.

It was easy to ignore persistent niggling doubts about some worrying signs when kept in stitches with a suitor's infectious humour, when the Lady was besieged by flowers (on two consecutive days – 30 in total) that ended up in my Director's office before finally landing on my office desk; when Cinderella actually played her part, obligingly getting her Jimmy Choo heel stuck in the floorboards of the flash restaurant only to be rescued by her Prince; when he carried her stilettos so that they were not drenched in the pelting rain on the way to dinner. Marcus had offered to carry her across but that was just not proper for the Princess, even if he was 6'4 and very strong. Then he wooed the Princess with passionate words, flattered her with romantic messages and phone calls and scolded her for not waiting for him to open her car door. Okay!

There are still Gentlemen of this calibre on the Gold Coast, though this is only his holiday home. Whist small in population, a large proportion of this city's residents hail from different states. The problem is their transience. If they stayed long enough, it might be possible to find a guy with similar interests to me.

Also, just how many were truly ready, willing and able, I certainly wanted to know. This serious suitor was relationship material.

I have never been a Woman's Libber and the fairy tale theme developed naturally through entertaining little incidences during the intense pursuit that kept a smile on my face for the first two and a half weeks. I was in fine spirits and my friends were already making plans for a day trip on his huge yacht, amongst other delightful soirées and functions to look forward to. Hey, hold on a minute! Give me a chance to catch my breath!

I began to relax and delighted at the prospect of a fine dining experience at Marcus' plush residence. The *pièce de résistance* was conceived to take my breath away. Marcus executed his cleverly engineered plan to woo me at his "Palace" on the ocean at sunset one Saturday night. As if the view and the thoughtfully selected menu were not enough to cause heady sensations, I discovered that Marcus was quite adept in the kitchen. In true Master Chef tradition, that I never watched, we sipped Champagne with the *Hors D'Oeuvres* he had prepared as we watched the most stunning sunset over the water. Right on cue! Strategically seated at the kitchen bench, (Marcus knowing that my gastronomic talents were temporarily shelved), with a glass of Penfolds' finest Cabernet Shiraz, I was perfectly positioned to observe his prowess in the kitchen. I was asked not to lift a finger.

Marcus had organised a sumptuous repast, course by course, beginning with an exquisite dish courtesy of a renowned Chef from Perth. We could not finish the four-course meal that sealed his culinary expertise, so, naturally I was invited to finish the last two courses the next evening, saving the *pièce de résistance* till last - a delectable medley of seafood. He had been very attentive to my tastes.

Wow! And they say that the way to a man's heart is through his stomach! What about the modern single Lady of today, whose epicurean talents are growing increasingly rusty. Mind you, we still need to consume small portions, especially when going on dates. "All about small portions, Mum," my daughter, Alessandra had reminded me.

In the heat of the moment I had forgotten the thorny issues, not to mention the prying personal questions, à la *Spanish Inquisition* that had begun to sour our friendship the previous week; and this, in addition to the arguments about previous relationships when they came up in conversation. The intense questioning style was becoming a feature of this dating journey and I was not impressed. We had been walking along the beach at sunset, but the romantic mood had swiftly evaporated. This was definitely a "no go" zone. Awkward, when an ex pops up in conversation. "No go" zones have a way of straining relationships.

That weekend was our fourth date and I decided to let my guard down. When the conversation reverted to the political debates about US policies and other troubling issues in Europe, Britain and Asia, I lost my composure. Our obvious disagreements, due to utterly opposing world views threatened to spoil what had been a magical start to the romantic encounter. Hard to think of romance when all you do is quarrel. It was becoming tiresome that every date revolved around arguments either inadvertently triggered by a *faux pas* or reverted to the political rhetoric of some of the most infamous megalomaniacs, world leaders, all of whom Marcus held in high-esteem, placing them on a pedestal as the epitome of effective leadership globally.

My disillusionment was palpable because our core values were at odds; where was the compassion for those less fortunate than ourselves? We held disparate views on the plight of the Syrian Refugees, on growing ethnocentricity in western cultures, on all things intercultural. I was an adopted Australian, an advocate for empathy, tolerance and acceptance in my profession. I tried to change the conversation to salvage the evening, but it was to no avail.

Animated discussions are healthy in a relationship; my ex-husband and I never voted for the same political parties, but that was not the reason I had ended the relationship. At this age, there was not much point in prolonging the agony if there was little hope of compromise between two people when core values were worlds apart. What compounded the problem was that the constant arguments about personal issues were provoking memories I preferred to forget from past relationships. I could not foresee a smooth, harmonious connection developing between us and I simply did not have the energy to continue. I left and was not returning.

This courtship had presented like a fairy tale romance, full of promise, until I had started to heed the worrying signs. It reached the dénouement a lot more quickly than anticipated.

Reflection

A little self-reflection is useful at this juncture. Never mind your disastrous introduction to internet dating Coco! How many lessons have you learned so far? You are an intellectual; Okay, internet savvy, still a struggle! Just cutting your teeth on that one. Prince Charming was not all he appeared to be. So what! Dust yourself off and move on! That was just a little speed bump on the road less travelled. Life's lessons along the road to the Palace. You know the score, "If you give up, you might as well check out!"

I had an amazing time for a couple of weeks with Marcus but unfortunately, the fairy tale did not have a happy ever after. I had to pull the pin.

I try to dismiss the folly of my substantial investment in readiness for an idyllic day on Marcus' yacht the week I broke up with him. This was to be the litmus test, meeting his best friends and seeking the tick of approval! Factor in that I had no experience in sailing, having been only once on a large yacht. I would have required at least two sea sickness tablets and my eyes strategically riveted on the horizon the entire day. Well! The designer swim suit, the light-weight, white linen sundress and beautiful new hat are still hanging in my wardrobe.

I really liked Marcus, but I guess that was simply not enough. I have a history of deflecting compliments, have not received many in my relationships, and Marcus taught me the need to accept the genuine words of praise that were proffered. Otherwise, he said guys would no longer bother; it seems their pet hate is a woman with low self-esteem. If some misinterpret my learned response to flattery and compliments as fishing for compliments, they are deluded. Upon reflection, I can see the truth in Marcus' words as I have witnessed a girlfriend's marriage fail because she could not accept herself. Her husband had an affair and moved on, leaving his wife with three children devastated and distraught. This beautiful, kind-hearted Lady has never recovered from this ordeal, lamentably.

One of my BFFs, Jessica, expert in her field, has witnessed the trait of deflecting compliments in many of our professional colleagues. She notes, the higher the credentials of colleagues in the echelons of an organisation, the more self-effacing they become. How interesting! I need to investigate this further. So, now, I consciously say "Thank you" in response, monitoring my speech patterns in order to avoid saying "but in the past ..." Live for today, Girl!

Authenticity is the most important trait, but the issue is to decipher which compliments are actually from the heart. If you can fake that, you've got it made!

I had a moment of weakness when Marcus contacted me once more with sincere words that I was pleased to receive.

Coco, if the fact that you are still online indicates you still haven't been romanced off your feet then I am greatly surprised and disappointed for you. Seems we are both in the same boat although the essential difference would be that my reasons are mostly to do with me and no one else... Hmm! But I do want you to know this ... There is no one online to compare with you and that is a compliment ... and I have not had the feeling of anticipation that consumed me when we met ... before or since ... and that is a compliment as well. Just thought it was worth saying ...

Marcus' words touched me, and I read them with regret for what might have been if we had had more in common and if our worldviews had not been polar opposites. I would have been a hypocrite had I pursued this relationship. As far as I am concerned, it takes a courageous male to admit to emotional issues that he had flagged during our dates. I sincerely hope that Marcus will meet a wonderful lady to share his life. Cannot live in the past. Move on! Step up the search! Not that easy when the pressures of work prevent a reasonable balance between work and play.

Giuseppe – that Italian charm again! Or not?

Aged 66, Giuseppe was 5'7 with brown eyes and a smoker. He was a hopeless romantic Italian male with whom I established a connection based on cultural similarities, but the meeting was lacklustre. I knew straight away but I was not going to turn him away. Being self-confident and ever so direct, as Italians are reputed to be, Giuseppe bluntly asked me, at our coffee date lasting 90 minutes, if we had chemistry. Taken aback, I was presented with the opportunity to end our contact, quickly and painlessly.

When he inquired as to why, I explained my penchant for guys in their fifties, closer to six feet tall (185cm), with blue eyes and non-smokers. He could not accept this and as I extricated myself from the awkward encounter, he continued to text me in the hope that I would change my preferences. He communicated with me in Italian. I have translated the message.

It has been an absolute pleasure meeting you. Not only are you a beautiful lady but you also have a brain that works. Very difficult to find these two elements in the same person! Height is not important for me but next time we meet, I will be ten centimetres taller (he had done that on one other date with higher heeled masculine boots). *Have a great trip interstate, hoping nothing happens with that other guy…*

Giuseppe was a really nice guy. The messages that followed revealed his sense of humour, a feature that most males hoped would override the tendency for women to select the tallest men. I wrote that his funny texts had kept me in stitches, lost in translation evidently when he sent me a "Please explain!" The exchange confirmed the stereotype of the overly confident, romantic Italian males but I was very familiar with that culture, after all. As he had appeared with grandchildren in his photographs, a feature of the retired males, especially the European contingent, he hoped to maximise his chances of attracting a woman who admired the family man that he personified, caring, attentive and generous. When he finally left off, he confessed,

I do not know to which Omnipotent, Supreme Being, Entity I should pray to, that this guy you are to meet interstate next week is a classic Aussie, not at all in tune with the values that you are looking for in a man – Me!

Wow! Italian through and through! I went to bed with a smile on my face and was pleased that I had not prolonged the misery for Giuseppe. I was really looking forward to my trip. I made a mental note to avoid meeting guys with whom I suspected there was only a weak connection. Forever learning!

The Effects of Flattery and Compliments

It is human nature to appreciate heartfelt compliments from those we believe are sincere, and perhaps those we really like? I have finally begun to witness the change in my physique, personality and behaviour; definitely a work in progress. The persistent problem for me is that I remain sceptical of the image projected in the eyes of some suitors. But not all these suitors are sycophants.

I still worry about the nature of compliments, if they are real. If authentic, it is a pleasure; if false, I feel damaged. How do I know if the remarks are authentic? Can they glimpse my real identity behind the façade of the makeup and the clothes that I wear? Or do they judge me at face value? Would they be ultimately surprised when my vulnerability is revealed to them? I simply do not see myself as many of my suitors see me. They admire my physical appearance but, so many harp on their preference of my look without makeup. This continues to annoy me immensely because the most "attractive" image I have of myself is when I am "dolled up," made up and dressed to kill.

Why do so many guys hate women wearing makeup? It makes us look good and hides our imperfections so well. I have always worn makeup. I blame my upbringing; my mother, my sister, my daughters and I rarely leave the house without at least a modicum of makeup. The rampant ageism in society has no doubt impacted on this behavioural trait. Going out *au naturel,* without a skerrick of makeup is simply not an option for me.

So, well-meaning comments about my makeup will simply misfire. This is one aspect of my physical appearance that I am happy with and changing this habit is not negotiable. They say less is more, but based on what I see in my *Mirror, Mirror on the wall...* this simply is not so. I am right, and they are wrong. I do not fish for compliments. The mirror – and my perception of what is in that mirror – does not lie. Although, the positioning of mirrors in conjunction with lighting makes us look fantastic in some mirrors and horrid in others.

Where can I find a magic mirror that will make me think I am Okay?

My reaction may appear bizarre because when I receive compliments from a guy who believes I need no makeup, I privately accept these kind words and am secretly delighted all at the same time, but only momentarily. At the same time, I am mortified at the prospect of leaving the house without makeup. Old habits die hard. I accept the blame for the intergenerational transmission of this behaviour to my daughters. Truth be told, neither my mother, my daughters nor I, feel that this is a bad thing. I admit, finally, that if I do not accept the complexity of this issue, the contradiction, the conundrum and conflict of others' perceptions of me and my own self-perceptions, others will perceive me as perverse, a little bit obstinate, and likely to be difficult to please. But I am not like that at all…

The truth of the matter is that I do not accept some men as my *Magic Mirror*. They tell me I am beautiful, but I think they lie. It will indeed take a "Magic" Mirror that enables me to see myself as others see me – reminding us that beauty is in the eye of the beholder. Clichéd, I accept… Am I only ready to accept compliments if I really like the guy?

When I reflect on the recurrent resolution to concretise a new relationship, in essence, skipping the due diligence that is mandatory for a committed and lasting union, is it because the void caused by former relationships induces us to behave like this? Or rather, is the grass greener on the other side? When individuals are ensconced in a committed relationship, they can look at the menu, but they cannot order. Or should not, because they have evidently chosen, and consumed. When individuals are dating online, there is a tendency not to waste time on someone who might not fulfil the stringent specifications and attributes we have engineered. This is the last time for some of us to find love, or so some of us believe, and we wish to enjoy the best time of our lives, unencumbered if children's school fees and mortgages are no longer an issue, to travel and really enjoy life. If it is not right, if there is no chemistry, animal magnetism and compatibility, we move on quickly to the next prospect. Such is the nature of online dating.

I have been tempted to sail away into the sunset, temporarily of course, with a couple of suitors in their sixties, as you do, all jousting for top position as to who possesses the biggest cruiser or yacht, but somehow the prospect of seasickness always brings me to my senses. Not to mention my career; I am blessed to love what I do. Having said that, I have since decided to face reality. This is all conjecture, but if the man of my dreams were to offer me the luxury of sailing away with him, with all the time in the world to devote to my favourite pursuits, I may just be ready. I have never considered this before.

Remodelling my identity

I continued to check my IN Box, just in case that mysterious Soulmate was hiding around the corner. What a letdown! This stupid site – No messages? Really? What an affront! Is it my photos? My messages? Am I too supercilious? I hope that is not what my profile conveys? Hmm... Must ask a few suitors for their opinion. What am I doing wrong? How many times have I adjusted my profile? My cyber identity is continually changing. Identity remodelling is, after all a dynamic process.

NO! No dramatic changes, for now! I will not lower the bar because I believe that the right guy will appreciate the honesty and integrity of my descriptive entries. I shall make slight adjustments but nothing that compromises my integrity.

Seriously though, I am beginning to understand why I seek guys who are less available. Am I finally coming to the realisation that I am perfectly happy in my own space? Am I leaning towards a long-distance relationship where I could enjoy the benefits of both worlds – independence and attachment when it suits us both? Do I really want him to share my life 24/7? Am I too set in my ways now? It is plausible then, that a long-distance relationship might just work in the end. This guarantees the space we both treasure (if we are on the same page) and the honeymoon period that never loses its lustre. Granted, travelling alone has lost its appeal because I need to share my experiences. That would be the exception.

So, have I followed this convoluted path only to discover that my remodelled self, finally contented with the ameliorations that I have integrated, is just where I need to be. I love the serenity I have achieved and the freedom to do as I please. Is this what I was searching for all along? If this is true, what is still missing in my life? Damned if I am giving up the search. At least I have a clearer idea of what I want now. Let's see what transpires!

My timetable is rather inflexible, but fate has a way of upsetting the applecart. The best laid plans... we all know the drill. I must be getting tired. Three clichés in a row!

What is wrong with my profile if nine out of ten guys tell me that my photos do not do me justice. What are they thinking? These are my best shots. I resent the negative comments about my personal photos, but I continue to take the negative comments on board along with the positive reinforcements and progressively amend that profile. Here I go again! What am I thinking? Can my self-portraits be interpreted as 100% images of me? That would be impossible, so, why am I wondering why the guys perceive me differently? I am asking myself the impossible…

I remain resolute in keeping images that represent different role identities in my life, a balance of sophisticated and professional and more relaxed poses. If they cannot accept me the way I want to be perceived, then so be it. Move on! Next!

The Complete Make-Over

The more I compared my image from my personal mirror with that of attractive women my age in the media, the more it induced me to review my dietary and physical regime. The Endorphins that sporting activities create is undeniably beneficial. I do not have to spend hours in the gym watching some of the Millennials preening in front of their mirrors. That is, quite clearly, counterproductive. In fact, I hate gyms, even unisex ones. I choose to go outside and enjoy nature, cycle or walk around my neighbourhood.

It is evidently time for a script that encourages friendship and leave it open ended - "Let's see where this takes us…" Mystery is good, keep them guessing! Perhaps a new photograph that makes me appear less professional might work. Now, the pose is important but posing is never a good move, in my opinion. Hard to appear natural though; what should I portray - cheeky, sexy, serious, fun, pouting, smiling, full bodied or head shots? This is hard. Bright colours are good. My favourite colour is red and that is very significant, psychologically.

Red is attractive to the opposite sex because whilst it denotes power and strength of character, scientific studies show that red makes men more amorous toward women, though they remain blissfully unaware of the role red plays in their attraction. Biological and behavioural studies indicate non-human male primates are attracted to females who conspicuously display red, particularly when they are ovulating. Interesting! Not quite my motivation… remarkable to discover that my penchant for the colour red, that has always empowered me in my career, may have been sending out some very questionable signals in my work place! Recent reports indicate that wearing red in a job interview for instance, may go against a woman. Imagine that!

My new strategy seemed to work for a while, incoming messages displaying the widely-travelled candidates proudly identifying the location of my images.

My objective is to attract a naturalised Australian of European descent, who might at least speak one foreign language. Tough ask on the Gold Coast where the hegemony of English is firmly entrenched. The images reflected from my online mirrors on my first dates gave rise to some serious navel-gazing. Have I fought so hard to reach the educated echelons of society in this country only to discover that it is proving to be an impediment in my quest to find love? Have I succeeded in rising above the racial bullying that defined my younger years in a culture that had ostensibly abolished the White Australia Policy, only to end up alone? Many of my school friends had suffered similar indignities; we, the Southern European contingents formed close bonds and our narratives are similar in so many ways.

I refused to believe, though it plagued my existence, that having boosted my domestic and international professional profile signified that I was still a fish out of water on the Gold Coast and could not meet a guy with whom I shared the same world views, cultural values and priorities. Or if I did, there was insufficient chemistry. The passport that had brought my family to Australia in the sixties was relinquished for Australian citizenship shortly after our arrival. It was so easy in those days. Australia is home, so searching for a partner overseas is not really an option. Focus on the here and now, Coco!

Okay! Desperate times… desperate measures. So to speak! I was quite comfortable in my little world as a workaholic, thank you very much. Until my children decided to impose an intervention. Nearly four years remonstrating that "Not ONE of my friends had deigned introduce me to an eligible bachelor" was wearing a little thin on my children. "You do not want a doctor, do you? And the lawyers are no better. The specialists are worse?" "Hold on a second! Could someone, anyone, give me the chance to make decisions as to whom would be suitable for me?"

My attempts to instigate changes in my physical appearance took on a strange turn on this unprecedented journey to find love. I began to pay far too much attention to female celebrities and actresses with my complexion, on television programs, advertising, magazines; of course ignoring the fact they were airbrushed images. They are beautifully made up and gorgeous. I constructed a brand-new image of myself based on these glossy portraits from the media. I succeeded I believe, if my date at a formal function is anything to go by. Until of course, I heard *ad nauseam* by that stage, that I look better and much younger without the makeup. Damn! This is not a cheap exercise. And let's face it; being fully made up is not part of my daily ritual and I do not attend many formal occasions. I have become minimalistic in that department, finally! Hope the makeup will not reach its used by date before I can use it again.

Changing my hairstyle was innocuous enough, nothing too dramatic. Lightening my hair colour or darkening it sporadically and letting it grow longer were apparently appealing. Easy! I realised that I had a distinct advantage finally, being olive skinned with dark hair and dark eyes because spray tans were not part of my regime.

The power of eyes

To my utter delight, a fascinating, natural transformation was taking place with my dark brown eyes. My irises turn grey when exposed to bright light. Whilst, on this count, I revelled in compliments from my suitors about the "mesmerising eyes that adorned my olive complexion", (creative language from some of my Beaux), this was the first time I accepted the compliments without reserve. I volunteered the fact that alas, the change in eye colour was just a sign of ageing. When my friends reiterated that my eyes dazzled in the romantic mood lighting at a dance, I was fascinated and quickly integrated the positive feature as part of my new identity. Made me so happy. Unfortunately, there was no way of accounting for this dual eye colour on the online profiles, in spite of a compliment confirming just that, from a lovely Gentleman on the Gold Coast. He evidently saw "gorgeous blue eyes in one photo". I laughed because I could not see that on the posted image. The power of eyes had an extraordinary effect on my psyche, a massive influence on my well-being.

Twelve months earlier, the discovery of my grey eyes had begun the transformation toward my positive self-image. Whilst waiting for coffee, a colleague had noticed the change in my irises. I had always admired Jenny's vibrant blue eyes and to think that now, I too could enjoy this embellishing feature, causing great elation, until that is, I visited my female ophthalmologist to ensure this anomaly was not sinister. Her sardonic remark took me aback and threatened to deflate my newfound joy, "It's only age, Coco!" she exclaimed, laughing. At least they were not cataracts. No action required! No one need know really but I delighted in telling all and sundry. They found me ridiculous but, I was not going to allow my ophthalmologist to burst my bubble.

Another positive to add to my dynamic image was my adherence to my ideal weight. I exercised every day and ate very well, considering cooking was no longer in my routine. It seemed that many single women these days ate out or lived on quick meals at home. That was a more appetising habit than concocting rich, time-consuming dishes for one! I hoped that the object of my affections was adept in the kitchen. The good news is that this seems to be the case for the cohort of guys I am meeting. Or so, they boast. I have tasted the proof of the pudding but twice and can confirm that the guys are brilliant chefs - promising signs for the quinquagenarian and sexagenarian sets of both sexes who have acquired a wonderful balance between their Ying and Yang qualities.

Next, teeth! I had long wanted to enhance my smile that, although no one had ever noticed, had ALWAYS strategically been photographed from what I considered my best angle. I had a crooked smile that most people did not seem to notice, vestiges of a broken front tooth in primary school, caused by a boy throwing stones, accidentally hitting me. I refused to smile until the crown could be inserted at the age of 16, when the tooth had matured. The retracted smile had originated from the age of ten. Once again, I was surprised that others did not see this, whilst the odd person found it charming. How uncanny that two of the most significant candidates on my dance card, also had a crooked smile. And I found it charming, whilst hating my own. A little odd?

I have always sought approval for the way I look, the clothes I wear, my actions, "Do I look fat in this dress?" I have to admit that if individuals suffering from *Anorexia Nervosa* can imagine their bodies are enormous when everyone else sees an emaciated frame, indeed my internal processing of my reflection could be flawed.

A disastrous experiment with charcoal toothpaste provoked a quick dash to my dentist, where I indulged in a clinical whitening regime, adjusting my smile in every possible way, gaps duly crowned. Within a couple of weeks, I could produce a winning smile once more. Inexpensive exercise, surprisingly! Success at last! I could not stop smiling.

The tick of approval

John, 62-year-old, retired and wealthy, flew up from Sydney for a lunch date with me, with no encouragement, confessing afterwards the trip had been worthwhile, if only to see me smile in person. He was from the Gold Coast but was spending three months in Sydney on a project. This was further validation that the three-dimensional image that we present to the world was far more appealing than still photos.

After an amazing lunch and John's full assurances, "You know that you would never need to work again, right?" I reaffirmed that I was not willing to abandon my career to retire with him and sail around the globe. Besides, there was no spark! John returned to Sydney, sad that he had not captured my heart, but delighted that he had spent three hours with me. I donned my counselling hat, recommending that he search for women who were closer to his age and not career-oriented professionals if he really wanted to find a partner. Hmm… message in there for myself as well? It was clear to me that he was still in love with his ex-wife. I felt for him. This was the third time he had approached professionals with the same response.

After consecutive meetings with guys confirming that there were essentially no real problems with my posted photos, I began to accept the fact that the camera hated me.

Accepting this provoked an interesting change in my behaviour online with promising leads. I was on a mission to charm the prospective partner in person as quickly as possible. This had to give me a much better chance in this game. Integrating the positive reinforcement, I started to relax, becoming a little more self-assured.

This was a fascinating outcome. I was beginning to enjoy this internet dating game, riding high on my roller-coaster. Wearing my "favourite first date outfit" produced the desired effect. Funny, it was not even red. I had up to five dates in one week. The kids and I were over the moon, even if some dates did not pass "Go." The second and third outfits were ready also, red featured of course, until the season changed. Never fear! Sheer stockings and stilettos despite the cold that was setting in, especially on a date interstate, was just the ticket. I love to wear stockings and heels.

Reality set in! I had to factor in a little exhaustion by this stage, as a fulltime, demanding career waited for no one. The weekends on the other hand had taken on a distinct flavour of fun and excitement. I was starting to lose my "Workaholic" status, a challenge that many guys had volunteered to undertake. Life was very good.

Reflection

Unfortunately, whilst I had psyched myself into this superstitious, lucky behavioural pattern, believing that wearing a "winning outfit" would entice the right man, the prospect of a relationship did not go beyond two or three dates. I had to admit, reluctantly, that this was entirely my fault. Why did I consistently have to worm my way out of future dates, sometimes becoming more embroiled in the existing dramas of the suitor before pulling the pin on the hapless Gentleman. I was seriously beginning to question my motives on these dating sites. Was it fear of a new relationship with all the complexities that this entailed, eventual co-habitation, joint financial arrangements, children, pets, idiosyncrasies on both sides etc., that prevented me from proceeding with the suitor or was this far more intricate than I cared to confess? All of the above?

7

At a Smorgasbord, it's tough to eat only what you should

My interim report induced me to revert to the first site that classed itself as a professional agency. I shall not divulge the name, but I suspect it is not difficult to identify sites such as theirs. I had ignored this site after a couple of weeks for its appalling use of algorithms to match applicants. I fared just as badly with the other sites, but I paid dearly for this one, so I returned to check my messages periodically. Internet dating is addictive and the urge to push further is constant. Surely, I am not the first person to find the prospect of falling in love intoxicating; but then I have always been a romantic!

It was already 11:00 PM. I had an early meeting the next day. Hard to explain, but such an amazing array of profiles to choose from misled me into believing that I had the time, the inclination and the opportunity to secure exactly what I was looking for, with a measure of patience, of course. That intangible trait again, or lack thereof!

I began to operate under a misguided sense of security, if, for instance a guy took my fancy but did not meet my standards. I stuck I to my guns; I felt that I could afford to move on, hoping that the algorithms would send the hot guys six-feet-tall and above, to my IN Box. I fooled myself into believing that I could still reach the goal post before my competitors.

Media reports revealing there was still a man drought in Brisbane alone, did nothing to appease my increasing despondency in the pursuit of Mr. Right. Still, I forged ahead. This was nothing like dating in the old-fashioned way in bars or private parties, where physique, personality and non-verbal cues played a significant role in determining whether to pursue a prospect that intrigued me. If our eyes were to meet at a party or night club, we would lock on for a few seconds and if the chemistry was ignited, we would find a way of initiating a contact.

However, how many times had I been attracted to a guy until he opened his mouth, lit up a cigarette; or did something so embarrassing, so stupid that I lost interest immediately? The laws of attraction, love at first sight, chemistry and pheromones were evidently more complex than they seemed.

How could this dating game get any worse? Subscriber beware! Especially as I was unaware of the automatically reoccurring payments. With a firm resolve to avoid disappointing guys unnecessarily, I had congratulated myself on finding the professional dating site that resonated with my needs, based on recommendations, but each time I returned to this site, I was even more convinced that I would crash and burn.

Most sites offer generic rubrics, *gender, desired age group, level of education, travel experience, main interests etc. your income* – supposedly to match you appropriately! Wonder how many people divulge this information? I suspect many just ignore it. Some were irritatingly less specific, creating more work for members and leaving them more vulnerable to verbal abuse. This was so frustrating. I had been advised to select 'divorced' because 'single' implied concerns about sexual orientation and 'separated' generally signified there was too much 'baggage'. Wow! That learning curve kept getting steeper. With algorithms allegedly guaranteeing a perfect match, in conjunction with the psychological tests I had believed useful at the time, I thought I stood a good chance of finally meeting like-minded guys, hopefully on the Gold Coast. I thought I was ready for this journey.

I was still fuming because the scheming internationally-based professional company managed to extract an extravagant sum of money from an Internet account on an iPhone App that I had set up. I had not waited for the kids to help. I was not used to Apps. Conflicting fees contributed to the confusion because of a discrepancy in information. I was committed to six months with this agency that immediately revealed its total inefficacy; not to mention the psychology tests. From limited multiple-choice options, they had the nerve to analyse my personality. I was not about to waste my time by indulging other sites to psychoanalyse me! One pedant went to great pains to critique aspects of my personality based on erroneous assumptions made from such tests. I was, by that stage, infuriated with the company but three weeks of attempts to resolve the issue and reinstate the funds into my bank account proved futile! My back against the wall, I delved further into the world of Internet dating. I convinced myself that there had to be at least a couple of guys who might take my fancy from there. I had paid already, so I might as well continue the search.

Dating sites – making tricks from their trade

Heavens! What was the point of the search criteria? I persevered nonetheless, as you do, fully intending to cancel the subscription early. Only one response to my brief expressions of interest on this professional site where 95% of the members were everything but. I was in no mood to respond to invitations to 'chat' or meet with guys with whom I found no connection, especially that by then, I realised these guys were probably not real. Being a self-confessed Luddite, I discovered after a week that many of the profile photos resembled each other. A disgruntled email accusing the company of fraudulent behaviour revealed that the 'poor guys' who did not wish to reveal their true image were encouraged to select from a range of air-brushed images of attractive male portraits, a.k.a. Hollywood heartthrobs! Encouraging *Catfishing*? That was a good one!

I was incensed by this because women had not been offered the same privilege and could only blur their images; we could release them upon request, whilst the guys chose glorified images to enhance their profiles. It was a tedious process if I became intrigued by the few profile descriptions of other supposed professionals. I had nothing against blue-collar workers; they happened to be the hottest guys on the sites from what I could gauge, but intellectual pursuits were an important consideration. A balance was, on the other hand, clearly necessary. The guy I was searching for did not need to be erudite because Tradies (the beloved hot Australian tradesmen) were often intellectuals who may not have completed Secondary School.

Some have become millionaire entrepreneurs with the gift of the gab and could put professionals and educators to shame. It was all about connection, attraction and compatibility; at least to begin with.

Click, No! No! No! Wow! As I navigated my way around three sites, I hoped that the algorithms would live up to the hype, but things were not looking good if these "matches" were anything to go by. No! No! No! The first profiles to hit my IN box did not match at all; not even close to my criterial selection. This did not augur well for my search that was lacking in enthusiasm by then.

No matter where I searched online, I was bound to come across cheeky suitors who would throw their hat into the ring. Some sites were obviously deceitful, and these agencies were clearly capitalising on the broken hearted whose dreams were constantly shattered when subscribers did not find acceptance.

The problem is that on some sites, there are no filters unless one pays additional sums of money to upgrade, hide profiles, discover whether messages have been read, and the list goes on; all clever marketing ploys engineered to make members disburse more money.

The poor guy below was but one example of the inefficacy of some dating sites that preyed on the susceptibilities of individuals. The agencies gave them hope, only to pull the rug from under their feet.

A 68-year-old Bikie named Bob perched confidently on his Harley, displaying his wide semi-toothless grin. His shiny, sunburnt, bald head gleaming in the sunlight and long white beard down to his chest were proudly exposed as he continued his search. The image displayed his sleeves – full arm tattoos to be precise! His headline read "Incredibly Cool!"

Each to his or her own, but I had a type, and Bob's description did not come close. I sure hoped he found a woman who loved tattoos… In what capacity did that match the parameters that I had so painstakingly orchestrated for this stupid dating site for Professionals? I wanted to find a kindred spirit who enjoyed at least some of the pastimes that were dear to me, but the site kept presenting members with offers that were far removed from my prescribed choices. I was beginning to have serious doubts about this dating caper. Scary thought! I had been so excited about this process. Next!

Father Xmas, appropriately named it would seem, 68-year-old male, white beard to match the persona, would not take "No" for an answer, reiterating the same message several times because I could not block him, "What a stunning woman" (a rose attached). "Thank you. Best of luck in your search" I responded eventually. "Thankyo ma'am..." followed by "Still stunning ha ha" to my lack of response. This Bloke decided to push past the barriers, "I still find you drop dead gorgeous! Meet me for a drink!" Perseverance did not pay off and finally, he gave up. I did not want to engage in a chat as I did not want to offend him. I felt for him because he was subject to the questionable practices of the agency.

A couple of months down the track, a new contact from Brisbane, hailing originally from Northern Europe, claimed to be new to online dating. Likely story! I decided to give him a few words of warning as he learned to navigate the site, suspecting from the start that he was only too aware of the tactics being used. After several messages that lasted three days, Sven gave me his name and wanted to chat on a free messaging app that I had not heard of. It needed good internet connections and in my area my service provider was woeful. When I suggested speaking on the phone for that reason, asking him for his number, his answer really surprised me, though it should not have.

"If your not happy with that [his suggested app] you can cry over it. Men should always put there number online?? Have a lovely good morning." Sven was telling me where to go, in no uncertain terms! My way or the highway! Wow! How many bullets was I going to dodge on this journey? You can imagine my choice of words, still dignified, of course, in response to this obnoxious man. Water off a duck's back this time. Or so, I told myself. It was hard to remain polite when some users rubbed me the wrong way.

We could find ourselves on these sites for years if we felt obliged to respond to every single notification, message, or other means of generating interest online. Polite messages deserved a response, though. It was not my intention to remain on these sites one moment longer than necessary. I would turn into a recluse, or a frog, rather than subject myself to an indefinite period serial dating. Incidentally, I discovered that this was actually the case for some of the guys I had met. Ten years on one site, really. One Italian guy sure did the rounds; and he was not the only one.

Fred, aged 63, was one guy who was keen to find a younger woman and was not shy to approach those with whom he perceived he had a connection. Nothing ventured, nothing gained! Clichéd, but, in spite of the huge discrepancy in his profile entry and his photograph, who knows how many women he ended up dating.

Fred looked like an 83-year-old, not one word of a lie; but he still thought that we had a lot in common. When I read his brief profile, there was not one iota that matched my principles, but he still deserved a polite response.

> *Hi there. I think you'll agree the criteria you speak about applies to me just the same. Perhaps you wouldn't mind having a look at my profile and if after reading it you felt inclined to share* **a coffee I would love to hear from you. Best wishes. Fred**

It is deplorable that so many dating sites appear to have but one objective; to profit from some poor souls who struggle to communicate in this medium and those who may never find a partner. Yet, like the demographic that is addicted to gambling, alcohol or drugs, are they capable of stopping the search? Just in case; you never know; just around the corner. We all know how it goes... like the common tactic children use to stay up a little later, "Just five more minutes, pleeease..." I suppose that looking at the bigger picture, internet dating might appear a little less costly in the scheme of things. However, if we factor in those who show signs of multiple, concurrent addictions, then society needs to address the social issues that are increasing exponentially in many cities.

Hooked instantly on the Smorgasbord of superficially "eligible" men, I clicked on a few profiles but became more annoyed at the matching process that continuously sent visitors ranging from 23 to 78 years of age to my IN Box.

Ray – reruns and repeats

How could I not do a double take when opening my IN Box to find this message posted in 62-year-old Ray's profile? The clever words were intriguing and I felt spell bound and "Read on"… as I was commanded to do.

> *The conversation was boring. I ordered a Martini and stood*
> *sipping it in a kind of stupor, my eyes aimlessly scanned the*
> *room .. and then I saw her. Our eyes met and in an instant*
> *I knew our lives would never be the same again. Read on…*

Sounded original, but I had seen this line before. Still, I had a good chuckle, and even so, I responded to Ray's approach.

This little vignette contains his comprehensive list of attributes. What more could I ask for? Perhaps a six-foot-three Adonis with blue eyes? Had he left anything out? Hey, he said he could dance!

> *A gentleman, young at heart, a thinker, amateur artist,*
> *novelist, web designer, real estate marketer.*
> *I'm easy going, a good communicator, happy, respectful,*
> *appreciative, reliable, loyal and true.*
> ***Emotionally available…*** *i'm searching for you!.. Always*
> *well presented, comfortable in jeans or a suit, sensual with*
> *style, I can mix in any social circle, down to earth and*
> *practical. Can dance …widely travelled, recently purchased*
> *an investment property abroad. Perhaps we can go together*
> *and have a romantic adventure?*
> *I am philosophical & left leaning, artistic, green, a*
> *conservationist, a friend to the planet & all its animals. I like*
> *to entertain, love movies, theatre, wine & weekends away.*
> *A giver not a taker, i'm looking to share romance & mutual*
> *lifestyle expectations, someone to complement not complete or*
> *complicate my life…*
>
> *Attracted to; intelligence, creative, attractive, happy, down to*
> *earth people. A natural elegance a definite advantage, never*
> *underestimate the power of a smile.*

I wonder how many women Ray managed to woo with this approach. He may have borrowed lines from the internet and included attributes possibly derived from female profiles but it was at least a start. I did not find his profile credible but persevered with the exchange. You want to woo a woman, check out her profile to see what she is looking for. *Et Voilà!*

I decided to chat for a little while. In answer to my brief response, "Hello. You are an early bird like me. It is only 4:00 AM", Ray's witty reply arrived immediately, "The early bird catches the worm!" Interesting... He wanted to play. About to abandon this game, my curt answer, "Or not! You are suddenly a man of few words" piqued his interest, or his ego, sparking a conversation.

I expected him to ignore my comments or to send a cryptic retort, but I was surprised when he showed interest in my profile and investigated further. We chatted online about our mutual interests but the glaring discrepancy between his profile entry and his messages alerted me to a possible subterfuge. When he suggested catching up to explain the intricacies of his work over coffee, I knew that it would evolve no further. Ray appeared with his three-day growth in most photos and a beard in another. I have a penchant for clean shaven men and did not want to encourage him to the Coast just to verify if he were real and if so, to try to change his personal image. Hmm... visions of shaving his beard whilst he slept... I felt it safest not to pursue this lead. Ultimately, I simply did not find him attractive. He did not persist in sending pointless messages because he could see it was going nowhere.

Self-Defeating Male Profiles

The gender divide is obvious when it comes to structuring profiles online. Where women prefer not to focus on their negative traits, personalities and behaviours, guys traditionally point out their shortcomings, believing this to be a good strategy. It does show they have a self-deprecating sense of humour I guess.

By posting minimalist profiles in too many cases, are many women too lazy and too busy to inquire as to the redeeming qualities that may lie beneath the Spartan male entries? Social media is rife with assumptions based on experience and simply gossip. How much truth this contains is anyone's guess. Are some discerning, educated women too quick to judge male profiles, on the presumption that they are not well-versed in literary pursuits and styles that might attract their cohort? If multimedia sources attribute the success of males on dating sites to brawn rather than brains, is this unfounded when we are constantly reminded that this is, after all, the playground of Millennials, and sex rules? The older demographics are said to be enjoying the ride just as much. Does this account for the increasing number of women who are now actively seeking sexual pursuits also? Anecdotal reports suggest this is approaching parity with the male counterparts. The traditional stigma of men and women registered expressly for sexual hookups seems to have vanished. If it works, why reinvent the wheel? If both sexes are satisfied, each to their own! No judgment from me. It is just not my thing.

The internet undeniably affects us and how we understand ourselves and our attractions. Whilst some individuals realise they cannot find everything they want online, they can find about a million videos of people spying on the neighbours or flashing in public if they so choose. They can satisfy their desires in many sexual ways that cannot be satisfied in a marriage (or in any relationship). So, if they watch these videos, it almost builds the fantasy.

It appears that a lot of random hookups are a big fantasy and now, fairly conventional, and online dating sites provide a mechanism to explore that. It is certainly an intriguing feature of this playground.

Competition is becoming rife between good and bad; brain and brawn; fake and genuine. Guys who are weary of the status that profiles engineered for hookups have earned them, are keen to outwit the proud *Bogans* by evoking creative, humorous, witty, honest and passionate headlines that demonstrate their intellectual abilities and spontaneous personalities INSTANTLY. This is a competitive world. These titles are supported by clever words to attract women of their ilk even if the spelling and photos do not always match their verve to stand out in a crowd. Their objective is to vie for the best women available, but they claim they need to eliminate the Gold Diggers first.

This approach had a degree of success, in my case. The clever strategy deserved consideration. Even if I was not attracted to the photograph, I was drawn to the message because of the humour, wit or genuine messages showing respect for women. Albeit, I was a little worried when I discovered the proclivity for voyeuristic tendencies in some aspirants. I responded courteously, encouraging them to keep on searching. I lived in hope, so why decimate their hopes and dreams unnecessarily? Where possible, I tried to build their self-esteem and I am happy to report 100% of these guys appreciated the response, rare apparently, and the advice, in most cases. 59-year-old Joe was a case in point.

> *hi miss C hope all is well in your world?? Thank you for your kind words. Lovely photos indeed you truly have won first prize in the beauty contest in the eye's of this beholder!!AWSOME profile as well i often click on this and admire your words … Hope you had a wonderful day and maybe we can chat sometime?? Cheers Joe… P.S. im always a little inquisitive into what BOXES are ticked in ones life journey and what remains to find fulfilment?? Cheers Joe*

I did not pursue the conversation for long. I had several exchanges over a week with Johnny, a lovely guy from Brisbane who was much younger than me and who found an older woman more trustworthy. Distance and age were no issue either; the positive trend showing promise. Johnny's profile was worth investigating because he was a good guy with Christian morals and his values resonated with mine. I was feeling disillusioned by yet another episode where I had been played, when I answered Johnny's message. I had not seen it coming. So much trickery! This usually induced me to put my heart on my sleeve online and show my wounded pride to those with whom I communicated at that time. I curbed this knee-jerk reaction after this because of the feedback I received, "Ouch! Hope you are not lumping us all in that basket!" This type of response usually reined in my criticisms and emergent cynicism and I bounced back quickly when I came across unpretentious guys like Johnny.

I am sorry you got played, but you see I was last on online date site over 6 yrs ago and to be honest its still same, you gotta be lucky to find a 1 in 100 decent person who tells the truth. I'm a lousy liar and would probably forget the lie so better to just please GOD as well and be Honest from first contact, besides life is way too short, if someone is going to put there Heart out, why tell crap… I believe at my age it takes 3 or 4 months just to become good friends to build trust etc as well before the rest of the icing if you understand me, I remember a 3rd date and was asked to stay over I declined and boy the next day I copped abuse even called a Homo etc. but you see I'm in no Hurry as I want a lasting real relationship this time not a player. Haste as Dad used to say is Waste? I believe he was right. btw just in case here is my number...

I enjoyed the online and phone chats with Johnny because he had a good heart and it was clear he was a man of integrity whose respect for women was imperative in a relationship. I ended contact after a week because there was no longevity, thus no sense in pursuing the lead. He proved to be a little too "religious" for me and we had too few things in common.

Craig's profile rang true. The sincerity of his words encouraged me to contact him, if only to let him know that I appreciated his profile. He was from Northern Queensland and that precluded a connection, so there was no harm in approaching him. We had a heartfelt chat over a couple of days as we shared similar sentiments.

> *After a short time of being on here and reading many profiles...I am almost saddened.*
> *What have I found? A field of broken dreams? People not needing anyone but just wanting something? Warnings against unscrupulous men.....and so on and so on.*
> *Isn't there strength in being vulnerable? Is it only men that break hearts?*
> *For me...I want to feel everything... even if it hurts...I know nothing is guaranteed except death so I am busy with living.*
> *To hear the words "You are my world"*
> *Come not from picking someone...but by someone choosing you.*

The Cheesy Pick-up lines

The majority of the cheesy, cheeky or clever one liners (or two) that appeared in my IN box are derived from the 50+ age group. The following vignettes provide some insight into the enormous variety of messages that brought a smile to my face even if they went no further. They demonstrate a healthy sense of humour from the clever wordsmiths. Or not? Some guys say just the nicest things that warm the cockles of your heart, if you dare to believe them. We can just have a good laugh. It is good for the soul!

love a woman with ideas, who is sure of their worth, and 'quirky' in one of the many ways that can be ... Oh, I want to do Adult things with you too. Like .. lodge tax returns, take the garbage out and (whisper it) chat about our day over dinner.

Looking for someone who enjoys a laugh. Who makes me want to get home quickly and leave slowly!!!

No pressure, no expectations. I don't mind if it's at the Ritz or the local milkbar [convenience store]. It's not where you are that matters - it's who you're with.

Good morning Coco sometimes things just have to be said you have the most amazing face ...

Lovely eyes beautiful smile i must say

Thank you for responding. Need to say you don't look 👀 your age I first thought 44 😊

hi thanks for the reply There was something definitely intreaging about you and your profile. and why im sure you would get several views each day. eventually love and happiness in cupids eyes will find a way. well deserved im sure. cheers ...

I think your profile is perfect. You know what you want about live and partner. Intelligent"

you must be a career woman, who would divorce a woman that looks as good as you? ... sounded a bit corny?, whoops lol.

A good helping of integrity, a big dash of honesty, a healthy portion of success, no limitation on humour, well packaged and ready for export!

> *I seek a woman who enjoys to do simple things and who rocks*
> *a frock, not a princess but on that has that" je ne sais quoi."*
> *We will know when it happens and the chemistry is right.*
> *You are tactile, have a wonderful combination of depth,*
> *compassion and style. Enjoys a good laugh and a glass of wine.*

I confess. I am a Drama Queen! Okay, so I am sometimes a Princess too! Some of us can rock a frock but I would love to have the certain *je ne sais quoi* that those Parisian Gals possess.

Some of these headlines were entertaining. Aged between 49 and 65, the introductions are worthy of mention. Teeth were certainly an important consideration for the sixties cohort.

Who wants to wake up to a partner's false teeth in a jar on the bedside table?

> *Botox-free, own hair and teeth*

> *Sorry but I dont have any photo's of me holding a fish* ☺

> *Not your average guy – I do Pilates. And I have my own teeth!*

> *Passionate man. open minded, educated, funny. Love life ...*
> *I am a gentleman and know how to treat my lady. I find*
> *beauty in and am attracted by, individuality, personality,*
> *humor, self esteem and confidence. You all have it. Maybe*
> *you don't let enough of it out at times. Maybe I can help with*
> *that but it's there.*

> *Looking stunning in your professional photo – classy and*
> *alluring at the same time* ☺ *... geography is but a feature! ...*
> *Rather felicitous! Two European intellectuals on a dating*
> *site* ☺

> *I have found doing an Ironman triathlon a somewhat easier*
> *journey and somewhat quicker than finding my Soulmate.*
> *Mmm.. I guess thats why so many of us try this site. Am I*
> *in the wrong country? I dislike ego centrics and look at me's*

(unless they can entertain a big crowd). Oh, and I have all my teeth...

Alan's entry below suggested some thought in the construction of his profile. He sounded philosophical, which correlated perfectly with his musical talents and career. He was a deep thinker who saw beyond the hum drum entries that everyone found so boring. I was pleased that mine stood out. This positive reflection was most gratifying.

I think you are Beautiful and I wonder what lies beneath the external Beauty. External Beauty is a Bonus. I am naturally attracted to that, but I'm not too interested in China Dolls. I want to know who someone really is, what makes them tick. I would be certain that you aren't any China Doll. I hear people talk of Fun, travel etc.etc. I wonder if that is all about not wanting to be with themselves. I don't hear you saying that and find that refreshing. I seek contentment, which I see as all encompassing and nourishing to the Soul. Alan...

Alan's correspondence with me confirmed he was one of the good guys and I hoped no one took advantage of him. Such a kind soul, but he was much older and lived up north.

Internet dating does have challenges...but these are only created by the few "opportunists." I believe the majority are genuine with their intentions...but just aren't perhaps brave enough to show their true selves...open & honest I believe is the key...but I see the good in all...that's why my kids call me the "eternal optimist" ☯....

It was entertaining to witness the eclectic entries of some guys because they suggested a ploy they thought was very clever - cutting and pasting incongruous sections from other male and often female profiles and adding their own touch to it. Did they realise how common this was? Those touches in fact, tended to reveal the real person behind the mask, warts and all! When they volunteered their personal details immediately, saying they were widowers, we were warned online to beware of these red flags - the *MO* of scammers usually.

There were also some clever lines that denoted some guys had trouble collating the information from several profiles. This profile was cut and pasted a little clumsily.

> *A women that has strength and individuality to be herself and carries true inner happiness. Has unclipped wings and ready to fly (again) Sexy from within, has a sense of humour with moral character. Has some depth but laughs easily. Is looking to create a special relationship.*

When a European Gentleman's opening line addressed me immediately, I thought he had potential. He only needed to find that intangible chemistry with the right Lady. It certainly caught my attention though.

> *I have to say I love your profile and look, I hope you don't mind me sending a message straight up but I couldn't resist. I do hope you have a weak moment and reply. I believe in old fashioned values, I guess a little old school but definitely not boring. Regards. L.*

> *It started with a kiss… Hello :) thankyou for responding, made my day,,, I feel I would like to know you better, may I ? :) … hehe ok, look forward to hear from you,,, just between you and me, I really won't mind if you wanted to stalk me, I would even help haha :)Love, Louis.*

In fairness to the fish in the Gold Coast pool, 55-year-old Justin, with whom I established a connection online towards the end of the subscription, was willing to talk but too busy to connect with me. This was a prime example of the tactic called *Benching* (Chapter 12). A little harmless flirtation might just keep you hanging in there for the next morsel from the fine Alpha male, or not!

> *Hello. Do I detect a bit of Spanish heritage? Mexican maybe? Would love to chat anytime! You definitely have "the look."*

By the way...your profile is absolutely perfect!

Not perfect enough to sustain his interest for long! After three messages with clever one liners, Justin was hoping I would be around to chat further when he was ready. You snooze, you lose! I terminated my subscription before its expiration date and had no intention of renewing it.

Some 50+ suitors who initiated reasonably clever lines often could not sustain the exchange for more than a couple of messages. Perhaps the information that I provided when asked put them off? I believed they were intimidated mostly because their entry was based on fictitious accomplishments that did not correlate with their messages. This was often the moment I was *Ghosted* (Chapter 12*)*. The whole profile just disappeared! Much easier than admitting defeat. Was this a stealthy way of saving face? Or, were the more adept gamesters testing the waters before setting in motion their unscrupulous tactics to *Catch* and *Release* their prey? I had discovered by then that the online dating games were ruthless. I was warned, "Make no mistake, both genders are involved in despicable games."

One such character introduced himself as a Dag. His profile was devoid of ANY information except for the few mandatory boxes identifying the candidate. These were very common. His one photograph presented the iconic beach bum with a t-shirt over his head, but at least he was showing an attractive, sculpted figure from the back. Oh Well! Good luck with that! All brawn in my opinion, and although he did cut a fine figure of a male model, I doubted there was much substance.

There were three messages from 60-year-olds. They did not miss a trick; the first came complete with *Emojis* and interesting syntax.

Hey uDO FIT my criteria just right u beautiful sexy chickybabe & not far away. MMMWAAAH XX 😝

Hi Coco join me for a cuppa date ...Yum yum bubblegum... OMG darling your gorgeous

Ideal date *- Whom notices i do the little things... Hmmm maybe a little fire a little hot plate some little tasty*

> *morsels and a pair of chop sticks so could feed my lady as she*
> *pleases and some wine*

The last entry I checked was from a guy aged 63 this time and his message sounded sincere. He was sweet, just not for me.

> *Hi, C. I'm Michael and want to compliment you on both*
> *your choice of photos and your story etc,* ***You appear to have***
> ***class & style a great deal of substance between the ears.***
> *All attributes I seek out and am attracted to. Hope you have a*
> *great day and if you are comfortable chatting me, that would*
> *be great, otherwise, I understand. Ciao :-)*

He even made the effort to sign off in Italian! It certainly helped to view myself from the eyes of a culturally similar individual who appreciated that I "have class and a great deal of substance between the ears." "Look me in the eyes!" I said.

Recidivists – Figuratively speaking

Then there were online aspirants who would just not go away! If the dating site did not register a request to remove profiles that were rejected, I was obliged to grin and bear it. Eventually they disappeared but the recidivists only needed to see my image on the carousel and the litany of inane messages picked up where they had left off – one liners just to let me know they were still "in love" with me. The following excerpts were but the tip of the iceberg for some males who were persistent hopeless romantics or just bored.

> *Good morning gorgeous can we please meet I find you*
> *absolutely gorgeous. regards*
>
> *i like you xx* [three days of the same message]
>
> *I would like to learn more about you. Hope there is something*
> *in my profile sparks this curiosity you seem to have for*
> *experiencing interesting connections..at least..!*😉😊

Who said chivalry is dead? I will open the doors for you..

How the guys fare on dating sites

It is most gratifying when, from my perception, some guys "get it right" when they display eloquence in their profile descriptions. Admittedly, this was mostly reflected in the cohort of males in their sixties or late fifties. Their educational background was unmistakable even if their occasional, contrived entries suggested they had gone overboard.

It is seriously not easy to conjure up just the perfect profile. It is in fact impossible because human nature is what it is; extremely diverse and quirky identities with vastly different attributes and expectations. You could easily find yourself re-writing your introduction ten times, let alone construct the perfect cyber identity to please the "right" individual who will read, react to and respond to your messages. The words we use, the photos we choose, the wit and humour we convey in our missive will either succeed instantly or fail miserably.

In this dating game, it pays to understand that if a suitor does not do it for you, you move on. Reminiscent of the words of my dear friend, Joseph, "My Dear, you will kiss many frogs before you find your Prince, but you will find him!" If there is no chemistry visually, from my experience, it does not magically manifest during your first encounter. Unless of course, you are a Gold Digger!

Incorporating the Lessons

I must admit that this journey has had a profound effect on me. The guys I met have provided a different window on the way I view myself; self-actualisation and self-awareness altering my identity in a positive way. I am attempting to be less assertive in my dealings with the individuals on and offline, becoming more soft-spoken without losing too much of my exuberance for life and allowing others to express themselves and to really listen. This deliberate exercise in fact requires that I alter the façade that I embraced at the beginning of my career in order to survive the bullying and psychological abuse I endured, but in some contexts, this is still a work in progress.

I have realised that the remodelling of my identity is indeed a mammoth task with no guarantee of success because each and every situation demands that I interact differently, showing an alternative facet of my personality. Identity is an extraordinary concept and once I begin to unravel the potential for changes to my behaviour and my emotions, I understand the confronting nature of the challenges.

I have discovered that this process is largely irrelevant for many Millennials. Alessandra confessed that during her online dating venture lasting one year, she did not change a single detail on her profile. So interesting. I am delighted that she is so comfortable in her skin. And so, she should be. Oh! The beauty of youth!

Which strategies should I adopt now? What is the way forward? I try to rein in my high expectations, promising to curb my impatience and vulnerability. I try to remain cheerful through the process even if scepticism is threatening to destroy any hope I have of ever finding a partner. Thus far, the tally of positive reinforcements outweighs the negatives. I have endeavoured to deflect unsavoury episodes, relegating them to the back burner. They are nonetheless, lessons to incorporate. I try to avoid the disappointments caused by guys who abuse me online or who reject me by instantly removing their profiles from the dating sites. I have my suspicions that several males who have contacted me (without a picture), are actually guys I have previously rejected. Once they have contacted me, they pull their profile. The need for tit-for-tat approach is sad, even despicable.

I have also discovered that this self-judgment is completely subjective. My close friends mock me, gently mostly, when they perceive that I take life a little too seriously; when my accent is too "English"; when I use "big words" to explain my points of view in a social context; when I say or do quirky things they find incredibly bold and inappropriate in their eyes, and so it goes.

I am still the butt of everyone's mirth. It seems that no amount of time spent in Australia will ever make me totally *au fait* with Australian wit and sarcastic humour. I still bite so easily when goaded and I take offence most of the time when I feel cornered, in the nicest possible way, I am assured. "We only take the p**s out of you because we love you!" Taking the mickey out of a friend is a favourite Australian sport but remains for me a bizarre, even obtuse way of showing support and affection. Many of the guys I have dated also attested to my inability to process this backhanded humour that they revel in. I think I have a sense of humour, just not the same sense as them.

I know exactly when to turn my back on those who are ethnocentric and racist, who do not share my values, knowing that human behaviour is hard to change. Leopards do not change their spots and I have neither the desire nor the energy to attempt to change anyone. I remain resolute that I will never compromise on my code of ethical conduct and my core values, not for anyone. Some aspects of one's personality are not negotiable. I am proud to reveal that I have succeeded in eliminating some negative aspects of my personality during this process. I have discarded the heavy armour that I held securely around my heart and replaced this with a softer shell to protect myself from abuse, humiliation and heartbreak.

I have in some measure become more dispassionate when facing disapproval and criticism. I have learned to deflect the negative sentiments, paying attention only to constructive criticism if I deem it warranted, firstly, and secondly, if it can be construed as useful lessons to be integrated in my psyche. I have not become a cynic, an angry, bitter, twisted and untrusting individual but I remain circumspect and non-judgmental. I am savvier in a variety of situations and proud of it and a much better judge of character. The most important facet of my transformed identity is that now, I have learned to trust my instincts; and I try not to second guess myself.

8

Cubs need a mother not a lover

There was a thrill when ten or more profiles appeared in my IN box in an evening. But the thrill was even greater when it contained a few men who were 10, 15, even 20 years my junior. Typically, these Cubs were looking for a Cougar, and while I confess my preference for the younger guys, I find myself asking sometimes how young is too young.

I suddenly had a wicked idea. What if I amended my wish list based on the brilliant lyrics by American County Singer, Brad Paisley, entitled *ONLINE*?[12] Perhaps a Cub is what I need... I could emulate the lead character's attempts to find love; reconstruct the lyrics to build a perfect image of me, and *Voilà!* My 6'3 Stud would turn up just as prescribed.

> ...*But there's a whole 'nother me*
> ...*'cause online i'm out in hollywood*
> *I'm six foot five and i look damn good*
> *I drive a maserati*
>
> *I have a black-belt in karate*
> ...*It turns girls on that i'm mysterious*
> *I tell 'em i don't want nothing serious*

---

[12] Paisley, B. Online. https://www.youtube.com/watch?v=UE6iAjEv9dQ

I'm so much cooler online...

Just toying with that idea... Fun, have to admit! This song is perfect for the medium of online dating.

How bizarre that, at the start of my journey, I had found it perfectly acceptable to envisage a relationship with a guy who was in his late forties. In the space of a few months, the feedback I had received from some of these boys and their reaction to older women had a sobering effect on me. What gave me the idea that I could snare a younger man once again? Those tempestuous days were long gone... Yet, I regularly turned down persistent Cubs in their 30s from Brisbane and interstate, ready, willing and able to travel down to meet me. Go figure!

Marco

When Marco, aged 49, with teenage children, was a match, I erroneously assumed that he too may be looking for a monogamous relationship. Long-distance to boot! Melbourne is a long way away but this was not a deal breaker... I was delighted but wondered if I were even more deluded than usual... When I approached him, Marco's response made me feel very silly...

> *Hi Coco. Now what can I say? First of all most woman in there mid to late 50s that contact me are generally not after anything more than a fling because I think they get that a younger guy is most likely just going to enjoy the moment which tends to be a mutual thing to be honest. Now you've pointed out that you're not interested in a fling which is cool I guess I just assumed it would lead to that. So I'm sorry if I gave you the wrong impression. Marco.*

How could I have imagined that he wanted anything but a fling? I was embarrassed, but this guy had not led me on. He was not after a relationship. That age gap becomes gargantuan as you get to 50+. Hopefully he would be more empathetic once he entered his fifties.

Thank God this was online dating, with no one to judge me or witness this episode. I thanked Marco for his candid response and confessed my daft illusions that he could have been after more than a fling. Why? Just because he had young kids? Stupid! I told him that there was no point in communicating further as I was intent on establishing a serious relationship with someone, even if it were not forever. I was becoming more realistic day by day. FOREVER is a long time!

Marco's quirky response, "So you don't like a bit of tutti fruitti?" indicated he wanted to play but I was not going to indulge his fantasies. However, my ego demanded that I reassure him that I was not a Nun, just not into one-night stands or flings. I told him I was a one-man Lady. Oh! These Italian boys! From that day, the late forties were out of bounds for me, as I was intent on avoiding further awkwardness. Well, that was the plan anyhow!

Before this episode, when I was more detached, I had a bit of fun with the Cubs who approached me, jousting with them online. Even when I was reticent, I was surprised that a few could be quite tenacious. There were a number of young men who made my day, for instance, a 24-year-old, two 30-year-old guys and others. In some ways, they were like any of the others – statutory spelling mistakes, tall promises. What distinguished them was their openness in searching for a Cougar, and how that especially flattered me. None of them ever said anything about wanting a relationship. Funny, how I had never expected the Cubs to want anything more. Yet Marco, I considered eligible. More fool me! Phil's approach was inviting to some, perhaps?

> *good evening lovely lady. Im Phil. very nice to be hopefully finding a connection on here. If your looking for a fun younger man then dont be shy. im actually 37. Am a **Cute Cub** looking for a cougar ... And if it's not to much information Passionate long lasting kissing is highly underrated. I could literally kiss all day*

I continued to copy and paste the pat responses that were intended to avoid pain, irrespective of age; until that is, they became too irritating. This was usually also highly contingent on my moods, admittedly, frustration increasingly taking precedence over excitement and patience.

My enthusiasm was waning fast. On that occasion, Phil's retort was worth noting,

> *by the gods you are one hard women to get to talk. if you dont adore me. just tell me to get on my bike Coco. my lovely goddess*

Funny, I was convinced I had done just that. Well! Well! The next guy, a 32-year-old declared,

> *I love documentaries about ancient and modern history and i have an interest in particular antiques from ancient times to 1945 so I guess I'm not your typical Aussie bloke **however i do have a nice Ute...***

I wondered whether I should respond at all. Sure, he liked all things ancient, but did he view me, an older woman, as ancient?

Things became more interesting. A 36-year-old and another 32, posing as a 50-year-old appeared in my IN Box. One entry I chose to exclude was disgusting, head tilted, half-cocked; this guy seemed to think his tongue hanging suggestively to one side was a winning look. It was clear he was not from Planet Venus. I was not going to dignify his entry by responding. Yet, the dating site had allowed his image, like so many others of this type.

The following partial entry from a youngster had the hallmarks of snippets copied and pasted from an older male's profile – a common occurrence. Could he have included any more clichés? Still, his profile may have attracted some! It was interesting to learn about what the Cub hunters were looking for.

> *I will treat you with respect & caring. I will hold your hand, give you a shoulder to cry on if you need it. I will make mad passionate love to you. We will do everything together and have some of our own space when needed. Life is short lets get our party started today... I am a genuine man.....What you see is what you get. None of us will ever find a perfect match....But we can mold each other Like we all have done in past relationships....*

He did not miss a trick. How could any woman turn him away? I had to give him some credit though. He certainly included an eclectic mix below that was sure to entice some girls...

> *A loving caring woman. No neurotics need apply. I prefer a lady i can hold, trust & love. We will share the highs & lows together. A lady who will bring out the best in me & vice versa. We will just enjoy being together, Beach, bush walking, stargazing, candlelight dinners etc. Work together as a team. I would like a lady who also enjoys hot lovemaking & passion. Whatever my lady desires...your choice...I am easy going...Just communication is all i ask*

One of the Cubs, a little older at 42, chose to dictate the terms of his future dates. The rest of his entry suggested he was actually being serious.

> *I'm ready... I'm on here to find that one true person. No mind games. And it's a real turn off to know how much of an a***hole your Ex is...I am what I am. Believe it or not there will be some ladies on here who do not find me cute and irresistible (go figure).*

A 47-year-old attempted to woo a few women with his professed attraction to the more "natural woman" with style, personality and curves. This guy may just have consulted his female friends.

> *I don't do the Cubs & Pub scene so at 47, would like to search for that profile and pictures that attract to my liking. I'm not looking for the typical GC Barbie doll stigmatic person. Attracted to style, personality and curves. A 'Real' woman has shape.*

Doug, who professed to be a doctor was in a class all his own. Determined, I had to admit, but I would hate to end up in his care. He remained a bit enigmatic. Doug contacted me and kept me intrigued for three weeks until I was relegated to the *Slow Fade* file, another popular ruse. The only reason I replied to the 38-year-old doctor from a busy

Brisbane hospital was because of his musical talents as a saxophonist, my favourite instrument, and hoped one day to hear him play in his band. My fault, for loving the Saxophone. Kenny Gee is an old favourite. No other ulterior motives, I swear. I was growing increasingly realistic.

What amused me was Doug's interest in "the older woman" that I did not take seriously but I was curious by his initial brief or quasi monosyllabic messages. That was the first signal that I was being played. I forged ahead to discover more. His penchant for constant travel was the second. I was not fazed by this and I played along, akin to trapping a fly in the honey trap. I responded to his weekly messages that held little interest as he rarely answered questions I posed about his role at the hospital. I wondered when he had time to work. As he traipsed from Canberra "for a week's conference," to Tasmania for a quick trip, amongst other escapades, I was quite entertained and wished to discover why he was bothering to message me. I never actually found out. Bizarre! After commenting, "You certainly do a lot of travelling for a doctor," Doug responded,

> *I just got back.. I got up at 5 Tassie time which is 4 qld time and got here at midday and my mates summoned me to the golf course. Naturally I was very excited and got there and went to the 4th hole to catch my friends and then it started pouring so I had to wait under a tree for half an hour and watch the course turn into a river then I walked with my tail between my legs without hitting a ball argh how are you going*

> *had to do 7am shifts which is a bit rugged for a night owl like me lol have to go to syd tomorrow to do a locum down there would love to catch up with you when I get back*

I was in no hurry to meet with Doug when he suggested we catch up after his locum trip to Sydney, but I said, "Okay" nonetheless. He responded, "Ok Sounds fab x" and this is where the messages stopped. No harm done! Just weird. His comments in fact had a soporific effect on me.

Young Karl saw no problem in breaching the distance between the Gold Coast and Brisbane and was ready to drive down the next day to meet me. The fresh-faced Cub was only 36 and very, very keen. Funny how the "eligible" 50+ males managed to find an impediment to pursue women who were outside their post code, logistical issues overriding desire. And I, of course, also found driving long distances a challenge.

One of my favourites was cute 29-year-old Damian who told me that I would need to show my ID to order a coffee, let alone enter a night-club with him. In fits of laughter, I told him the age of my eldest; he said he nearly choked and asked if she was available. That was a quick switch! Damian asked me if I was Christian, interesting, and said that he had always wanted to date a Christian professional Cougar. On a serious note, I provided moral support for Damian when he confessed he was dealing with a challenging issue at work. The next day, he told me he had made a decision and was grateful for my advice.

It was not surprising that some of these Cubs should be approaching older women, given the antics they discussed with me about some of the young Prima Donnas on these sites. I learned interesting things. These boys confessed to being heartily sick of the games and the demands the Millennials and X Gen daters made. They attested to preferring some conversation after a romp in the hay. Hmm... They wanted a woman who understood them and could teach them a thing or two about love, but, they were happy to play until it was time to settle down with the X Gen member who matured a little.

I indulged in some laughs with a 28-year-old, but cute Mattie, 30, who approached me early in the dating game, was persistent. The gorgeous Gold Coast Tradie (comes with the territory here in Queensland) would not give up and I thought there would be no harm in having a chat. I decided to humour the young man after turning him down several times, just to see where this may lead. It would be harmless enough to have a drink in a public place I thought. So, the youngster, fully aware that I was his mother's age, agreed that this was just a drink. He arranged a date for the evening of Good Friday, with four days to enjoy his Easter break.

He proceeded to cancel Friday because of office drinks that he could not possibly miss. When I declined his invitation to have an innocent drink on the Sunday because I was bored by then, I called him to cancel, feeling rather foolish. Mattie confessed to having just woken up, extremely hung over after a Work day out at the races. Instead of taking no for an answer, the youngster suggested I come to his apartment for a beer and a "quiet" afternoon, watching the football on his couch! Seriously? I thought it best to give him some advice about dating older women. I guess I was never to find out what these Cubs had to talk about when the mad stupor and the alcohol dissipated. Thought I might leave that demographic well enough alone!

It had become clear to me that a Cub needs a mother not a lover…

Antonio

Antonio, a 35-year-old, could not decide which age to lie about and which tertiary degree he preferred. He regarded himself as a true gentleman, with young children; an international businessman with an array of adventurous extreme sports. That he could indulge in such pursuits with three young children rang alarm bells. For a tertiary educated man of this calibre, I would have expected fewer spelling mistakes but then his first language was Greek. Antonio was searching for an equally adventurous and athletic partner "who dont take herself to seriously because that's so old fashion." Our brief exchanges include only my two responses.

> *1st response: Hello Antonio. Thank you for contacting me. Whilst I am flattered by your attention, you are a great deal younger than me. Pity! In what area is your advanced degree?*

> *Second: It is strange, Antonio. Initially, you were 58 in your heading and 37 in the body of your profile. The second time I looked, you were 42 with three kids. You might need to decide on an age and stick to it; also, decide which profession you prefer and whether you have kids or not. You will get caught out with these lies!*

I never heard from Antonio again, but his profile was visible to everyone. I noted that he at least managed to fix the anomalies in his entry. I wonder how many women had fallen for his ruse.

Antonio led me to consider offering my professional services to the dating agency. By then, I had provided advice, solicited by three suitors. A charming gentleman of 63 contacted me very early in the piece saying,

"I imagine you have been inundated with requests to chat. May I ask you please to read my profile and let me know how I can attract genuine Ladies? Thank you." My profile must have given them the impression I knew what I was talking about. Perhaps I could start moonlighting on some of the sites as Accidental Counsellor.

Reflection

A 65-year-old guy contacted me thinking he was being very complimentary in telling me, "You look pretty good for an old girl!" Smarting at this, my ego-driven riposte was to object with a sarcastic reply; to which he retorted that he thought people in their fifties were actually old! Vestiges of my former partner who delighted in talking about me, in my presence also, as "The Old Girl!" He had convinced himself this was drôle!

It amuses me when some younger guys approach an older woman online and their selection criteria ranges from 50 – 67 years old. Wonder why they select this range? I was generally not willing to find out and declined the invitations to chat. Interesting, when such guys believe that they have posted a clever heading also. Sadly, crass is crude, in monosyllabic entries or long diatribes. If that is supposed to attract the right woman, good luck with that!

The confident behaviour of at least some of this younger cohort of male daters is seemingly much less prevalent in conventional dating. Could it be because many of these Cubs are likely to be rejected outright when an older woman has had a good laugh and a little boost to her self-esteem? Then again… Perhaps if the inebriation gauge soars above the limit, they may just indulge the whims of the youngsters? Who knows? Now, when they reject me because I do not want to "play", the experience dissuades me from heading in the direction of the Cubs. Suddenly, a *Silver Fox* in his late fifties or sixties seems rather fetching.

Strategising, yet again…

Wow! This process of devising clever strategies to catch my Prince was proving more challenging than I cared to admit. What about those personal adverts - lists of *Dichotomous Propositions,* requiring a pre-questionnaire?

I could have a bit of fun with these, and ultimately discover a lot more about a potential partner than through regular checklists and actual dates. Let's see… this could prove enlightening… The sequencing is, of course, subject to interpretation and key to determining the wit, quirky humour and personality of the guy I am looking for.

Steak or Salad?

Speed or Comfort?

Cocktails or Wine?

City or Bush?

Real or Fake?

Talk or Listen?

Manual or Automatic?

Stilettos or Sandals?

Resort or Wilderness?

Give or Receive?

Boats or Cars?

Big or Small?

Classical or Modern?

Silk or Cotton?

Sunrise or Sunset?

9

Old widow(ers)

Seniors, Nyppies **or** *Owls?*

I am not convinced that many pre-retirees want to be called *Middle-aged* or *Seniors* any more. Some of us will simply not have it, and social trends are reflecting the opinions of all and sundry. I thought that the term had become obsolete until I heard a 50+ speaker use it to designate his age group quite recently. The French, on the other hand continue to favour *Seniors*, in English of course!

If anyone thought the online dating venture was going to be easy, think again! It is not for the fainthearted. There are clear advantages on the other hand. It is a sure way of getting to know oneself better as internet dating provides incredible insights into who we were, our transitional identity, and who we become at the end of the journey.

Dynamic changes to our identity, our personality and behaviour continue their relentless pace whether we desire it or not. Some are subtle, some are not. They are not irrevocable! Our emotions will continually go through the wringer, but we will emerge on the other side with a shiny new identity, more internet savvy, less inexperienced and vulnerable and we hope to be better off for it.

Current debates on the terminology of age groups provide new trends that are ephemeral or become fixtures depending on the traction they generate on multimedia platforms. The consensus is that *Middle-aged* or *Seniors* tend to be pejorative terms that do not adequately describe the current members and I, personally, refuse to adhere to their erroneous connotations. *NYPPIES (Not Yet Past It)* is another term proposed for this group who look much younger than their antecedents at the same age, just as patronising, in my opinion.

What an insult! I refute this uncomplimentary term. Some of us over fifties and over sixties are no longer old; we are the new over forties and fifties; we are not elderly; we are not past it! Quite the contrary. We are the new breed that increasingly looks much younger than our chronological age; we are still working, active, intellectual, young at heart, fit and very busy, quite entrepreneurial also; we are largely well-educated, often well-off, well-travelled, liberated and have become experts at multitasking, especially when expected to assume the care of grandchildren.

Who would prefer *OWLS (Older, Working Less, Still earning)?* I quite like this one as it conjures up the Owl, *Archimedes*, in *The Sword in the Stone*, Walt Disney's famous cartoon. Some individuals in these cohorts may well boast that they rival the Millennials, beating them at their own dating game. Very imaginative minds out there. How about the *Boomers*? I perceive this as less offensive.

Despite the scalding blows to our self-esteem that academic and journalist, Bernard Salt employs to decimate our character, I prefer to look at life with hope and optimism. This is not escapism; I simply prefer Positive Psychology. What does he know anyway? Salt[13] may be going through his mid-life crisis. Grumpy old man!

> *Well, I have news for you. Fifty is not the new 40; 50 is 50. Fifty is the end of youth. There is no escape from Planet Fifty; it is inhabited by middle-aged people, by people who don't look young any more. Sorry… Fifty leads to 60 and then on to the great abyss 70 and beyond.*

---

[13] Salt, B. (2011) No, sorry, 50 isn't the new 40 **http://www.theaustralian. com.au/business/opinion/no-sorry-50-isnt-the-new-40/news-story/ ff1d87778e8cb0bc6657e057a25ed8e4**

Ouch! That dose of reality is not easy to swallow and the pessimist hits even harder. Watch out Coco! He might be *Maleficent* behind your mirror.

> *Sure 50-somethings can dress up the situation - teeth whitening, hair plugs, liposuction, groovy clothes - and convince one another that they're actually living on a younger planet, but they're not … Beyond 50, boomers catch glimpses of themselves in the mirror and are shocked by what they see. Is that me or is that my dad?* (Salt, B, 2011).

Salt (2011) argues this Boomer obsession with ageing is because we are the first generation to possess a good photographic record of our parents in their 50s. Prior to this, we did not have access to the gene pools of the middle-aged stage in the life cycle. This may be so, but I still believe that this negative perspective is likely to do more harm than good to the ageing population.

We must remember that the longevity of the human race today is unprecedented in history and there will be more challenges of this nature on the road ahead. We might ask ourselves about the incomparable advances in science that have prolonged the lives of human beings who have no desire to subsist on their own, most especially when their Soulmate passes on and ensuing illnesses set in. If they are in very poor health and dire financial circumstances, they see little point in going on. Society, on the other hand, continues the contentious debate on Euthanasia, adequate health care and housing. We really need to configure inventive ways of caring for the ageing population so that they retain their health longer, finding inventive ways of keeping them active and occupied at home.

Fit and fifty

As I continued to periodically scan the dating sites, by then, the process becoming rather tedious, I began to analyse the types of males I was trying to attract. The choices of 50+ male profiles I made were based on the following taxonomy,

> *Professional; Medical; Intellectual; Cultured; Stylish; Well-travelled; Athletic…*

These categorisations could easily be subsumed under larger umbrellas, but they fit quite well under the age brackets I had selected. I communicated with many of them but dated very few.

I am highly selective, not interested in meeting guys with whom there is no future. I know, I know, I had considered 49-year-old Marco in Melbourne! I must have been at a low point in this dating game. I admire a man in a tailored suit. Cannot help it. I could spend hours in a busy business district in Rome and London just watching the elegant men walk past. The problem is, when I click on the profile of the "suit", often I find it is simply packaging, with very little substance beneath the cladding.

A snippet of the content of profiles that led nowhere provides insight into this feature of dating. I was attracted to the package, but it could not hold my interest.

> *My story? I tell stories for a living, and they are all true. Reserved, outgoing, intelligent, ebullient, inquisitive, circumspect, iconoclastic. Always do things in polysyllables;-) Actually, not really, but I just read what I wrote.*

> *Sapiosexual.... But aren't you? Underestimate me, and that'll be fun ... No Clichés though*

People who consider themselves "iconoclastic" love to challenge cherished beliefs and traditional institutions. My conversation with the sceptic who posted the above entry was interesting but I could not handle the esoteric discussions that led nowhere. He became a little over-bearing and after an hour I had to let him go.

As for "sapiosexuality", if a guy deemed intelligence to be the most sexually attractive characteristic of a woman, I wondered if he could accept her other qualities as equally worthy? I needed to determine if this dating game was turning me into a sapiosexual but I knew that I need a balance in my life. Did I want too much?

One guy tried to impress with his words, using French because he knew it was one of my languages. That was pretty cool, but there was nothing else that induced me to contact him.

I'm a writer. Never written a book. But I love words although often I get paid to use simpler words rather than le mot juste.

Fifty and unfit – for me at least

The 50+ group of males who showed interest in my profile professed to be in their late forties or early fifties, but the first meeting consistently revealed them to look closer to their late sixties. They may wish to age gracefully but it is too late to reverse the damaging effects of the sun... so, they continue to challenge the odds.

This confounds me, and I can rarely tolerate such a cavalier attitude towards their health. I know of very few guys who have resorted to the knife, believing plastic surgery more the "female thing." There are other ways of restoring their damaged skin if they take the time to research this. However, the popular trend for males in other countries, such as South Korea, is an entirely different story. Competition in job interviews induces many young South Korean males to wear makeup daily, in the process, improving their job prospects and their self-concept.

Some women have openly confessed they do not wish to fall in love with a much older man only to end up being his carer. In my experience, many guys in their fifties and sixties are very stubborn and their continued irreverence toward their health simply drives them away. A great many are scarred by a significant number of skin cancers, melanomas, moles and spots that have been excised or frozen in the hope that they will not prove to be Squamous or Basal Cell Carcinomas. That is to be expected in Queensland, the State that is often touted to hold the title of skin cancer capital of Australia, thanks to the life style. The dangers of UV rays were not understood for decades. However, the incorrigible sun lovers who have grown up without sunscreen, now fully cognizant of the toxic effects of exposure to the Queensland sun, still refuse to protect their skin. I am baffled by this and I end up nagging them to apply it, at the risk of being labelled a Nag. Or worse, controlling. Lose, lose scenario in my opinion.

The Sexagenarian Beaux

Analysing these groups of men, I hope to be able to convince myself that my objectives are not futile. Many guys are looking for love, companionship or lust and some are involved in multiple affairs interstate if the anecdotes from the males I have dated are to be believed. This overwhelming and damning view is irritating, and it comes predominantly from the mouths of other males. It makes it even harder to trust online suitors. This makes my quest to find a partner more frustrating.

Ironically, the women are not perceived in a flattering light either. Is this perhaps an obscure way of cracking that glass ceiling? In fact, some bitter and malicious females are said to be rivalling the men at their own games; but often, other innocent women become targeted victims. More on this in Chapter 13, on Infidelity.

The difference in cohorts is interesting. Now that many of the sexagenarians are retired, they are increasingly conscious of their health and their mortality and a few at least are anxious to move forward, to fill the void created by early retirement in some cases and often to redress the perceived wrongs from previous loveless relationships by settling down with a good woman. They are tired of the games they profess are ruining the online dating scene.

Some of my dates have disclosed details of past indiscretions for which they are contrite, but they are prepared to redeem themselves by vowing to be faithful in future relationships. Can a leopard change its spots? If I believe that the guy is remorseful and sincere in his revelations of prior affairs that wrecked a marriage, then we can begin with a clean slate. It takes two to Tango, so everyone comes with baggage, whether we admit to it or not. The issue is to determine if we are still angry and revengeful or whether we have moved on. It is up to me to sift out the con artists from the aspirants I consider are genuinely interested in me. Not an easy task.

What is it about many of the guys in the sixties bracket? My investigations revealed an interesting paradigm. The astute businessmen, many of them retired on the Gold Coast, are fully aware that they need to protect their investments and have hopefully secured their assets in robust Family Trust Accounts. Believing these important financial measures to be bullet proof, many of them are likely to boast of their fortunes online, posing in front of the Yacht Marina, with their European cars, their beautiful residences, their beautiful horses. And they wonder why they are inundated with interest from scheming Gold Diggers. When prompted by a few to give advice, I humbly obliged, suggesting they be honest without advertising their financial independence online and wished them luck.

Guys in this cohort tend to display certain characteristics that can be construed as stereotypical to the less discerning. The guys on my radar, irrespective of who makes the first step, are extremely self-assured, proud of their old-fashioned values; they are chivalrous; cool and collected, and laid back; not unexpectedly, as this fits the apparent privileged profile they present. Divorced or widowed, their financial commitments are generally less onerous, and they live the life of luxury where they can indulge in water and adventure sports that befit their social class. I am beginning to wonder if they all know each other and how much time they spend comparing the size of their yachts, and no doubt their exploits of online dating! I picture them as subscribers to an exclusive *Male Divorcés' Yacht Club*. Some have even indicated that they are prepared to relocate "for the right Lady." Money does not appear to be an issue; they are quick to point that out. Inviting proposition but fortunately, most of the guys I have chatted with are not so desperate that they would jeopardise their hard-earned fortune on Gold Diggers. These guys are in a class of their own and I have really enjoyed their company.

So many of them appear much older than their advertised age, though. A 69-year-old guy from Melbourne sent me a message that I politely refused. He looked at least 82. Could some guys from this cohort be feeling the desperation that characterises the dating process if they remain online long enough? Do they perhaps prefer companionship at this age? I really do not know. I wish them well, but it fills me with sadness. This is an indictment of our societies where everything and everyone appears to be disposable.

No one is indispensable! Many individuals have found that out the hard way. Are the 50+ daters suddenly being classed, along with the Millennials, as an "entitled" generation? There are signs that many of us are now endorsing this behaviour. We want it all, and we want it now. Life is too short to wait. Live it to the fullest now! And in relationships the same paradigm is emerging. When else in history, have we been able to click on a few images and *Voilà!* The person of our dreams appears on our screens; the onus is on the individual to decipher the authenticity of the profile, however. If this person turns out to be fictitious, NEXT! NEXT! And on it goes.

Clearly, many of us also miss the intimacy, the affection, tenderness and the enjoyment of simply sharing the same space; holding hands, walking down the street as a couple, watching television together etc., and just hanging out with that special person. We miss chatting about our day, (Okay, the Ladies do) with someone who has greeted us with a welcoming, meaningful long kiss to indicate that we love each other, not the cursory peck on the forehead that so many of us experienced when former relationships lost whatever magic they had. We cannot ignore the fact however, that tapping instantaneously into an infinite source of "candidates" to fill the void lies at our fingertips. As this exciting world of potential partners beckons, we date other people and our friendships either grow stronger or fizzle out altogether.

Binding Financial Agreement (BFA)

Quite early in the dating cycle with a Lady, some astute men are keen to discuss a potential *Binding Financial Agreement (BFA)*, just in case the encounter evolves into a committed relationship. This wise move is not always welcome by all female contenders, from what I have learned, as it is perceived as a euphemism for the dreaded *Pre-Nuptial Agreement*. When I was in my prime, I did not go on dates. Married very young, I met my ex-husband through my sister. It was clear in those days that women were unimpressed if a suitor presented them with a *Pre-Nup*. It implied that we could not be trusted.

Today however, I see it perhaps as some men see it. I am more financially independent and savvy; I remain adamant that my hard-earned financial freedom will not be decimated by greedy and predatory partners. And so, I find myself leaning to adopting the financial strategy of the *BFA*, heeding the horror stories of my cohort whose inheritance for their children has been ravaged by avaricious partners on a hunt for wealthy women.

For the males I have dated, divorce settlements have sometimes been halved or almost decimated. I feel some sympathy, but less for those whose divorce was fuelled by their infidelity. I may admire their honesty, but not what they practise.

Regrettably, many of the men with whom I have communicated online readily confess that a wealthy woman is the means of recouping losses suffered in previous divorces or separations. In this, they are no different from female Gold-Diggers; love is rarely factored into the equation.

We, the mature male and female internet daters of this Millennium, now need to be prepared to sign a *BFA* because those who are judicious are intent on leaving their legacy to their grandchildren. Why would we not?

I imagine some lonely and desperate aspirants may have a different agenda however. Loneliness is crippling, and it is conceivable that a state of depression could provoke irrational decisions that could see hard working individuals, of both sexes, losing their entire fortune.

Divorced, desperate & dateless

I have witnessed a trend emerging on this journey. It has become clear to me that an increasing number of older men and women find the dating game challenging. To compound their problems, conventional dating has become a relic of the past. If they are needy and forlorn, they join online dating, but the majority struggle to compete with their younger counterparts. Wealth is – if they have it – a potential trump card if they are internet savvy and lucky.

However, relationships are changing at all levels of society. While the young are reported to subscribe to a "sexual hookup" culture, some older individuals of both sexes seem to be opting for the status of Friends *with Benefits* rather than cohabitation with a partner. Some newly entering the dating scene at older ages may find this prospect confronting. My girlfriends are vehemently opposed to resuming the role of the traditional housewife that they willingly accepted during their years of "wedded bliss" - cooking, cleaning, ironing, washing a partner's socks and jocks – these days are long gone. Most are focused on their career.

Are some career women choosing *Friends with Benefits* to avoid any claim to their wealth? That would not be farfetched. If they are financially secure through their professional experience and good management, their reticence to risk losing it all in a relationship that may fail, is comprehensible. The foolishness that is often attributed to young love is much less likely to be present in older love. I, however, remain resistant to this method of relating, notwithstanding my desire to protect my own financial interests. Quite simply, I cannot envisage spending the rest of my life alone.

Reflection

Rationalising to myself that I am not engaging in frivolous activities, the interim report of the time I have invested in this online dating exercise represents, in fact, a veiled attempt at disguising my true feelings about the dramatic effects internet dating is having on me. I genuinely hope that I will find a partner with whom I can spend the rest of my life; but I have become somewhat irresolute, in tandem with my growing disillusionment. I vacillate between abandoning my quest for love and living in hope that I will find the "One" who will fulfil all of my desires.

Trust issues are at the forefront of my mind and I remain constantly vigilant, bordering on cynical. Life is so transient, and love can be ephemeral, ever so fleeting! Philosophical reflections help to map out the trajectory that destiny has plotted for me and the road that lies ahead. If I understand this, if I put everything in perspective, I inadvertently place more pressure on myself to secure a good outcome as quickly as possible. In the process, I may make hasty and imprudent decisions that may come back to bite me on the butt. Been there; done that! A bit of a conundrum!

Considering this, my renewed strategy is to establish in the first instance, friendships with guys in their fifties or sixties who can accept companionship first. I am consciously attempting to take things slowly, enjoying the journey when a date shows true potential and simply moving on if there is little promise of longevity. Should a friendship quickly turn to love, then it will be a victorious outcome.

If not, *C'est la vie!* In the long run, others will benefit from my experiences. I sometimes feel like I am taking one for the team! Still plenty of fish in the sea, but how viable is this proposition? How long is a piece of string? Only I can judge just how long I can withstand the peaks and troughs of this journey.

When I discussed thoughts of giving up online dating with a male colleague, explaining that I was perhaps too discerning, not on the same page as the guys, he acquiesced, saying that so many guys were on dating site for easy hookups only. Why on earth would they contemplate a relationship?

I would just have to keep looking for that needle in the haystack. But for how long…

10

Some princes turn out to be frogs – he may look good, but nothing may be better

I have learned – the hard way - that dating sites can generate false hopes for anxious individuals. They are engineered in such a way that daters are presented with a carousel that presents the best face forward of the profiles of hundreds of adherents. But looks can be deceiving – and have at times created in me, a great deal of despair, angst and distrust. For instance, I have been accused at times of having viewed someone's profile (which I have) yet criticized for showing no interest when they have contacted me. Yes, I looked. But no, I am not interested, hence my non-response, or perhaps lukewarm polite response.

I'm pleased you are still looking at my profile .. I thought after your last message you were being polite indicating you were not interested .. may be I'm presuming more than I should now ... your main photo your look holds such deserving passion .. I often wonder what your thinking

This old chap's profile provoked pathos, empathy and even a sense of guilt in me. Was I wrong to read desperation in his messages? It certainly felt palpable to me. Perhaps I was overreacting; perhaps I read into the profiles what I myself had at times felt, but I perceived the pain, despondency and disillusionment just beneath the surface of some outlines. It was not my fault, it was but a reflection of our society, a view of an underclass of lonely individuals that I might rather believe did not exist in this lucky country. Before online dating, I was perhaps so engrossed in my own life, my head stuck in the sand, that I was not aware of, or plainly ignored the plight of those whose paths I never crossed.

These individuals are not illiterate, but their confused or unintelligible entries suggest they are not well educated; but their effort to find friendship and love online is tangible and real and easy to read in their lines.

> *Good day Pretty Lady, love your profile which shows the smile you have hidden within the profile you have put up… caught my attention … I am an interesting man or Guy, simple, down to earth, understanding, caring and romantic who take his woman serious… want to share my hobbies like camping, cooking, swimming, fishing, canoeing and sometimes golfing with my woman… I am a widower, has no kids and works for myself … because of interesting you are I would love to get to know you to build a continues communication with you to see where it leads us. Please email me to the respective contacts given below…*

Harry was a 65-year-old chap whose strength was his persistence. However, his sometimes-incoherent entries made me wonder if he may be inebriated. I ceased to communicate with him quite early, but he did not give up. I felt exasperated such as the following messages from Harry suggest.

> *Hi how are you?Nice to meet you?March 5*

> *Hi Nice to meet you…"I have read your profile and I think you are nice…"Thanks for reading my first message.Im a Cook. What you do?March 6*

> *Whats your name may I ask,Iam sure is sweetMarch 7*

I Think your a a nice Lady who knows what she wantsMarch 7

Would you like to reply and chat a little,pleaseMarch 7

WOW,sound perfect suits you niceMarch 7, 2017

Humpty Dumpty is my name remember that rime,hahahaMarch 7

I like your photos, especially the one in Red, that's my favourite colour. I like your sexy eyes, I think you're very specialx😀July 13, 2017

Hi princess how are you? I think you are very special.Any romance princess 😊? Yeah good luck to you 😮July 27, 2017

It was heart-wrenching to observe the despair that I believed defined some of the hopeless romantics on dating sites. Again, it was but my perception. Day after day, night after night, some appeared to trawl the pages of these sites in the hope of communicating with someone, anyone, who might just notice them. Even after a long spell with no contact, Harry sent me another message,

Hi gorgeous what are you doing this weekend anything fun? I wish I had your company today go out for dinner have a laugh with their exciting weekend. August 12

I can only wonder how many hopeless souls, male and female, are searching for human contact online. I wonder, even fear that internet dating may offer some hope in some superficial way, but ultimately, provokes anguish and is potentially harming many lives. This is a double-edged sword that poses infinitely more questions than it provides solutions.

Who will love the unattractive?

The online medium for dating is unforgiving, especially for those who are not handy with words. It is a medium that offers suitors only a few lines, a few words, a few images to woo the unknown male or female they seek. In old-fashioned dating, we might have had cause for concern for the less beautiful people – a commonly held assumption is that this is less an issue for men than for women. This problem still exists in the online environment – although those with nefarious objectives can at least get to a meeting perhaps by posting fake images. But in the online environment, the less literate are also likely to be punished. Perhaps they can borrow the words of others, but like the one that posts fake images, this presumably only works at the very first threshold. After that, their hands are up, but they are drowning, not waving.

It is distressing but, in this new age of internet dating there is a greater audience, and therefore, perhaps someone may just respond to a kind hearted old chap or old lady.

Literacy however, like images, can project a false image. Some individuals may kick off with a witty entry, but I would often find in the guys' profiles that reached me, that there was little substance beneath those words. Perhaps they were just using abbreviated internet language? They may have engaged someone to assist with building their profile. I cannot say. The problem is the ensuing communication generally precludes spontaneity and genuine interest.

Some messages tend to generate interest but if there is no chemistry, you just move on. The excitement fizzles out like sparklers at a party.

The Articulate Romantics (50+)

Many of the male profiles that caught my eye or those belonging to men who approached me occasionally displayed a measure of reflection and often included the statutory succinct and witty lines for effect. Some guys waxed lyrical to demonstrate their humoristic side but that was strictly contingent on the stipulations of the dating site. If they were not expected to elaborate on any facet of their personality or physical appearance, many guys limited their profiles to monosyllabic expressions or unimaginative phrases.

The following introductory spiels provide interesting insights into the workings of the male intellect when he is on the hunt. They are but a snapshot of what is available online, headlines from the guys who approached me. Some are on a mission to prove to the woman they seek that they are clearly not just another fish in the sea. No, they believe they are the articulate ones who hope to take the prize by appealing to the right kind of woman who will appreciate the formulaic platitudes they believe we, the Ladies wish to hear.

> *Position Vacant.......Subservient Female Required....Joking of course does such a creature exist :-) and how boring would that be?*

> *Passionate man! 60. Attracted to smart people and value intelligence over looks.*

> *Humor, reality, and a sanguine nature makes up who I am ...*
> *I am a good listener and 'all about Me' People turn me off very quickly, however I do like people who are eloquent and can engage in meaningful conversation ... I love intimacy and emotion and consider myself to be tactile and romantic. It is a relationship I want to pursue and yes... I am prepared for an organic process with time and commitment. I like to go out where you need to dress up but also like to dress down and do casual somewhere, so if you're good in a LBD and heels as much as a pair of jeans and you are fit and healthy we have a great start. My Photo's are very recent (2016 / 17) and so to be fair to this process I do expect the same from you*

> *One word Stunning!*
> *I would love to chat to you over a coffee soon. Are you interested, my mental age is way lower than my chronological age and I am fully house trained by a European mum and same with the ex. I am very fit lean and healthy and a born mischief... And I cook and fix things but having read ALL the right boy chick books wont try to fix you... I am very emotionally aware.*

> *I am retired by choice but sometimes do projects. I have chosen dating because a long term relationship evolves without being prerequisite for me. I have 31 years experience as a husband so understand what it takes and what my contributions should be as a partner. Communication is the key especially the ability to*

have the hard conversations and remain true to ones self. I am looking for a fun loving snuggle bunny who is spontaneous. If that is you contact me and join me for lunch soon.

Distance is no detriment to determination, I travelled 600 km each way on weekends for kisses in 2004 then married her to save fuel.:-)

I must say, marrying someone to save fuel is original!

The following entry from Nick was in reaction to my curt message thanking him for his interest and letting him know I had met someone I liked. I apparently sent him into a guilt trip.

Dear Coco, reading your profile my impression was that you are an impressive lovely woman.

Hello Nick. Thank you for contacting me. I read your profile and I am sure you will find someone who appreciates you. I am interested in someone right now and wish to see where this leads. Best of luck!

Me too I thought Id let you know, you're making me feel guilty. I just couldn't help myself. Nick

The next European guy appeared to have little self-esteem, considering his response to my interest.

Good morning. Im somewhat bemused as to how an outstandingly beautiful lady like yourself have an interest in a man of my calibre.... it begs the question??
Especially with the amount of approach I'm certain you're fielding due to your allure. You belie your age.
11/10 comes to mind... 💣
Clearly you're not all about/ into looks, I'm living proof of that "-)
Let me recalibrate, you've left me unusually speechless, stuttering at best....& once I settle I'll come back to you.
I'm not so cocky all of a sudden. Paulo

Well! That perked me up! Paulo graded me 11/10. Maybe I should have pursued him? Or perhaps I should be examining my motivation for persevering in internet dating? I do not doubt the veracity of some, emphasis on "some" of the words that several guys have employed to woo me. There are those who use fancy words that are simply misleading, but Paolo appeared to be a nice guy. We communicated briefly but discovered that we did not have much in common after all; but I had found his comment intriguing.

I believe many guys to be genuinely searching for love, who find me to be a worthy candidate, but this is my interpretation based on what they have included in their profile or ensuing communication. It is easy to make assumptions that they may lack self-esteem or be lonely, but this is again only my perception, predicated on my own experiences. That we do not all adopt the same mode of communication during social interactions, on or offline, is the result of personal preferences and differences in personalities. Is it possible that some of these guys who have been on the sites for a long time may be a little insecure? My male friends suggest this is not farfetched! It is essentially the impression their entries have given me; but when they make contact with someone who may just fulfil their needs, it makes online dating a worthwhile pursuit for them.

Fearful of being alone

Thousands are single but thousands are silent; i.e. don't talk much
My parents are in their 70's living separately and alone.
Who wants to live like that?
I don't!

So, spoke Sam. His words tore at my heart. He was not alone. The internet dating scene that I explored gave the impression that many men were lonely, exposing themselves and their loneliness to all those online. I imagine the situation for the female daters to be a close match.

Why are they online? I am under no illusion as to why I am here. Do these guys hope to find companionship? Or is it more, to ease the loneliness? I am new to internet dating, but many guys have confessed to having been *habitués* of various dating sites for years. Their needs are evidently met, on and off, given the ease with which this can be done in a non-judgmental way. Otherwise, why would they persist in this pursuit? It can be rewarding, certainly, but there are far greater chances of this venture being despair-inducing. This is just a snippet,

> *It is now at the point where I have to do something as all this loneliness is becoming unhealthy... so if you are a lady that actually likes the company of a man and want to make a relationship with a male of the species perhaps give me some consideration ..*

I am convinced, however, that this form of dating can be a panacea to loneliness, perhaps more than other social media sites. After all, dating sites, like the antiquated methods of matching people, were created to facilitate companionship, romantic or sexual encounters and not just a way of connecting with existing friends. These sites are not just there to share photos with family and friends.

Words can be powerful, but they can also disguise the real nature of the suitor. *Cyrano de Bergerac* had a gigantic nose that prevented him from wooing his beloved *Roxane* face to face. He used a third party as his face.

Perhaps we, online daters rely on the online platform as our third party? I sometimes feel like I am engaging someone – and he is wooing me – but sometimes it seems hollow. Mere words. But then I regather my skirts and rejoin those on the floor. I will have to dance with some guys with two left feet in order to find a partner for the rest of my life. If I am lucky, he might just be in the same retirement village or nursing home as me one day!

"A beautiful critter"

Then there are those who aspire to be *Cyrano de Bergerac* with a skill with words, but who fall hopelessly short. They are as challenged then as *Cyrano* – they may be physically beautiful, but clumsy in their words. One fellow, Ellis, called me a *"Beautiful Critter."* This guy made my day. His clumsy words made me smile – and at least he was trying.

> *You be about as pretty as they come …i recon very pretty. how*
> *are you …my name is Ellis*

I sent him a short note thanking him for his interest, but dissuading him from his pursuit of me,

> *You are a romantic. Thank you Ellis. Best of luck in your*
> *search. C. July*

But Ellis was nothing if not persistent. He sent me about five more messages that first day, and another dozen over the week or so that followed. But for all that, he patently lacked the charm of *Cyrano's* command of language,

> *Oh … dont worry …i just getting my daily inspiration ..just a*
> *little look at you and i feel like springing out of bed and getting*
> *stuck into my chores …**beautiful critter …x.*** 💀 *July 31*

I sent another note of dissuasion reinforced by telling him I had found someone, and he replied,

> *So you can settle for less than one in a million …lol …strange*
> *breed …you girls ..lol*

Ellis was well-meaning I believe. He looked about 75 and was from the North of Australia. It is perhaps his location that may partially explain both his ancient look (he said he was 56) and his failure to finesse me with his words. Still, if I can inspire old Ellis to trim his beard, *"I had a trim and cut my beard yesterday ….tell me what do you think 😳😳😳"*, and to spring out of bed to attend to his chores, I must be doing something right. And he did manage to get me to respond to his quirky messages. Clever fellow!

Reflection

As I sit and cogitate on this dating journey, I feel that I need to reassess the impacts of the online dating experiences on my identity. Some of the most promising dates I had were short lived; they gave an incredible boost to my wounded self-esteem. However, the fact that none evolved into a loving relationship left me quite deflated. I felt that they built me up only to let me down ultimately.

I had warned these guys not to place me on so high a pedestal, but it had been part of their strategy to woo the Lady. The motives of these guys did not include diabolical tactics; they did not represent a ploy, a demonic game to bring me down. However, underlying issues were instrumental in ruining a potentially solid relationship; and at times, we reached a mutual decision. The Boys were equally devastated that things had not moved to the next stage. Their intentions were sincere. Things had just not developed the way we had hoped. I trusted my instincts, something I have rarely done in the past. Despite the rapid demise of the promising relationships, I gained by trusting my instincts. I became a little less credulous!

I suspect we were simply not on the same page. For my part, I paid the price of being an incorrigible romantic, choosing to leave the rose-coloured glasses firmly affixed over my eyes until I saw the light. Realisation in the cold light of day...

The conscious decision to be prudent when starting a new relationship is fraught with doubt because I always try to be honest with myself. When I find the man of my dreams, whatever troubling issues he may be experiencing, I will be at his side supporting him... And yet, I say I will reject a guy I fall in love with if he has unresolved problems in his life. Rather contradictory, I realise.

I cannot expect to find a guy who will respond to my rigorous list of expectations at this stage of my life when looking for love. The likelihood of joining the members of the *Happy Divorcées' Club* is looking pretty certain. Or maybe I will become a discontented member of that club.

Unconditional love is what I am ideally seeking, and this comes by accepting "warts and all." I am on this journey to find love and I can only hope that the "warts" will not manifest as the indelible marker of a warlock in disguise. I like to think I am in total control and I hope to detect such an occurrence. But what if I am wrong? I do not wish to be controlling in a relationship, but I am intent on examining all aspects of a potential union to avoid falling into familiar traps. Otherwise, I will have learned nothing from past relationships.

In examining my conscience and my behaviour in both online and offline, I am left asking whether I share responsibility for the failure of the promising leads. But I cannot identify where I have erred. I consider I have acted with integrity of character.

There are few guys who have had a strong emotional impact on me. Mutual attraction is rare. While some guys are immediately infatuated with me, and they have offered a salve for my self-esteem, their overly-effusive attentions became overbearing and created a problem by being difficult to let down. I have reacted negatively to the compliments and flattery that they persistently showered on me; I sometimes found their comments insincere.

On the other hand, I am baffled when contrasting the unrealistically favourable images I project to the eyes of the suitors who fall for me so quickly, with the unequivocal rejection of my profile by other online daters whose attention I seek. Curiously, 90% of the time, this concerns males from the Gold Coast… Am I just like those I reject? I cannot reconcile these distinct perspectives. Is the hypothesis that I am a fish out of water on the Gold Coast proving self-fulfilling?

It sounds so self-serving, but why, when some are so generous in their compliments to me, that others will not even talk to me? Am I too strong, too independent for some of the Alpha males? Not sweet enough; fragile enough to be rescued? Do they want a Damsel in Distress? Are they too competitive? So many questions to which I have no answers. I think that they just need to understand the real Coco beneath the mask. Is this not a human speed trap when we choose to engage in the digital world? Once more, I realise that I am asking the impossible!

This leads me back to ask which guys are sincere in their pursuit of me, an issue that continually haunts me. When I fall for someone, I crave for every ounce of affection they can give, the compliments restoring instantly what years of emotional abuse have destroyed. If my affections are not reciprocated, the effects are devastating. I still believe in true love and I believe there is a Soulmate for me, somewhere out there. It is, I believe, human nature. It is, I am certain, this human's nature.

Trolls, ghouls and fairy tales with unhappy endings

Some of the guys I encountered online are simply not there for the same reason as me. Some are simply self-aggrandising, some are vile – but both can hurt me, and others like me.

The road to successful internet dating shines golden with promise, but is paved ultimately with broken promises, deceit, bruised egos and shattered dreams. If we are successful, we may find the "One," but inexperienced individuals blindly trust online posts, where real or fictitious photos of 'happy couples' have ostensibly found each other thanks to the clever use of algorithms. The antics employed by many predators on dating sites are transparent to the internet savvy but unfortunately the vulnerable continue to fall prey to the hype that is promulgated by social media.

The reality is that just when I think I can see the light at the end of the tunnel, how many times does this transmute into lights of the oncoming train? A pessimistic observation, certainly, but anecdotal evidence suggests increasing numbers of disgruntled adherents of several internet dating sites, of both sexes, end up in tears and become contemptuous and dismissive, vowing to give up the search. Yet, a glimmer of hope remains.

I persevered, addicted even to this avant-garde social dating medium of today. But each new ride seemed to offer an ever more vertiginous trajectory. I have my neurotransmitters, Dopamine and Serotonin to thank for that, as I continued to chase those promised rewards in the pursuit of happiness and love.

The promise of instant gratification, part and parcel of the Smorgasbord of profiles that awaited me filled the air when I began to surf the waves of internet dating. However, when I began to search through the "Zoo", many good guys were fast abandoning the game.

These honourable guys do not want their reputations tarnished by those whose instrumental objective is to satisfy their unquenched thirst for sex and game playing. Male profiles increasingly caution Gold Diggers who lack integrity and have not a shred of dignity, that they will not tolerate game playing. I can only hope that their female counterparts are doing the same.

Unfortunately, the damning criticism that is circulating, describes many women as vindictive and on a mission to challenge the males as common perpetrators of nefarious games and tactics online. The *Dark Web* or *Dark Net* is where these tactics thrive; other examples can be found on *Urban Dictionary,* where the lexicon is derived entirely from sex. It is a worrying trend that this is no longer the domain of males, as one might have expected. It seems the chances of being targeted have grown exponentially.

Given this scenario, for the Ladies who are too discerning, or let's face it, downright difficult, the road can be long and agonising if they are constantly rejected because of unrealistic expectations. Whilst some of us, legitimate daters stick to our guns and our principles, gamesters appear and disappear, gauging the odds of "winning" the game. If the odds are unfavourable, they may just slither away and wait for a more opportune moment to strike. This is not the stuff of fiction. Reality is oft said to be stranger than fiction.

I have witnessed a metaphorical tug of war online between the imposters and defiant males with integrity who take up the challenge when I have thrown down the gauntlet. They have proved to be just as discerning as I am; and consequently, claim to be a perfect match. The problem is, even when the profiles appear to match closely; even when they prove to be legitimate and devoted suitors, amazing, unpretentious guys, sometimes there is simply no chemistry. I cannot fabricate this! I cannot force the spark! It either does or does not ignite.

I prefer a little sophistication, even when relaxing, and I have found that the guys from Melbourne, Sydney and Brisbane have a sense of style. We have a great deal more in common. I get them and they get me. Guys can still be elegant and comfortable. Let's face it Gentlemen, you do not have to suffer to be gorgeous. At least you do not have to wear stilettos!

The worst male offenders are those who woo you and lull you into a false sense of security; lead you to believe they are genuinely interested. Within a few weeks or months, when the catch has been consumed, the shield is removed, and these individuals show their true colours – proud *Yobbos* or *Bogans* in the guise of distinguished individuals. They act so superior; yet, could this hide an inferiority complex? If they woo someone under false pretences, I guarantee this will spell disaster for the relationship because it is not only the lack of sophistication that is being dissimulated. I suspect there are many people from both sexes who have tales to tell about the despicable lies in relationships.

Catfish - Charlie

Cyber fantasy is attractive to those who have abandoned former norms of dating and the depraved individuals who lurk on the *Dark Web* have created an attractive playground for others of their kind. Make no mistake! These include both sexes.

55-year-old Nancy was a successful accountant who immigrated to Australia in the sixties. She enjoyed a solid reputation in a large international firm; was well regarded and financially independent. Lonely after a ten-year relationship soured, she was cajoled into internet dating. Nancy met Charlie very quickly, a charming and handsome 50-year-old who claimed to be a citizen of the US. Nancy was not adept with modern technology and after two months of online communication and weekly Skype sessions with Charlie, they professed their love for each other. Things quickly proceeded to the next level of commitment because, for all intents and purposes, they were compatible and were making plans for a life together, initially in Australia and then in the US.

As Nancy's schedule was inflexible, Charlie offered to visit her in Australia. When he confessed to being strapped for cash, currently waiting to start a new job, Nancy hesitated but decided to follow her heart. Charlie manipulated the situation stating the only way they could meet was for Nancy to transfer some funds into his account. Whilst uncomfortable with these plans, Nancy transferred AU$5, 000 to Charlie's account and waited for D Day.

Nancy, full of excitement for the anticipated joyous meeting, headed to Sydney airport to pick Charlie up at 6:30 AM on a Thursday morning. She waited in vain, with a sinking heart checking the flight details that had been sent via email, but the promised long-awaited rendezvous never took place. Charlie was not on the flight.

Devastated and embarrassed beyond imagination by the subterfuge, Nancy could only speak of this to her best friend who finally convinced her to contact the police. As it turned out, this *Catfish* scammer was being surveilled by US authorities for some time and with concrete details from Nancy, they were finally able to catch the perpetrator online, playing his own game. With her help, the common ruse by this scammer had been terminated and Charlie was at last behind bars, but her money was never reimbursed. Charlie had no intention of turning up in Australia because Charlie was in fact a scheming woman, a practised fraudster who had been pursued by detectives for years. She was a rancorous and twisted woman with a personal page that was totally fraudulent. All profile photos featured a male friend of Charlie's. The skype conversations had taken place with a good-looking male who had pretended to woo Nancy and the poor Lady had fallen for Charlie's puppet.

The practice of Catfish[14] that inspired a 2010 film and television series of the same name about the horrors of online dating has become the predilection of males and females who despair of ever finding a partner. It may well be that there is no other reason except that they are perverted. Catfish is a term reserved for predators or unsavoury stalkers whose ploy it is to ruin the lives of others. Detecting the perpetrators is not easy; neither is the onerous burden of proving your real identity if yours has been cloned

---

[14] Petersen, H. (2013). Daily Mail. Australia. 'Catfishing:' The phenomenon of Internet scammers who fabricate online identities and entire social circles to trick people into romantic relationships http://www.dailymail.co.uk/news/article-2264053/ Catfishing-The-phenomenon-Internet-scammers-fabricate-online-identities-entire-social-circles-trick-people-romantic-relationships.html#ixzz4wD0FWfc1

but reporting the cases of this abuse to the agencies and to the authorities is not guaranteed to work even if precedents exist. In the UK, cases such as these have been known to reach parliament. It was revealed that the police were allegedly ineffective, inciting lobbyists to finally approach the government. It pays to note, however that many such unconscionable acts of all calibres found on the *Dark Web* go largely undetected.

12

Fairy tales with unhappy endings - beware ginger breadcrumbs. Denizens of both genders

According to a recent study on the tactics used by the internationally-based site, *Plenty Of Fish*, published in the Daily Mail online in the UK,[15] 70% of the males on this popular free site have been found to indulge in inscrutable tactics, a ploy for the narcissistic hunter to strategically lead his prey (the credulous woman) up the garden path, only to release her after weeks of coaxing, flattering and praising her attributes. Whilst the sharks massage their massive egos, who knows if they remain entrapped in loveless relationships? I have just added some select new terms to my lexicon. This journey has proved revelatory!

Whilst this scenario has been published by one online magazine, some women are using their own tactics to obtain gratuitous sex and free meals, gauging from current affair programs and the bitter recriminations of some males with whom I have spoken. They target *Sugar Daddies,* engage in simultaneous affairs, visa scamming and more.

---

[15] Cliff, M. Have you been breadcrumbed? (Daily Mail Online 6/2/17) http://www. dailymail.co.uk/femail/article-4159250/Have-BREADCRUMBED.html

I have had the displeasure of meeting some male predators online who leave a trail of breadcrumbs for a woman to follow; but, for all I know, they could have been women. It is not hard to become cynical during this dating venture. This tactic is known as *Hansel and Gretelling*, better known as *Breadcrumbing*. Predictably an *habitué* of several dating sites, classic offenders promise to meet their love interest SOON (I now really hate that word); their pledges forming part of a daily ritual until D-Day arrives, when a precise location and time are required. The inevitable avoidance of the meeting leaves victims reeling, duped, embarrassed and disillusioned because the player has no intention of showing up. Only then does it become clear that a relationship was never on the cards. As these culprits emerge on several sites, some are too lazy and stupid to change their photos and profile descriptions, risking being caught out by a sarcastic comment from a former victim. If the site allows it, they can be denounced but the fact that some of these profiles keep resurfacing, suggests this measure is highly ineffectual. Undeterred, the narcissists simply withdraw for a while, making their reappearance when ready.

The following profiles depict some of the ploys utilised online. Hansel's tactics represent the epitome of the *Breadcrumber* of my chronicle; the other manoeuvres appear in diminishing order of dastardly incentives, with some people dismissing a few tactics as inoffensive. The definitions and vignettes found here are simplistic and perhaps naïve if compared to the significantly twisted versions that can be found on *Urban Dictionary*, but I have chosen not to delve into the sick and depraved world of the *Dark Net*.

Ghosting is another apparently popular sport, except of course for the trusting novice. The term, increasingly being used on dating shows on television, signifies terminating communication with a person without warning, essentially ending a relationship. Often, all traces of the profile disappear, along with any messages. *Ghosting* gives you closure and you are forced to move on, whereas *Breadcrumbing* leaves a window of opportunity and is more malicious and deceitful, as it perpetuates unhealthy communication.[16] It is easy to make promises to renew a liaison

---

[16] Sareen Nowakowski, A. (2017) Difference between Ghosting and Breadcrumbing. https://www.elitedaily.com/dating/difference-ghosting-breadcrumbing/2002092

as one leaves a first date but if the offender is not local or lives interstate, terminating the contact poses few problems. I can vouch for that too.

Slow Fade is a common ploy employed by those who feign interest in a hopeful relationship and slowly begin to withdraw contact and communication. If this is swift, it causes annoyance and distrust; if it is drawn out, once again, it hurts.

Catch and Release is a classic, popular game often attributed to men and women who enjoy the thrill of the chase and who get bored easily. Once caught, the release is swiftly executed, with another notch on the belt. This can be quick or extended, like the other tactics. The most painful part in these activities is when these impostors string their victims along for months, just a plaything. It keeps them interested without ever having to commit to a serious relationship.[17] In the meantime, the victims may discount all other suitors, investing only in the potential union.

Finally, *Benching,* a term commonly used in sports, is an effective way of hedging bets, just in case the new suitor does not meet expectations. There are usually several prospects forced to take "time out" during a match, literally put on the bench. I believe this tactic is a common strategy inadvertently employed by most online daters, often with no nefarious motives in mind. Internet dating encourages users to chat with several people at the same time until they are ready to connect with one of them. The Smorgasbord effect is responsible for this. It becomes problematic when suitors set out to communicate with several people at once telling each one they are the only love interest.

I am determined to remain empowered and will never again surrender that power to any man. This is not a failsafe strategy because I discovered that scurrilous gamesters became more expert in their tactics as my journey progressed. The following vignettes recounting the disturbing episodes that occurred early on my cyber journey may have discouraged those with a feeble constitution from persevering in their quest to find love, but not the feisty Coco! The more challenging this pursuit became, the stronger my resolve to achieve what I set out to do on this voyage of self-discovery and love.

---

[17] Cliff, M. Have you been breadcrumbed? (Daily Mail Online 6/2/17) http://www. dailymail.co.uk/femail/article-4159250/Have-BREADCRUMBED.html

Hansel, Epitome of a *Breadcrumber*

Hansel's outline immediately resonated with me. He, because I believed him to be a male, approached me, ostensibly secure in the knowledge that his carefully structured profile would achieve his shameful objectives. His personal page exhibited four photos with the *Ray-Ban* sunglasses firmly affixed to hide his blue eyes in all shots. He exemplified the image of the flawless, suave and sophisticated wealthy businessman from Brisbane, proudly promoted on the dating site.

51-year-old, dark and handsome professional, close-shaven, *distingué*, with only the hint of grey hair above his temples, 6' Hansel was impeccably groomed. He spared no expense in fashioning his profile to attract like-minded women. In one image, posing in his tailored suit and white business shirt, unbuttoned seductively to show a relatively smooth chest, his chosen stance denoted the end of a long, satisfying day at work. The next photograph depicted the casual Hansel, seated at the wheel of his Prestige 4x4, construing the image of the debonair, well-to-do Australian male poised to enjoy fabulous weekends away (a feature reiterated in his written introductory message). The next photograph was engineered to show his sense of humour, portrayed through a Selfie, posing with a Kardashian pout. Lame, I agree but I was ready to forgive him anything. The final photo, in a t-shirt showing his abs and six-pack, was posted from a bedroom with a sardonic smile on his face, completing the image of a quirky, athletic male, still sporting the sunglasses. How could I possibly resist even if I hate Selfies, with a passion!

Hook, line and sinker! I fell for this guy and after a couple of messages online, Hansel quickly volunteered his phone number so that we could both get off this "Zoo." Fascinating insights into the typical language used by *Breadcrumbers* follow. Fortunately for me, half way through the month-long interchange, the article on these tactics was brought to my attention. I played along for another two weeks before confirming the ruse, whilst hoping, just a little, that I was wrong. Ever the romantic. Certainly, the eternal optimist. I began by asking for a photo that showed Hansel's blue eyes.

> *Hi there Young Lady. You do know you are the lady of my choice… exquisite, refined and delightful. Would welcome*

the chance to meet you… My eyes are blue/green. You can see for yourself soon ☺

When I concurred that dark hair and blue eyes were an attractive combination, Hansel needed no further encouragement, stating,

Seriously, you are the refined princess I seek. Love the complexion. Love your pronunciation of the English language, correctly and accurately spoken. Love your look. So very attractive to my eyes 👀*Catch up SOON!*

After a little while, in answer to my text, "Enjoy your day", Hansel grew more brazen as the days progressed. The ensuing messages went up a notch, "Hi Sexy! You to, my exotic dream xx." When I became sassy, responding, "That's funny! Why don't you hurry up and meet me then?" Hansel added, "I hope young lady I do hope there is an amazing connection as my lips are so lonely ☺."

Trying not to throw up by this stage, this last message confirmed, sadly, that Hansel was actively engaged in his Oscar-hopeful winning performance he probably believed would go the distance. I began to wonder if Hansel was in fact Gretel? No proof of course. I continued to play along, curious to see how far he would go. "The little boy in me wants your hand in mine. The man I am desires you. Exotic Princess… a chance to taste your lips is all I ask for now… H. XX."

Emboldened by the tone of the text messages [with no encouragement from me], Hansel was on a roll and decided to step up another notch, sending me a message in Italian, "Tu sei una bella donna☺. Yes, we need to meet please, very SOON Exotic Princess." When I responded in a complex message in Italian, Hansel was lost and reverted to English.

I am about to drive sweet. But thought I would make you smile with my message xxx
Oh and p.s. I WANT YOUR LIPS ON MINE♥*I will not be coming down today (as promised). I will come tomorrow xx*

I kept up the pretence. All in the name of research. This was tantamount to a harmless version of a honey trap.

The "long awaited meeting" was for the following Tuesday. Hansel apologised for the fourth time since our first chat, saying that his crazy schedule precluded a visit to the Gold Coast. He had visited his son on the Northern end of the Coast on three consecutive weekends but had not found one hour to meet me for a coffee. He evidently took me for a fool.

> *See you SOON Dream Girl. You are Devine. The primal*
> *man within desires you strongly beautiful xx. Kiss me when*
> *you can!*

My last text, after a month of this contrived and ridiculous tone of exchanges, convinced Hansel that the game was over, finally, as he had no intention of showing up. "That will depend on you during our first meeting…" were my last words. The rest is history as they say, because the expected rendezvous never took place. When Hansel resurfaced on another site, my sarcastic and dismissive remark was enough to scare him off for a few weeks at least.

> *Well, well! Young Hansel. So, we meet again! Or not! What?*
> *No more breadcrumbs?*

Although this quip was most satisfying, I was by that time disillusioned by the games that I witnessed online and was on a mission to warn other unsuspecting women; hence, the release of this personal chronicle. I refused to allow this disheartening experience to dampen my enthusiasm in my search for love.

I will not tolerate the attempts of any individual, male or female, to extinguish my trust in human nature. My resilience and spontaneity will help me find my bearings.

Hansel turned up sporadically on three different sites, resolutely complicit in perpetuating the ugliness of the lies and deceit in which he revelled; he was no doubt trying his luck on women who were more easily duped, enjoying the tease and the fantasy. The control freak was too stupid to change his photos and profile entry. Why? Who knows? Bizarre! Did he feel insecure to be playing these games? Was he trapped in a loveless relationship, too much of a coward to break free? I have heard these versions from guys I have befriended.

Anecdotal evidence increasingly suggests that individuals such as Hansel could be social delinquents, perverted sadists who need to go to such lengths to cause pain. They may have a distorted view of women; misogynists who enjoy messing with women's brains. At any rate, raising awareness of the antics of some online daters of both sexes became an important objective of this journey, especially after confirmation from a few of my dates that these ruses were widespread.

Well! I live and learn! I am getting so much better at washing my hands of the degenerates online. Move on, I say! Besides they will just become the antagonists of my narrative! I have no intention, however, of identifying these low-life individuals. Only they, and perhaps the victims who have been duped by them, will recognise them through the typology of the predators, gamesters, narcissistic and unfaithful players that deserve to be ousted. I hope to have saved lonely people a great deal of heartache and embarrassment.

The tactic of *Ghosting,* especially if the partners are interstate, becomes the choice of predilection and the relationship ends on a sour note, the woman usually left in the lurch. I have met sexagenarians who have been enjoying the "pleasures" of internet dating for many years now, touting the brilliant medical wonders of Viagra. I wonder when they will decide that it is time to end the charade. This mode of dating is unprecedented, precisely because its instantaneous advantages and subsequent effects are so attractive; the members of the Boomer generation could well be the pioneers of these questionable practices in the New Age of dating, sex being a fascinating drawcard onto the playground of Millennials.

Casper the Ghost

The magician appears… again and again. A suspected perennial gamester on dating sites, Casper, is adept at playing mind games with unsuspecting women online by posing as a debonair, tall and handsome gentleman in his early fifties. His obsequious charms left me holding my breath. Again. Just when I believed he might actually be real, he pulled the rug from under my feet. When I thought I had recovered from the deceitful tactic, Casper reappeared, bearing a different name and completely different profile. This was the *MO* of the typical online dating Ghost.

Feisty as ever, I refused to give this fool, Casper, the satisfaction. I caught him out three times. I was watching out for the signs. How could I allow myself to fall into the trap of the wily Casper, who used well-practised ruses to lure his prey? Using a photograph in the genre of the original post, with a carefully engineered profile once again, he could relax knowing few women would save his attractive, fictitious image on their phones. I was onto him. I saved the photo. If you are gullible and naïve, you are a sitting duck.

Casper's well-conceived new pranks, reinventing himself time and time again, were sure to see me fall for him instantly. The overwhelming feelings of foolhardiness and shame began to envelop me. I berated myself for my folly. Self-flagellation was threatening to become a permanent fixture of the dynamic remodelling of my identity… I was fighting it… Thoughts of removing my profile kept resurfacing, but once more I told myself, "Do you really want to let him win?"

There are few words to describe the feelings of emptiness, despair, embarrassment and disgust when I admit that I have been played. It is disquieting, to say the least, especially as I am supposed to be an intellectual. Does it ever get any easier to detect the fraudulent behaviour of sociopaths online? Just when you think you have outsmarted the despicable scoundrels who have nothing better to do other than play with your heartstrings, they come back to bite you on the *derrière!* Is it possible to ever grow thicker skin to endure these moments of distress? I thought I had succeeded.

How many profiles was I prepared to probe in seven months? This imposter was aware of my penchant for the type of look and personality he arrogantly portrayed. He had certainly done his homework. As this online dating journey progressed, I became shrewd at searching for the kind of guy I wished to attract. The only redeeming feature of this episode, to restore my self-worth, was the personal growth that I experienced. I was on to him but lamentably, it did not diminish the sense of disillusionment that encompassed me when the ruse was cut short. I expected no response. It did, however, give me some insight into what trolls enjoy.

Casper's last game lasted only two days because the niggardly voice at the back of my mind was telling me to stop pussyfooting around. I asked him for his phone number to avoid disclosing too much information online. I was trying hard to curb my impatience but considering the tactics employed by so many guys, I was disinclined to give the suitors the benefit of the doubt. Survival of the fittest became the name of these *Online Hunger Games* because I was on a mission to outsmart the internet dating clowns. I wanted to become adroit at outwitting the ignoramus who tried to play me, outsmarting him with the written word.

Never underestimate the power of words! Oscar Wilde's words when challenged to a battle of wits are spot on in this context, "With pleasure, but I will not take on an unarmed man!" Spoken words are transient but printed words and images remain indelibly embossed on paper or computer hard drives and iClouds today; they come back to haunt us time and time again. Pays to heed what we divulge online and to whom. Nothing is totally erased. Nothing is sacred these days. Big Brother is everywhere and always watching. I figured though, that having done nothing wrong, I had nothing to fear.

Okay! It was time for me to examine the perpetrators! I recognised the guy I rejected a few months earlier and I saved his image. I was quite pleased with that idea as I also began to keep a copy of the profiles I liked because I did not want to misconstrue the information they contained with the others. Too late to denounce this despicable, ignoble individual who was in the habit of igniting such hope and promise, only to pull the carpet from under my feet, but I vowed that if he were to resurface elsewhere, I would be quick to report him.

The technique of these players tended to vary; at one stage, Casper, the Ghost decided to erase all traces of his identity – all messages and his one photograph gone; my messages included. He unfortunately knew my first name. The night before, we had a preliminary chat online and I retired early to bed. Casper was fishing to see if I had found the man of my dreams. Pretty standard for daters to pose that question. I told him that I was still chatting with a couple of guys on the site, but my profile was hidden to the public because of the verbal abuse I had received. "I am on to you, Mate!" I think he got the message. As suspected, the next morning all traces of Casper, the Cyber Ghost had vanished.

Casper had attempted to trick me again, for what I hoped was the last time, posting his profile under the new name "Jimmy." On that occasion, I was responding to the advances of a very attractive, albeit shorter, dark and handsome individual from across the border, thinking that the distance would not be an impediment to a coffee or lunch date. More cautious on this occasion (listening more to my intuition as the journey progressed), I responded to Casper's monosyllabic message, refusing to reveal my name so quickly for a change. I no longer wore my heart on my sleeve and did not wish to engage in *Catfishing* with these perpetrators. A fine balance was needed.

Marauding as "Jimmy", the supposed widower (one of the first signs of the scammers) was judicious this time, or so he thought. It became obvious that when the only information these profiles contained under several categories was, "Ask me!" that they were into games – Arrogant narcissist! I was not going to be fooled again, or so I hoped… Casper's one photograph was reminiscent of a Hollywood aspirant's. It guaranteed instant success. Interesting that he stopped short in his *Catfishing* tactic, of glorifying his height. "Jimmy" was 5'10. Becoming a little wary of being caught out, I would think. I dispatched him instantly, refusing to waste time on Losers. I wondered how many of the same women became ensnared several times before giving up.

Recidivists on this site were becoming easier to detect. The profile disappeared in just 15 minutes. Record time! If this were to happen routinely, how satisfying would that be? However, realistically, how is it ever going to be possible to eradicate trolls, narcissists, predators and scammers on internet dating sites? I fear this is a losing battle. But we Amazons are on a mission and we are armed, we will fight through the losers to find the keepers.

Slow Fade – Josh, the Naïf

Josh, a supposed hopeless romantic, blond 52-year-old in a very fetching uniform was in my Match box - guys in uniform will do it every time, for some of us, at least. And they do not all have blue eyes. A Brisbane candidate, and so, within range? This character, adept at the game of *Slow Fade*, was back on the dating scene, disgruntled that the last experience had not lasted the distance. He appeared to have aged exceedingly well, boasting "a full head of my own hair" and six-pack in the gym. Josh announced that he was after "a meaningful, monogamous loving, giving relationship... that's it!!" Wow! The first male I found who actually mentioned monogamy. I told him so and it evidently caught his attention. Having given up his former career to spend quality time with his children, he was reluctant to tell me their age. After several evasive answers, he confessed they were under ten, as I had suspected. His response was classic, "Run, she says." His sense of humour at least resonated with mine. Rare on these sites, as I usually seemed to miss the point. We played the game for a little longer and I was not happy but had to confess that I was older than him with much older children. "Run, he says."

Josh declared that he,

> *loves life; intelligent people and conversation, science, politics, current affairs (err... not the TV show) the arts, theatre, music, camping in my Jayco campervan..... and love.... and being in love.....and being loved.*

If the select quotations I have inserted in this chronicle do not offer sufficient insight into the calibre of candidates one can encounter online, newcomers will have to trawl through the murky waters to verify what I am saying. Just in case I was not convinced that Josh was legit (tongue firmly in cheek), these few lines really left me enthralled. Not!

> *I look after myself and care how I look, as should you. I keep fit and I have no yucky teeth haha. (I read some girls profile that said no yucky teeth... pretty funny!!). I am tactile and love holding hands and cuddling... try and stop me!*

Okay! Get the gist? It deteriorated from there, with fewer messages until he stopped communicating. He had nothing left to offer, so he took the easy way out. It is not hard to say that you are moving on. This classic little gem was interesting, "Importantly... I don't want someone who has mental issues, is an alcoholic, does drugs, is a play station gamer, has tatts, has a Harley or a pair of Staffies."

Poor puppies! Well, good luck if Josh matches other women's prescriptive lists. Each to her own. It does, however, pay to be cautious in dealings with guys who are probably skilful at outsmarting innocent

Ladies. It takes practice to detect the individuals who are playing games, but even then, unfortunately, women only need to fall for their wily tricks once before learning their lesson. Or maybe be tricked twice, or thrice. If the guys volunteer their phone numbers after a few exchanges, there is a chance that they could be authentic, though that is not fail safe. Hansel, the *Breadcrumber* should serve as a reminder. I wonder if he has a second mobile phone… Alternatively, they are pretty daft if they think some of us will not catch them out.

Catch & release – Hunter

Profiles where suitors are encouraged to pay for well-intentioned "gifts" of images, in the guise of large *Emojis*, caused me to lose patience and I usually retorted with terse words to cease the bizarre communication. It was clear to me Hunter was enjoying his fishing expedition, especially adept in the challenge of catching the biggest *Marlin* and swiftly releasing it. The dating site reaped the money and the suitor sent a picture of a rose, a bottle of Champagne, a stuffed Teddy Bear etc. How charming! I received a few of these from the supposed intellectual, pictured in a suit. You can dress them up… I assumed that Hunter was articulate, given his profession but it seems he was much more focused on tactics. The last attempt to communicate produced the third large heart in *Emojis*. I could just picture him sniggering. The easiest way to handle these was to keep on deleting them as they could not be removed permanently; at least I managed to work that out. He was a local, so not difficult to imagine that he could be involved in a relationship and did not want to divulge further information. Yet, he was on the site looking for a serious relationship. It was all about the game, but Hunter could well have been a woman having fun too. These tactics were really doing my head in and I was close to giving up.

Those who are duped are generally incorrigible and idealised romantics who are flattered by the attention and apparent affection of the online suitor or the interlocutor on the other end of the phone, or the email communication. As the adulation intensifies in tandem with the predictable reaction of an unsuspecting individual who succumbs to the persuasion of narcissists and scammers, they could resort to tactics that lead to identity and financial fraud, if we allow them to. This is a perennial concern for dating agencies and social media users online as the offensive behaviour escalates. These predators become emboldened and empowered, professing their "love" for the victim; they begin to use selected *Emojis* and symbols interspersed throughout their comments. Sexual innuendoes begin to appear and depending on the reaction of the target, they can intensify to sexting and other obscenities if encouraged.

Irrespective of the degree of *Catch and Release* tactic, it leaves the innocent victim despondent and cynical.

Benching Ben

It has become apparent, from my contacts on and offline that *Benching* is becoming a feature that is entrenched in internet dating. As adherents increase their activity exponentially, locally or globally, it is more practical for time-poor individuals of both sexes to chat with several people at the same time, deciding which one to favour when ready. If one approaches this exercise from the premise of truth and integrity, no one gets hurt. Some gamesters are not that concerned. It is an easy game to play and if the innocent target does not catch on, it can go on for months.

I wondered whether I had inadvertently been involved in this practice when dating Ben. My penchant for the British Beaux was sure to attract trouble for me. 6'3 Ben, 55-year-old, the British Bodyguard was not shy online, disclosing an eclectic mix of medical, professional and creative talents that he brought to different professions; and, he lived on the Gold Coast. Was this a sign from the universe? Oddly enough, he had recently moved out of my neighbourhood to relocate 20 minutes down the road. Check, Check, Check... this was promising, something quickly confirmed during our first date lasting four and a half hours.

We were acting like silly teenagers in the bar/restaurant where we met, laughing and enjoying each other's company. What can I say, those blue eyes again? What a pair! Embarrassing, clichéd, quirky, Over the top? All the above, and we made no apologies for it. Even the unappetising pizza we obligingly ordered (nothing else to our taste on the menu) could not destroy the magic of this meeting. The waitress had brought us wine but returned like the proverbial penny to take our order. We did not want food; we were too engrossed in our banter and laughter to eat. We learned, alcohol without food was not allowed. Seriously? Would have helped to know this beforehand. Seemed stupid to leave just for that. The pizza arrived. Ben and I both stared at the small pizza, "Where is the Mozzarella; pizza without cheese?" It was only on the way out that we noticed the Vegan sign. Diners beware! Need to pay more attention where I meet my Beaux.

Ben's initial online comment, "So, what do you do apart from breaking men's hearts?" would have fit perfectly amongst the vignettes depicting massive egos in this chronicle, if Ben had not been an intellectual, clever author; authentic, respectful, romantic, humorous, a man of integrity. His attributes correlated very closely with my prescriptive checklist, but it is crucial to factor in other subtle and desirable traits that can only be revealed face to face, and over several dates. Important to avoid embarrassment and losing face by declaring too quickly that "this is the One." I had learned from my mistakes.

Ben's redeeming qualities became apparent immediately through the quick repartee that infused our banter, confirming him to be a perfect Gentleman with the most honourable of intentions despite some very cheeky text messages. The façade of the perfect joker shielded a proud, devoted, sensitive and pragmatic father in his mid-fifties. The codicil attached to the above quip was that, "breaking men's hearts comes from there being only one of you and so many men who would be interested but ultimately disappointed as only one will manage to capture your heart!"

The consummate charmer declared far too eagerly and way too soon after our first meeting, "I have found the lady with whom I wish to spend the rest of my life." I began to feel quite uncomfortable. I did not know him. The magic was fading. He introduced me to his daughter very quickly also and she was delightful. Ben's gorgeous daughter and I got on famously, and I made a mental note that this would be the perfect match if my daughters also liked Ben. Our sentiments were mutual, but it was too much, too soon and Ben's cheeky sense of humour landed him in trouble. His daughter and I ganged up against him because he had embarrassed both of us when he blurted out that we had already decided to be married on the first date. Awkward! The look on his daughter's face was priceless, as it was on mine. Ben was being a little overzealous for my liking because I was trying to take things very slowly. We were both locals.

This British Gentleman, thankfully, was not intimidated by a woman's intellect; we were on the same wave length; and he was relieved that

I was not into indiscriminate hookups; not into games; he knew that my intentions were honourable, as were his. Our apparent compatibility was established within hours. The chemistry was real, but we wanted to tame these bourgeoning feelings to see if we could base a relationship on friendship first. There were other cogent issues to consider, and our geographical match presented us with the opportunity to resolve anything we considered might be deal breakers.

Despite the immediate mutual attraction on many levels, the pressure to make everything gel was too great, and I withdrew to reflect on the effect this was having on me. I was confused and needed time to regroup. I felt rather scared, trapped really, in spite of liking Ben. He was fun and happy to be my friend. I thoroughly enjoyed our dates as his maturity and intellect shone through, even if he was the biggest kid on the Gold Coast, literally, considering his stature. Ben understood immediately that if he did not allow our friendship to blossom gradually, he would lose me altogether.

I had become a little more wary by then. How could we get to know someone without doing the hard yards? Living on the coast gave us the chance to test the waters of that theory.

Ben was happy to give me all the time in the world, so long as I ended up with him. He was my date at a formal professional function where my colleagues and the hierarchy were present. He was the image of the suave and sophisticated man about town, from head to toe in his evening attire, and his crowning glory –a number two haircut. "Don't touch my hair!" he told his daughter and me. "Okay! Got it." Ben's self-attributed title of Bodyguard, whilst hilarious the first time, became a little embarrassing as the evening progressed and more formal introductions were made. Our connection was strong, and we had a wonderful evening. Ben had mastered the art of wooing a Lady, blending affection, respect and steadfastness perfectly. The Bodyguard caper was not working though…

That the potential relationship was left open-ended had nothing to do with Ben, and more to do with the dating process after several months. The roller-coaster ride had surprising effects on my self-esteem. I really enjoyed Ben's company. He was so patient, and I admired his forbearance and resolve to win his Lady's heart. There was absolutely no pressure. I did not give him false hope. Our friendship was predicated on truth and integrity. We learned a great deal about each other, touched base regularly, whilst mutually respecting potential partners as we dated other people. Peripheral pursuits kept us busy though, on top of our careers. We had a lot in common, but subtle barriers still prevented a commitment.

Our friendship grew steadily as I turned to Ben when a potential relationship disintegrated as it struggled to progress to the next level. Ben and I could discuss current and past relationships candidly, without judgment or embarrassment. We had become very good friends. How amazing! This was certainly a promising outcome, a solid foundation for a lasting relationship, should the stars align in the end...

Perhaps, stepping back and focusing on our friendship was working in our favour.

Ben found two of my personality traits difficult to understand. My restlessness; I could rarely just chill; and my panic to pull the pin on a potential liaison because I still suffered from low self-esteem. Conceding that this dating process had reinforced the deficiencies that I had thought eradicated, Ben took on the mantle of correcting the anomaly in my character, saying, "Still don't get how someone as gorgeous and intelligent as you can have self-esteem issues and have decided it's my mission to alter that situation."

At that point, the reflection from my own mirror had only just begun to correlate with the images emanating from some of the nice guys I had dated. I still could not see what he saw...

So, was I also effectively involved in the *Benching* tactic? Upon reflection, my conscience is clear. I always confess to the guys I date that I am still chatting with others. They are harmless, superficial conversations that often revolve around the trials and tribulations of this new world of dating. I am genuinely searching for love, and in the process, I am uncovering interesting paradigms in online dating. All my energies and time are devoted to the guy I am dating, my family and my work that are all-consuming; not always an appealing thought for the guy I date who expects a lot more than I am able to give. My intention is not to play with the hearts of men.

Ben and I remain good friends. It really pays to take my time, even if in this race, the tortoise may just beat this little Hare. The truth was that there were personal issues that were not easy to resolve, proving difficult in the formation of a committed relationship. Sometimes, that is just the way it is. For this reason, our mutual decision to remain friends was a wonderful outcome.

The emperor's sycophants

It is reasonable to assume that the end game of Internet Dating for many mature-aged singles of this century is to eradicate loneliness and feelings of abandonment and desolation. Evidently, finding love is not the objective of all daters. It would be naïve of me to think that most of my suitors endorse the premises of truth and integrity that define my dating experience. I have discovered too many incongruities in that line of thinking and have revised my stance on the issue. However, despite the tarnished reputation of internet dating for provoking despair, this form of courting continues to attract some daters who live in hope that they will find the "One".

For the individuals who do not find love, the dating game continues, depending on their resolve. A Daily Mail survey found that six in ten men profess to "punch or bat above their weight." Contextually, this idiomatic expression categorises the woman as more attractive than they are. The most common reason behind this is apparently to boost their self-esteem and to create envy in other men. This tactic is also meant to endear them more to women as they pride themselves on possessing more commendable attributes such as a great sense of humour and sensitivity to women's needs.[18]

Is this practice of placing someone on a pedestal engineered from a premise of sincerity or posturing? Frequently accompanied by exaggerated flattery, the barrage of compliments begins to wear thin after a while and smart people can see through the ruse quickly. At the nexus of sycophancy (flattery) and compliments, we all need to gauge the authenticity of individuals who appear well-versed in the art of wooing and accept their overly-effusive charm or bring the praises to a halt. If suitors have integrity of character, they will cast their ego aside for the sake of the new love interest.

On the other hand, I cannot deny that I find it heart-warming to

---

[18] (Daily Mail Read more: http://www.dailymail.co.uk/news/article-2515925/Six-10-men-punch-weight-relationships-pair-better-looking-women.html#ixzz4j6S1N9s8

receive an unpretentious message that contains the expressions, "Hi Babe" or "Ciao Bella."

Many members, from both sexes abandon the chase, but many more cannot extricate themselves from the fast-moving pace and magnetism of Internet dating. Let's face it. This can be just as addictive as most obsessions. It is not harmless, but the ability to quit this game should be a little easier if a dater stops searching when he or she has found the "One." Why would you want to continue this single-minded compulsion? Unless, of course, you have ulterior motives? For those whose objectives are far from honourable, it is not difficult to imagine that every chance they get, they are online, checking their messages, a broad smile lighting their faces as multiple 'hits' appear in their IN Box; they know that the unwitting victims are attracted to a fictitious image. That is, no doubt, what propels their sociopathic desires. Does narcissism increase in tandem with increased interest from suitors?

Rex, the Narcissist

Narcissists are not gender-specific, but men tend to score higher, whilst women and men differ in terms of their personalities. Psychiatry research describes this personality disorder as the patient's grandiose idea of his or her own appearance and abilities and an excessive need for admiration. It is in the context of internet dating that the psychoanalytic theory emphasising the element of self-directed sexual desire in the condition becomes most pertinent for this chronicle.[19]

My communication online has revealed that the initial euphoria of this dating game often turns to dismay when subscribers witness the results of the inaccurately woeful mismatching of the algorithms. Rejection, sometimes polite but increasingly abrupt and rude, can contribute to decreased self-esteem. Dating fatigue sets in, and members are not impressed when they have paid to send messages.

I soon worked out that an evasive tactic for uninvited approaches required some subtlety. I prided myself on doing the right thing, but this sometimes landed me in hot water.

---

[19] Begum, R. (2017). Digest if you can. Exposed they stand. http://thephoenix postindia.com/digest-can-exposed-stand/

The first episode made me fume. In response to an unsolicited advance from a guy I was not interested in, I politely said that I was chatting with someone on the site, with whom I found a connection and wished to see where it led. His bitter retort really upset me, "Sure you are!" I saw red! I sent him a sarcastic reply that kept him away from me in future, "In fact, I am chatting with two guys, and guess what? You will never be one of them!" Only words, I know, but really? How dare he? That fragile ego is just something else. What upset me the most was that he had managed to push my buttons. The inability to curb this predictable reaction was quite concerning. The next guy really got to me also. Some really play on your vulnerabilities.

When responding to Rex, who had approached me on another site, I used one of the pat responses that are engineered to curtly end a potential lead and wished him luck. I had not been prepared for the nasty message that appeared in my IN Box:

> *I don't appreciate you chatting with me when your supposedly chatting with someone else. Not one but two! Two-timer! If us guys did this, we would be abuse! Why is it Ok for you woman? I'm not interested in frivolous chats while you play the field. Don't contact me again or I'll report you! Better still, get off this site.*

I must have missed the memo on the unwritten decree stipulating we had to chat with only one individual at a time. At this rate, we could be on these sites for years. That is what you get for being nice? I had only responded to this guy's message because he had paid to communicate with me, one individual at a time for a whole month - a stupid system that meant he had wasted his money. His profile information had initially made me smile but I wondered how many Australian women would understand his attempt to woo someone in French language. I have translated sections of the following French entry from his profile, *literally* to demonstrate the effectiveness of *Online Translator* engines. Or not!

> *Romancier, guitariste, entrepreneur … forme athlétique, en bonne santé, contour bien éduqué, financièrement*

indépendante et resiliente. Une veritable légende dans mon pantalon! Je suis fidèle, tenace, bon ma parole et s'efforcent de toujours faire de mon mieux. J'admire le courage, de charité, de gentillesse et d'abnégation. Conflits du cœur et de raison peuvent troubler moi. **Novelist, guitarist, entrepreneur… athletic, healthy, well-contoured? well-moulded? Financially independent and resilient [in feminine form]. A real legend in my pants! I am faithful, tenacious, true my word and [they] try to always do my best. I admire courage, of charity, of kindness and selflessness. Conflicts of the heart and of reason [mind] can me trouble.**

I was still smarting at Rex's previous rebuke and thought to myself, "serves him right", especially as I like to think that the pompous, egotistical and obtuse 60-year-old would have had trouble attracting other than women fluent in French language. He may be accomplished in his own eyes, but I decided to rebuff his supercilious attitude. "Willing to relocate for the right person…" that was a likely story for a professional with a good position on the Gold Coast. Good luck trying to find "an attractive woman for a lasting, mutually supportive and loving relationship" with his abusive attitude. I continued my internal rant. "Selfless"? Seriously?

Unbeknownst to him, French women would have immediately recognised the literal online translation of his fabricated list of values and attributes, dismissing his profile with derision. Rex should have enlisted the help of a French friend to check the entry. His tactic was laughable, backfiring because it made him look ludicrous, unlike some guys who only utilised the odd catchy French or Italian phrase to attract European women. Nonetheless, this episode really affected me, I had to admit. I immediately deleted his profile and messages, but his vitriolic attack had done its damage.

Reflection

This episode, provoking a knee-jerk reaction at a vulnerable moment when the roller-coaster was careering downwards, had brought out the worst in me as I employed biting, unkind remarks because Rex had pressed my buttons, trying to intimidate me. And he succeeded. Attitudes such as his were, in fact, what had triggered my decision to write this book, to alert unsuspecting women about the antics of some males on dating sites. From what I have learned, it seems that some guys may also appreciate becoming aware of how vindictive females now rival the males in these games. I concluded that online dating could make a toad of Princes but more appropriately, a little Frog out of a Princess. Not happy!

Many individuals are reputed to resort to familiar tactics to catch their prey. Can disenchantment turn people into cynical beings; into perverted control freaks, misogynists or man-haters in unhappy relationships or problematic marriages? Difficult separations and a lack of sexual gratification amongst other issues can provoke a state of dissatisfaction that could ostensibly be appeased by online games to ensnare the unsuspecting party. Could they simply be lonely or bored? Whatever the scenario, the machinations of the minds of sick individuals are sure to cause heartache, humiliation and loss of dignity and they do not only reside on the *Dark Net*.

Harold - Heartbreaker

Given the propensity for game playing in online dating, is it unreasonable to expect the broken hearted and the disconsolate to retreat and fortify their souls, before relaunching their profiles, usually on alternate sites? The games move up a notch as both genders play the field, adjusting their profile and posting remodelled identities on three or four sites. Whilst it is common practice to react to feedback and re-construct profiles, many daters are said to employ additional tactics they believe to be inspired. Honest participants on the receiving end perceive this to be disingenuous and despicable. The information gamesters post uncannily coincides with articulate descriptions often employed by the opposing gender. By reiterating what a man or a woman wants, the self-assured dater is confident of being inundated by messages; that is, until they are expected to reveal their true identity; and communicate further on the phone; and so, the game begins again. This tactic usually smells of a rat, often a rejected member whose insecurities and deflated ego will not let things rest.

Believing themselves to be clever, there is always a degree of transparency in the inviting one-line heading and extended profile that is often incoherent, usually replete with grammatical errors. If we are wary of *Catfishing* or when our curiosity gets the better of us and we respond, requesting a photo, this is customarily when the profile is swiftly removed, and the following message appears, "This member has decided to take a break for a while." As those who have been caught in the web of deceit become shrewder, they recognise the offending dater on another site and the predators are caught out. At that point, the profiles tend to disappear rapidly, probably forced to become voyeuristic as they continue to trawl through the new site, undetected.

What are the ulterior motives of predators? There are of course lots of motives. Some get the same superficial pleasure from this online dating as I did at the start. Whereas I moved beyond, some are stuck in this stage. That is their choice, but it is annoying because it creates an obstacle to what I want.

Is this mere power play? Has their unrequited love or lust turned them into bitter and angry individuals whose duplicitous strategies for retaliation is to play sick games that leave a trail of destruction and broken hearts in their wake? Is the motive revenge? Do they act in a sadistic, reprehensible manner only to hurt others as they have been hurt or simply to massage their fragile egos, to boost their self-esteem? Irrespective of the objectives of such predators, voyeurs, stalkers, players, the resulting disillusionment is the same; broken dreams and feelings of dejection, foolishness, shame and inadequacy. I imagine these sick, twisted individuals could be afraid of being caught out by a spouse or partner. It makes little sense to me. They can only massage their egos for so long...

I am not afraid to employ language as an instrument to decimate the ego of depraved individuals, whether they are marauding as male or female narcissists, because their predatory games are destroying the lives of innocent victims online.

I make no apology if my words belittle those who merit such treatment. It is probably water off a duck's back anyway, but awareness of bullying tactics online is of paramount importance as online dating is here to stay; this, despite announcements to the contrary on multimedia platforms at regular intervals. I cannot see some of these impostors being lured away from this Smorgasbord of potential prey.

The playground of Trolls and Narcissists

It is imperative that I continue to strategise to engineer a better outcome on this dating journey. As if the preceding insights on the nefarious aspects of internet dating were not enough to scare me, I braced myself and buckled up more securely. I did not want to hook up for casual dating; I was not prepared to indulge in mind games; find friends with benefits. This was ideal for some individuals who endorsed sex without intimacy and could only envisage a liaison without commitment. I remained focused, actively searching for a committed, long term relationship. The key was to constantly re-examine what I wanted exactly because this journey was provoking deep-seated changes in my thought processes. With a sinking heart, I had, by that stage, discovered that where I had started was where I may have been ultimately happiest.

A word of advice to myself; if exposing my heart guaranteed ridicule from many sources, espousing honesty and integrity could have its drawbacks, clearly; especially when this dating game exposed the vulnerabilities of all involved. The feedback on my candour was likely to incite a re-evaluation of my perceived ethical behaviour, if some choice comments by sceptical male suitors were anything to go by, but I restrained myself. When I was *Breadcrumbed, Benched* or caught up in other tactics, cynicism and thoughts of self-sabotage threatened to destroy my wavering moments of serenity. I had to remain vigilant; stay one step ahead of gamesters.

I had to become aware of internet trolls and ghouls that were front and centre on these sites, perfect for undetected abuse, as many had evidently duped the organisers and psychologists at the helm of the agencies. Blocking offensive messages or reporting abusers proved futile in many instances, and certainly an ineffective deterrent, as offenders returned time and again to plague the existence of users with abusive language. This was fertile ground for narcissists, their over-inflated egos easily detected through their arrogantly-worded profiles. Like their namesake, *Narcissus*, from whence the Greek myth originates, some of these individuals, both male and female, spurn the love offered to them and fall in love with their own reflection. *Narcissus* was a young man who fell in love with his reflection in a pool and drowned trying to reach it…

Some intellectual males, whose objective it is to distance themselves from the narcissists that thrive on the sites, choose to employ clever lines in their introductory spiels to counter these nefarious practices. I found this one refreshing, "Buff, handsome, Adonis, god's gift to women might apply to some of the guys here but I'm average Joe with, at least, a sense of humour..." Effective, admittedly. And, I can vouch for the veracity of Jonathan's words. I chose to include his poem at the start of Chapter 14.

If online daters are not pedantic, they will ignore the typographical errors or the overabundance of incorrectly positioned apostrophes in the profiles. A Brisbane guy who is a grammatical pedant like me, detests the errors that abound online and in text messages. His frustration was exaggerated but this headline was a classic, "Quite honestly, I'll marry the first woman I meet who knows the difference between *your* and *you're.*"

The abusive comments from online tricksters who are rejected by honest daters are enough to discourage reserved individuals from continuing the search, retreating from fear of being shamed, embarrassed or stalked online. Why, we may wonder? To what end? Is it simply because stalkers can and generally love to dissimulate their identity? This is a practice that goes largely unheeded; could they have been rejected or jilted, or are they mischievous gamesters, or sociopaths? Whichever shoe fits... the effects are still devastating.

Predators need little excuse to indulge in scams, much like the infamous Nigerian variety that prey on innocent victims. The situation escalates when scammers often hailing from other African countries, plan their requests for funds to be sent to their bank accounts so that the couple can be together. The extraordinary thing is that, sometimes, highly educated women have been caught out and would only, under duress, confess to having been fooled; I know of one such professional and very few people know that this has happened to her; disclosing this fraudulent act is shameful in her culture and losing face is unconscionable. Women such as these, and those even more vulnerable, elderly people, have been known to disburse huge sums of money until they acknowledge the fraud. Police intervention is usually ineffective in these cases because it is virtually impossible to trace the funds offshore.

A metamorphosis tends to take place when those whose prime objective in life is to profit from others. If they join dating sites under a pseudonym, employing modern technological tools to create fictitious personas, such as *Catfishing*, anonymity and often impunity are generally assured. This is no joke. This is the playground of predators. Cybersecurity protocols, including password encrypting measures, irrespective of how sophisticated, simply cannot be guaranteed and Big Brother can rarely detect the convoluted schemes that perpetrators utilise to lure their prey only to defraud them of their credit card details, their savings and ultimately their identity, leaving them destitute.

Equally devastating, one's self-esteem can easily be destroyed along with all trust in human nature as some poor souls lose all hope of ever finding love again after dreadful tactics used to deceive them. Hacking is a perennial concern, inducing loss of dignity, lucrative careers and family loyalty as people's fantasies and sexual preferences are disclosed to the public. Layers of encryption found in sophisticated programs that create a thriving underworld of the *Dark Net* promises anonymity in a playground fertile for despicable online predators. So, we need to remain prudent. Keep our eyes opened and our wits about us.

13

Discerning the truth in online dating / lying vs wishful thinking

Infidelity. Why do couples cheat?

How can online daters of both sexes determine the truth of what a suitor is suggesting is a good idea? Are there glaring tell-tale signs to warn us, or, are the subtleties likely to confound the issue? If there are reportedly so many individuals involved in affairs online, then, it seems that we are indeed at their mercy.

The specificity of choice is undeniably important in the context of online dating... and probably encourages infidelity. The option of having whatever you want is pretty intoxicating for some.

The disturbing thing is that the inducement for infidelity that traditionally defined female adultery is now archaic. A recent article has debunked the myth that women stray if their emotional needs are not being met. Dogson [20] unveils some home truths about the ways and the reasons women cheat. The claims are predicated on sociologist, Alicia

---

[20] Dogson, L. December 4, 2017. 5 of the biggest myths about the ways women cheat — and why they're not true. Business Insider. http://www.thisisinsider.com/the-biggest-myths-about-the-ways-women-cheat-2017-12

Walker's book, *The Secret Life of the Cheating Wife: Power, Pragmatism, and Pleasure in Women's Infidelity* [21] as well as interviews with members of the *Ashley Madison's Dating Website*. Unearthing the misconceptions about women's rationale should make a fascinating read. We may learn a thing or two about the males in the process.

Dogson [22] reports that women no longer indulge in extra-marital affairs to get out of their marriage. They simply seek to "outsource" their sexual needs, and they do not restrict themselves to one partner. They are skilful in dissimulating their affairs, working on the premise that if no one finds out, no one gets hurt. They consequently rarely get caught... Unless of course, hackers release damning evidence on adherents of *Ashley Madison Married Women's Dating Site* once more. The resolution to cheat is based on methodology and pragmatism; this is not at all a rash and impulsive decision. The women involved are not searching for love; in fact, they shun liaisons where there is a potential to fall in love, opting for compatibility instead.

I have spoken with some males in their 40s and 50s who espouse exactly the same sentiments, particularly when they consider just how much they stand to lose through separation and divorce – financial and affective (emotions) dimensions at the core of their decisions.

Another recent report, *Why do couples cheat?* [23] on Australian Television, tackled the subject of infidelity following findings of a study on British habits. Dr Michael Carr-Gregg, one of Australia's highest profile psychologists shed some light on the cheating habits of men and women. This report gives credence to Walker's revelations, confirming that women are actively engaged in more extra-marital affairs than men. This would not raise eyebrows in some European cultures as anecdotal evidence suggests this role reversal has been in place for quite some time now. The British study found that more women, lonely housewives especially, cheat on their husbands regularly. They are lonely, bored and complain of a lack of communication and curiously, sex with their partners. They therefore

---

[21] Walker, A. 2018. The Secret Life of the Cheating Wife: Power, Pragmatism, and Pleasure in Women's Infidelity. Lexington Books/Fortress Academic, USA.

[22] Ibid.

[23] *Why do couples cheat?* Australian Television, Channel 7 Sunrise (01/08/17)

indulge in daytime sex and are subsequently too tired, if satiated, to talk when their husbands come home.

Think about it! I do not know too many guys who would complain about a dearth of nonsensical chatter in the evening? They are likely to remain blissfully unaware of the infidelity of their wives for considerable time I would think. How often do we hear guys complain about the paucity of their conjugal rights anyhow? If this is true, it probably does not dawn on them that their partners are seeking sex with no strings attached. Just think of the number of divorces and separations that occurred when the *Ashley Madison* site was first hacked.

In a 2013 article in GQ online magazine, Teddy Wayne posed an interesting question about the infidelity paradigm change,

> *In the real world, with greater professional equality between the genders and third-wave feminist sexual liberation, are women cheating for the same reason that men have throughout history ... that is, to sate their sex drives and gratify their egos? ...*
>
> *In the spirit of this gender reversal, I invite you to picture me as Carrie Bradshaw,* [Sex and the City] *sprawled out on her bed with her PowerBook G3, as she voice-overs, "I couldn't help but wonder: Are unfaithful women the new adulterous men? Has Casanova turned into...Cassandra?"* [24]

Interesting conceptual changes that I suspect many individuals are frowning over... Or perhaps, are they rubbing their hands in glee because they know where to locate compliant candidates for their lunchtime escapades. Who knows? It is not a stretch of the imagination to suggest that easy internet access to so many dating sites encourages extra-marital affairs. Instant debauchery at their fingertips. Some men and women do not need additional reasons to cheat today, but Dr Carr-Gregg suggests the recognisable traits of the male cheat can be traced back to the typical

---

[24] Wayne, T. Ashley Madison: Online Married Ladies Seek Immediate Offline Boinking. P.1. https://www.gq.com/story/ashley-madison-affair-cheating-site

profile description, so we need to be wary. He argues we are looking at the consummate narcissist - tall, rich and smart. It is all about their ego, admiration, recognition, lust, arrogance. Their infidelity preferences remain 50% in the workplace; their reasons based on their need to find units of recognition after a long-term relationship; they need to be validated.

I am beginning to put two and two together and do not like what I have surmised from this report. Damn! Some of these characteristics match the good looking physiological and personality types that I keep falling for.

Heard of the seven-year-itch? Apparently, the secret to a great relationship is to achieve balance – *Balance Theory Relationship Ratio* – a master of relationship or disaster of relationship. It seems that the worst possible thing couples can do during an argument is to correct their grammar. Oops! Guilty. Who knew?

A recent report on France 24[25] confirms what French popular culture has always suggested, that "love affair" – translated as *une aventure* (adventure) or *une liaison* in French, are more tolerated than in many other countries, the most propitious times for indulging in affairs being 5:00-7:00 PM. This might seem peculiar to Anglo-Saxons as children usually arrive home from school around then. Let's just say, the stereotype of the French finding monogamy challenging, does not mean that they actually cheat more; they are simply less judgmental toward infidelity. Reports suggest half of French males and one third of the women cheat. The stereotype holds true in some measure as they are allegedly less hypocritical about cheating. Some Australians may have witnessed the commotion caused when an aspirant to the Socialist Party presidential primary in 2006 met his political demise. *DSK*, as he is commonly known, *Dominique Strauss-Kahn*, owed this to his indiscretions; financial and sexual scandals in the US that cost him the opportunity to lead France. He had been a contender, but global reaction had a lot to do with his fall from grace. I dare say, the sexual scandals were the least of his peccadillos in the eyes of the French public. That was of course, before the *Harvey Weinstein* sex scandal and the *Me too* global campaign.

I should heed these findings, but I am in far too deeply into this project to abandon the search, just yet. Considering this report, I am wondering just

---

[25] France 24 French Television News broadcast (12/08/17). SBS Australia.

how many of the men I have dated could actually have been cheating on their partner? How could I possibly know for sure? I believe I have become a much better judge of character but how does anyone really ascertain the truth in these situations? Trust is paramount in relationships and if we jump in too soon, we could easily become embroiled in an illicit affair. Extricating yourself out of that is guaranteed to be painful, so it pays to remain circumspect for a while longer until you really get to know the person you are with. This game is fraught with challenges that you could never have anticipated. These reports have certainly provided food for thought.

Trying to figure out how the online dating world works, we could think of the internet as a 'finder'. The problem is that it appears to serve a certain type of person. I can be extremely specific online – with a camera lens, I type in that I want a camera with wide-angle lens, plus all of the accoutrements, that weighs less than 1kg, and is less than $2000, etc. 20 years ago, my search would have proved to be a long and logistical nightmare; now it takes less than two minutes; and I can order it and have it delivered within two days.

Similarly, in line with findings on why couples cheat in this chapter, it is now common to find a woman, for example, who loves her husband and children but needs something else for sexual satisfaction. Years ago, she may have tried to pick up someone at the supermarket or sneak off to a bar at night or look for someone who just wanted casual fun, even put herself in physically dangerous situations. Whereas now, she goes online, and just say, that she only gets sexual satisfaction from muscular, well-endowed young men. She types in that she is looking for a guy with her specifications, 20-40-years-old, muscular, disease and drug free, for no strings attached. Oh, and the guy pays for the motel. Then she waits for 20 minutes and has ten guys to choose from; three are fake; three are fantasists; then she has four genuine guys who send pictures to confirm they meet the criteria. An hour later she is getting what she wants, and an hour after that she is back with her husband and kids.

The issue is that if people are interested in something transactional, the internet is great. Essentially, the problem is that the mechanism we are using has predominantly morphed into a quick, short-term transactional environment. Like Twitter and Facebook etc. I remember the days where people wrote long, involved, thoughtful blogs. There is no time for that anymore.

What I must keep in mind if I wish to continue on this journey, is that for every "one" like me out there, searching for a serious relationship, there is likely to be a guy thinking and feeling the same thing... at least I hope. Time out now. Need to play some sport to clear my head. *Ciao!*

Ghost, Cheat or Scam artist?

When a Gold Coast man asked to chat with me, he waited for my response asking him to supply a couple of images and suddenly, in a puff of smoke, no more profile. What kind of game was this one? For a 60-year-old supposed professional from a very good suburb, this was a little surprising. The dramatic change in style and syntax of the next two vignettes was a warning sign... I was immediately *Ghosted!*

> *Hi..Looking to share what life has to offer with someone very special who enjoys having great times, is a little cheeky, adventurous and is confident in themselves. Dinners, drinks, weekends away, visiting somewhere new, revisiting somewhere old. Love the beach and the sun. A positive outlook on life and a life that is to be enjoyed...*
>
> *I'm honest type of man and am also romantic, open mind, down to earth and having a great sense of humor. so much respects of other i have a million ways to make laugh and happy my beloved, i know how to treat woman. i have a big heart and a big love inside my heart, i really want to share this love with real woman i like animal sports,movies,music.....Looking to meet and share fun times with someone attractive, intelligent, independent, genuine, witty, confident.*

The second suspect profile was from an engineer, a foreigner who lived in Melbourne; it is possible therefore, that he had trouble expressing himself but the number of profiles with the profession of Engineer in the title was overwhelming, especially with *Fly In, Fly Out (FIFO)* attached. Smelt of deceit and scam but impossible to verify. This entry was skewed with parts probably copied and pasted also. For someone in a management role, one would expect a measure of correct grammar in a message. Should he meet with cynics, he made sure we were aware of his faith in God!

> *Being Optimistic and Open minded has always attracted people to me Naturally. I'm not the kind of man who base his feelings on the Outer Beauty or physical appearance. I believe in the Beauty on the Inside because I learn long ago. that character's and altitude's will determine the qualities seen in personality. i being passionate about environment is being in it by making people to achieve there goal. I am a goal oriented individual and mostly everything I do need to have a reason sense of accomplishment. I'm passionate about God and all His creation*

Seb, the unreal

I spoke to Seb the first time when he sent what appeared to be a genuine message. The most embarrassing exchange ensued on the phone. I managed to hold on for 15 minutes, trying to decipher the twisted story line that he was feeding me. The blond, blue eyed Stud and the voice on the phone produced the most incongruous image, leaving me baffled. I questioned him about his roots and he claimed to be from Papua New Guinea. I could barely understand a word he was saying. I became convinced that he hailed from Nigeria, infamous for scamming. Once again, without concrete proof, as he had done nothing untoward yet, I could not denounce him to the administration of the dating site.

This roller-coaster ride was so bumpy. Just when I thought I was becoming internet savvy, enjoying a smooth ride, I ended up getting it so wrong. Seb showed up on two different sites with slightly altered images and I was about to respond when my gut told me to back off. I was becoming a better judge of character – even in the limited cue world of internet dating.

Proud Princess or fairy-tale frog?

Is it you? Or is it me?

Men are like parachutes, if they are not there the first time you need them, you will not be needing them again.

Why do so many guys reject my profile outright? Have I aimed too highly, punching above my weight, so to speak, just like some guys have suggested that they do? Are they perhaps just looking for reinforcement of their charms and intelligence? Who knows? I sure as hell am not! After approaching some eligible guys, rejection is harder to take when there is no explanation or any attempt to soften the blow. My ego prompts me to make excuses for these. What calibre of men did I hope to attract? Were they out of my reach? I can hold my own, they just need to give me a chance. I am articulate, not opinionated. I can speak about anything, politics, travel, religion, sex, taboo topics that some cultures will not broach. We are in Australia, a tolerant society.

Four months of probing and see what the net brings up from the ocean? The games people play! Fascinating, I must say. Time to reassess... Get back to the drawing board, Coco! Need to be street smart. Now, how to reconfigure my profile to protect me from some of the insalubrious rejects trying to decimate my character. No more abuse!

Mirror, Mirror on the wall... Am I a Princess?

It upsets me to think that not only acquaintances, but friends and family, also perceive me as high maintenance. I set out to define the term and to gauge the opinion of those around me. A few were amused and reluctant to confess their real feelings. Michael (Chapter 2) was adamant that I was not. Phew! It was perplexing because of the dichotomous connotations this inquiry produced; positive and negative interpretations of the term potentially depicting most of the people I knew. Are we all, in some respect, tarred with this brush?

When my eldest daughter, Angelina also suggested that I was high maintenance, I reminded her that she too was the perfect embodiment of this personality trait; something she was quick to refute. This mirror image of me (we are two peas in a pod) went to great pains to point out that I was worse than she was. It was comical and therapeutic to dispute the degree to which the terminology was appropriate for each of us and we light-heartedly concluded that some of the characteristics fit us both to a tee.

I make no apology for the higher than normal expectations that I have, in full defence mode, reiterating to all who care to listen, that these unrealistic expectations are for myself alone. I have always set the bar highly for myself because I take pride in my appearance, my behaviour, my work and my actions and always, irrespective of context, ensure I look my best, coordinated if I can help it, and behave according to my social standing. Interestingly, my BFF, Jeanie answered my query in the affirmative, surprising me initially. She always calls a spade a spade. However, she exclaimed that my very high expectations were for myself. Relief, but Jeanie also added that I had high standards for the partner I was searching for. "I see absolutely nothing wrong with that. This is not a derogatory judgment," she said. Jeanie endorsed 100% my philosophy of "Better to be alone than with the wrong person."

I am not intolerant of others who do not act as I do. I already admitted that I am a *Drama Queen*; I tend to make a mountain out of a mole hill; Okay! I sweat the small stuff, something that constantly exacerbates my stress levels; I admit, more clichés. I seek affection in a partner, vowing to never again accept anything less. Is that tantamount to being an attention seeker? Some things are not negotiable. I am independent and discerning and like things done in a certain way; I am a self-professed perfectionist; this comes with the territory for my star sign. However, I refuse to perceive myself as challenging, even if others do… Why do people not understand that my exacting standards are for myself? I am accommodating and not judgmental. One more imponderable question.

…Just because I enjoy the finer things in life? That is crazy! So, what if I am a European Brand girl. I have never expected anyone to provide anything for me but when I am treated like a Princess, spoiled with gifts without *quid pro quo* intended, these are greatly valued. I am quick to reciprocate, and some of the Gentlemen I have dated have appreciated my gestures. It may go against the grain for some, but I am beholden to no one. Michael and I had fun fighting over who would pay for drinks and coffee during our short interlude. I have found this more endearing in these guys but giving has always been more important than taking for me. It makes me happy. It is also highly gratifying to witness that chivalry, honour and generosity are alive and well. These traditional, old-fashioned values endorsed by some of the guys I have met have not entirely been shattered with the *Women's Liberation Movement*.

Do guys prefer to be with a woman they consider to be high maintenance? Seriously doubt that… I must continue my investigations. I feel better after this exercise as I can confirm that a self-professed Drama Queen need not a high maintenance woman make.

Why do some people misconstrue in negative connotations, my exuberance for life, my passion for my career and my intercultural pursuits? I am a *Stress Bucket,* this is undeniable, but it irritates me that people cannot simply appreciate my passionate nature and accept me as I am. Why do they need to criticise me, become anxious that I will end up with a heart attack because I am a *Worry Wort* - always high on life, always restless; the adrenaline keeping me buoyant? Admittedly, many people not just online dating, have overwhelmingly identified me as a highly strung, strong willed and independent woman but whilst I am willing to work on the first two aspects of my personality, I refuse to relinquish my hard-won independence. Ultimately, a potential change in the intensity with which I approach challenges might make my life easier, but I plan to devise an effective strategy to incorporate my independence within a committed relationship.

Am I capable of this, *Mirror, Mirror on the wall…?* The answer is quickly projected from my reflection. At the root of the problem, fear rears its ugly head; fear of offending, of being alone, of giving up my personal space, of not being good enough, fear of not being able to please others, sentiments that make me second guess myself constantly. I need to unravel this paradox that has a great deal to do with matters of the heart and the brain. I must admit that at times, usually when I can predict that a budding relationship is not going to proceed to the next level, I find it easy to justify my reluctance to relinquish my hard-won independence. Yet, my heart strings pull me betwixt and between until I concede that my drive to be in a committed relationship with all the interdependence that this implies, still reigns supreme. These conflicting deliberations must be resolved. I tend to allow the heart to win over the brain. I am an emotional buyer; I am driven by emotion. It is no wonder I put my heart and mind through the wringer…

I am told by all and sundry that I should not care what others think; easier said than done when I have been this way all my life. I realise that if I integrate negative aspects into my psyche I run the risk of actualising self-fulfilling prophesies. I am trying to keep this in mind. Diminished self-esteem is the common denominator underlying the issues I am trying to resolve. I focus on this constantly. My feisty disposition, always on the defensive… this is effectively why I learned to assert my independence, why I became stronger willed and remain highly strung. Do I need affirmations to try to change such deep-seated characteristics that define my identity negatively? I am certainly keen to try but not convinced of definitive success.

SWAMPS, QUAGMIRES & OTHER CHALLENGES

Happily, not all online men were bastards. Some even felt the pleasure of the pursuit as did I.

Poem by Jonathan:

You're only a picture on the screen
looking for love it would seem
your profile reads like you're in my head
we have a lot in common
so I've read Cupid's bow was loaded and ready
he took aim, his hands were steady
a shot by that arrow pierced me deep
and because of it I cannot sleep,
my head gets drowsy tho full of desire,
the thought of you keeps the hope afire
I pray I can ask you for a date
but then I find out that I'm too late
you say you've clicked with someone already
and for a moment you feel unsteady
but what can you do but wish them well
and since that news has broken the spell
you return to the computer ready and keen
and you find another picture on the screen.

14

Seeking a Soulmate or friend with benefits?

My online dating journey has unveiled a curious paradigm. A huge number of internet daters are searching for sex, though anecdotal evidence suggests more males than females across most demographics espouse this behaviour. This is not for me, but I guess it seems as if it might be a highly efficient platform to satisfy these desires. Whilst they search for a mate for one occasion, I search for my Soulmate.

The challenges are numerous and all too real. Beyond my own distaste for this loveless relating, I feel that the whole system is unfair. Unfair because those who are seeking to satisfy lust seem much more likely to get what they seek than me. Love takes time to develop; there is an initial attraction, a chat, a building of attraction, a first date, an agreement to meet again, and so forth. The path of love is long and interlaced, the path of lust seems short and thin. Yet, nothing will induce me to hop on that band wagon.

An early assessment of the dismal results of my search for a Soulmate online did not improve my chances of success. I discovered that many guys were intimidated based on the education and independence of intellectual Ladies. Why was I being punished for being successful? Was I effectively less attractive to men because of everything I had achieved in my life?

Were empowered women so frightening? They say we have tough ovaries to fight out battles. Well, people say a lot of things! Am I turning into a sapiophile, only attracted to guys who are cerebrally stimulating? What about other qualities and attributes? Core values? I am undeniably attracted to intellectuals, if my dating experience is an accurate gauge, but I am not alone in preferring a good balance in my life. Is this asking too much? This is not to say that I find rambunctious men overly attractive either; a nice mix of quirky, witty, intelligent and cheeky is always a good start.

Some of the guys I chatted with proclaimed great interest in smart women who rationalise their arguments through logical thought processes. As I had an informed opinion about current world affairs, politics, diplomacy and religion, a few guys seemed to appreciate the spirited exchange; they perhaps believed that they had found their match. It unfortunately led nowhere.

Where some of my aspirants and I shared mutual interests, this generated vigorous debates and I enjoyed our discussions immensely, but my feelings did not develop any further, for complex reasons, the most basic of which concerned a lack of chemistry and compatibility. How long is this quest going to take? It is easy to forget that searching for love in the days of conventional dating, it took weeks and months to reach the stage where we thought we could have a life together. With online dating, it only takes two to three weeks to decide that things are not going to work out. And we move on.

Discussions that last a few hours are generally contingent on mutual respect for disparate world views, values and morals. The trick is to find a zone where we can discuss polemic issues, to not feel personally invested in our own views so that a challenge on a position is not taken personally. Incompatibility is often simply seeing someone's criticism of our views as a criticism of ourselves – and the latter does not necessarily follow from the former. The challenge is for that to be clear – and that requires cooperation from both sides. If we can enjoy the sparring, this could just form an interesting partnership, but compatibility is so complex.

My time is valuable, and I do not indulge in frivolous conversations online that lead nowhere. This is a feature of internet dating that allows me to move on if I feel dissatisfaction on any level. In my experience, if the guys are too opinionated and closed-minded I generally limit the encounter to a few messages. I am hugely attracted to guys with intellectual curiosity; but emotional intelligence is imperative if we are to move forward. To be quite honest, I must confess that sometimes, I am just not into them, for various reasons. The popular Hollywood film, *He's just not that into you* constantly crops up in my mind. I always recall this film when a guy rejects my advances online or when the shoe is on the other foot. It is a twisted salve to my bruised ego. The power of perspective once more to the rescue.

I decided after three months online to discard my fear of being alone once and for all. As I sat in front of my computer one night, I became convinced that adjusting my profile and honing the finer points that could potentially be deal breakers was the way forward. Okay! Reality check. Time to be honest with myself. It appears I am not what they are looking for, most especially on the Gold Coast. Is it really my fault? Am I too discerning? Downright difficult, perhaps? We shall see if my modified identity adjustments produce a more accurate and attractive profile. The feedback I was receiving was instrumental in the remodelling of my cyber identity.

The initial parameters for my first foray into Internet dating had clearly stated my search for my Soulmate, my expectations depicting the largely unrealistic image of the consummate Gentleman in his fifties or early sixties. These specifications had unwittingly set me behind the eight ball even before the search had begun.

The line: ***Seeking my Soulmate*** produced a great deal of mirth and sarcasm. Being laughed at was disconcerting but judging by my reaction to the first ignoramus who contacted me (below), I amended my profile quickly to avoid being verbally abused or totally disillusioned. Selected print-worthy comments include,

> *Soulmate? Sure, pull the other one! Most of you woman want the same thing as us! Stop all your BS! Searching for values and morals on dating sites? Good luck with that!*

> *The Gold Coast is an intellectual vacuum!*

> *Only sharks on this site luv!*

We like the GG barbie dolls. Your not blond with fake boobs!

Way to naughty for you Honey!

Too posh and educated for me Girl!

You are to high maintenance! You Gold Coast women are all the same. Never going there again! Good thing I moved to Brisbane! Not getting burnt again!

If you are cute and savvy, this is the only way you'll survive the games on this site. The men are all after one thing, Darlin! Get with the program!

A mate met someone on here once who described herself as the Gold Coasts answer to "Lady Gaga." The only bit that was correct was the "Ga-Ga" bit as she turned out to be Gold Coast's answer to Aileen Wournoss. :-) ... Then again I could be lying and my photos could be ten years old and not current, or not even me at all and I could actually be Adolph Hitler or Jeffrey Dahmer:-)

Prophetic words emerging from the last creepy entry. Strange way of trying to entice a woman to meet with him. If this guy thought that his knowledge of criminal minds was going to attract the right women, good luck! I must confess that I had no idea who Jeffrey Dahmer or Aileen Wuornos were until I Googled them. This guy from the Gold Coast, whose photos were hidden, certainly went to great pains to distance himself from the average Joe. Dahmer was better known as the Milwaukee Cannibal, a serial killer and sex offender. I did not need to find out any more. Aileen Wuornos Pralle was reportedly an infamous serial killer who shot seven men at point blank range in Florida between 1989 and 1990. Wow! If that is not enough to scare us, there are many entries where guys think they are being so very smart, only to fail dismally in their attempts. Sometimes, we are just not on the same cosmic wavelength.

I was excited when a French guy, Armand, who recently moved to the Gold Coast, showed some promise, even though I did not find his four-day growth attractive. I was not that shallow; had to pursue the lead as, perhaps he was not attached to his beard… There could have been an immediate connection, except that he now enjoyed the notoriety of being the first suitor to call off a coffee date the day before our meeting. Gleaning from the tenor of the messages we exchanged, his responses evasive and replete with incorrect French syntax, I understood immediately that he felt intimidated by smart women. Sharing common points of reference is not always enough to build a relationship and, as he was floating between jobs, the precarity of his employment posed challenges. We would never last the distance. No harm done! I can safely declare that I have at least never been stood up and that thought is comforting. At this stage of our lives, I was not prepared to support another person financially. I hoped to find men who were on an even keel financially or this was sure to spell trouble with our offspring.

Whilst I hope to find someone on the Gold Coast, the most eligible guys clearly appeared to be in Melbourne and Sydney; at least, according to my requirements in a partner. The Gold Coast that used to bear the title of "Retirement State" for many years has changed dramatically in profile; however, the insignificant number of high calibre professional fields does not appear to have attracted sufficient eligible men likely to interest many professional women living here. Some of the dating agencies have done their homework, enlisting psychologists to design their chemistry assessments and neuroscientists to work on potential rewards, as erroneous as these often turn out to be. To begin with, standardised tests produce generic analyses based on inflexibly concocted questions that are intolerant of ambiguities. They hone their skills on algorithmic formulae that ensnare the unsuspecting user into a false sense of security – "It's a Match! Our computers are working 24/7 to match you." Really?

Ever so polite, some sites boast of carefully structured replies that encourage members to be decent with unwarranted advances even from those whose language borders on abuse. Add to those, the number of gamesters who hedge their bets, all angles covered. The gamut of responses caters for predictable reactions to online requests, ranging from polite dismissals to engaging or suggestive witticisms to prolong the dating game, and in the process, fill the reserves of the dating site.

On your bike Squire!

Do I really need to walk on egg shells? I vow to remain true to myself. When I cast the line hoping my Soulmate will fall for me, hook, line and sinker, I know that I will need to gauge the situation based on whatever intel I have gathered during the first few dates. If he still does not bite, guess what? Plenty more fish in the sea! This is the balm to my bruised ego and my incipient sentiments that could just turn to love. What is a girl to do? I hope the guys do not destroy the tenuous links to true love.

Communication is imperative if we wish a new connection to proceed to the next stage. We need to tell each other what we need and what we want. I have agency; I have strong moral principles, I am available and ready to commit. I am equipped with the tools to create a lasting union with the man of my dreams. Just add water! Or perhaps, Champagne? I will tend to your needs too. It takes two to Tango.

The vignettes related to ***Seeking my soul mate*** gave rise to some serious deliberation, providing some fascinating insights to milk from the derogatory remarks. First, NONE of the senders of these messages expected a dignified response – making social network a misnomer. They offered very little that could be labelled as friendly and were seriously NOT looking to make contact. Second, the receivers of these messages, oversensitive individuals like me, need to develop thick skins. Point taken. I am still working on that, but I have thus far made little progress on that score. I am certainly not alone in this.

So, if these men expected no response, why give them one? Why even give them attention? Which leads to an interesting conclusion – why did I change my headline? These responses disqualified these people instantly and they were NEVER the ones I wanted to have any connection with anyway. And yet, they succeeded in pressing my buttons and I immediately put a stop to their ugly sentiments by either deleting their entry or using sarcastic language to dissuade them. My decision was clearly predicated on my fear of attracting further abuse of this kind; I chose to amend my headline, just in case… The strategy must have worked to a certain extent because there were no further retorts from this cohort.

This stage of my journey was discouraging but the interest my title page generated was certainly thought-provoking. Is that why so many guys are turning into Psychos if they fear coming face to face with such monsters as Wuornos? And are we, the women as fearful of attracting axe murderers or the likes of Dahmer? Scary! The guys I accepted to meet seemed so normal, decent, educated, but how do we know who they really are? I am not a quitter. I planned to give this quest a fair go. Besides, I was hooked.

What the hell was I doing wrong? It must be the photos. No, it must be my headline… no it must be my message. My God! Maybe I need to talk to my mirror. I had to get it right if I wanted to outsmart the Piranhas. I called in the big guns, the kids. They would know what to do. Why should the Big Fish even look at me? If I put down *"Professional, intellectual, sophisticated, accomplished"*, I sound conceited. This is hard, my identity is "Caucasian" but this classification online only comes in shades of white; vestiges of a time where Caucasian was synonymous with beautiful and very pale-skinned individuals. What about the ethnic groups that are Caucasians of various shades of brown, from Southern Europe, Egypt, Middle-Eastern countries through to India? Caucasian, but not white. Never an appropriate category for us. They could have used "Mediterranean." I was tired of selecting "Other." No wonder I have an identity crisis!

When I opted for "Caucasian" in the parameters provided on one site as an experiment, an ignorant fool's sarcasm got to me as he insulted me for posting false information, questioning my identity with the incongruous image. Where there was room for an actual national identity as well as social classification I was accepted because it explained my origins. Bizarre! This venture was tantamount to walking on egg shells and the continuation of this journey of self-acceptance proving to be quite a challenge.

The internal philosophical meanderings had become routine for me. A *mélange* of conflicting sentiments started to flood my mind.

> *Young at heart, fit as a fiddle, 50+ intellectual who has finally decided to discard the status of 'Workaholic'.*

Prophetic! Just happened to be during the full moon again, ebb and flow, ebb and flow like the tides… The recurring leitmotif of the full moon influencing my profile reconstructions was not promising for the rest of this journey into Cyberspace. Surely nearly four years of reproaches and self-flagellation over a broken heart were enough for a fine upstanding professional of the 21st century?

My mirror whispered to me, "You're no Spring Chicken, you know?" I needed reminding of that? Not!

I berated myself for acting too smart for my own good. The average fish would feel intimidated by my perceived strength, my independence, my newly-established self-confidence (Hmm... maintaining the façade was exhausting), my prowess with words, my education, my status... La di dah! I was not so hot, so why bother? I recalled what happened when I stopped responding to the guys who managed to sneak past the draconian barrier I set up in my criteria selection. There are so many layers to one's personality. Why do some guys focus on just one facet? I know, I know. They cannot see me at my most vulnerable. Silly question, again. Asking for the impossible. I could not show this online. When I was abused for being little *Miss too High and Mighty* and when they misconstrued my perceived confidence as cockiness, now, that hurt. I refused to dumb down. Not an option!

The right guy would appreciate me... Or perhaps feign to support me, nurture me whilst manipulating me. Have learned a thing or two over the years. I certainly know what I do not want... a refreshing change.

This self-examination sure was draining. The question was, would I fancy the ones who genuinely appreciated me? Let me see! Too old, not tall enough, not handsome enough, too introverted, overweight, now, that is shallow. Come on Goldilocks! Am I going to find one who is "just right"? I had to face facts; there was no accounting for chemistry, no substitute really for animal magnetism.

As a 52-year old astute aspirant wisely included in his profile,

> *You would not really know the "real person" until you have met a few times and if there is no chemistry what's the big deal you may make a new friend. :-). Or you could spend 3 and half weeks filling in a questionnaire on another site.*

Why was this sensible view not espoused by the rest of his cohort? He understood what I was talking about.

...and the list went on...

Are they not educated enough, too self-centred? Had I become so caught up in the games they played on the Cyber net? Could I honestly say I had not become an unsuspecting participant in these online games? Being honest to oneself is not easy. Were my expectations so high that this was a symptom of a more serious malady? Did I really want this? I believed this was my last chance at finding love in this crazy age of Turbo Dating, but was I furtively avoiding commitment? My values belonged in the last century. Hard to change the deeply-rooted lessons inculcated from a young age; the indoctrination worked a treat. Should I try to emulate the behaviours of the Millennials? I think not. Might need to reassess and tone down the list of unrealistic demands though. It was demoralising to get no interest in my profiles sometimes.

Times are a' changing. Had to get a move on. Where the hell are you my Prince?

Still living in fairy tales, it seemed!

Why do I hide behind a shield?

As I pondered on the synergistic counsel from my beautiful girlfriends who were instrumental in guiding me on the path to self-acceptance during a difficult period of my life, I was finally beginning to understand from Louise, that the veneer of my exterior self may be blocking, as she put it, the "genuine, loving, empathetic and most generous woman" she knew. I was deeply touched and humbled by her words. We were both in tears... Was I setting myself up for a massive fall? When the men I dated saw through the veneer, would they run? I started to see that the image I proudly displayed to the world of internet dating was essentially flawed. I had to admit to myself that every single date I had been on had confirmed that I needed no makeup at all, an abhorrent thought to me. Was it now time for the reverse? Time to turn back the clock, if I really wanted to appear younger? Be accepted?

Louise's views of the internet dating scene were astute. She perceived the concept as tantamount to a shopping expedition; a meat market where individuals, young and old, of both sexes advertised their wares, their products. Katarina was also of this opinion...

An early comment from a disgruntled suitor on one of the sites immediately came to mind, "Are you free, or are you expensive?" I found this incredibly offensive and did not dignify it with a response. How dare he? Just, because I was wearing professional attire? Seriously? Were we actually selling an illusion online? Did we want the prospective partner to buy the "gift-wrapped box" or fall in love with the real person who hid behind the cyber identity? Food for thought…

"Don't tell them I met you online"

I have discovered that one of the most significant challenges confronting the 50+ daters online is the perceived stigma attached to this form of dating. The focus of this investigation concerns the quinquagenarian and sexagenarian age groups. Could this be attributed to the escalating rates of divorce in many western societies in particular? It appears many lonely people tend to hesitate for some time but eventually, if the objective is to find a partner, if both sexes seek to indulge in gratuitous sex, find love or simply establish friendships, the first logical step is to throw themselves into online dating. This easy access to gratuitous sex is unprecedented in history. However, for some mature daters, only after having considered the degree of the social stigma attached to this form of dating. Once they join, it is not unusual for newcomers to become addicted, and even the simplest messages in their IN Box are likely to become a panacea to their loneliness. Is this not the "charm" of Facebook and all forms of social media and texting? Instant gratification! Facebook (and any other brands of social networking) is to social connection what *MacDonald's* is to nutrition.

Some dating agencies capitalise on the weaknesses of individuals who may be teetering on the brink of loneliness and the sites' questionable objectives enable depraved individuals to continue their games with impunity because it is impossible to monitor the behaviours of all users. Dissimulating profile photos and posting fictitious information is so commonplace. But, by the same token, this is a double-edged sword. Hiding a profile can represent a strategic measure of safety online for those who simply cannot cope with the stigma of online dating or those who just want to protect themselves from predators.

I went on a few dates with one guy from interstate named Paul whose wishes of remaining anonymous online I chose to accept because I believed there was a spark that could develop into something serious. I played the game, rather begrudgingly, when his family wanted to know how we met. His sister and family live on the Gold Coast, so it was inevitable that we would meet as things were progressing nicely. The problem with telling white lies is that eventually, one gets caught out and it could be embarrassing. The dilemma is whether to honour the requests of your suitor or to be true to yourself...

After two weeks, I decided that I could not live with this lie that was compounded by Paul's poor communication when he returned home. When I read between the lines, examining our email and text exchanges, I decided this potential relationship held very little substance. I cut him loose and opted for personal integrity. Not surprisingly, he was not all that perturbed!

The issue of stigma for those in their fifties and above is substantial and continues to pose challenges for both men and women who contemplate this journey. I spent a great deal of time considering dipping my toes in the murky waters before diving in.

It is extremely difficult to simply discard your traditional beliefs, values and behaviour, to let go of fear and to expose yourself to potentially soul-destroying experiences online. These appear to outweigh the chance of finding the "One." Some individuals simply refuse to change and cannot embrace this new form of dating; they fear being judged by their family, especially, their colleagues and friends; they worry that their reputation will be tarnished, that their social circles will denigrate and ridicule them. One of my suitors from Perth explained, "I only joined this site recently... I think its really crappy and cheap, this whole dating thing online is degrading and I do not believe much of what people say... I will be quitting this site for good soon. There is still a stigma attached to it."

This is sadly, a popular refrain.

The reality is that when some manage to overcome their fears and join a site, with trepidation, they post profiles with hidden images. The lucky few may attract someone without revealing photos, but chances are slim. The Smorgasbord of images seems infinite; so why bother to play a game of hide and seek; plenty more fish in the sea. They could be reported as fraudsters and scammers and are likely to end up on the lonely heap if they do not change their mindset and follow the rules.

This is where an exceedingly complex situation emerges. When one joins a site, the degree of 'eligible mates' becomes disproportionate; this is admittedly, a highly subjective and emotionally-charged term; and impossible to prove. There are claims that the males outnumber the women by a high degree, effectively facilitating the propagation of tactics employed online simply because of the quick sexual fix it promises. Decadence breeds depravity, but now, both sexes are contributing to the nefarious image of internet dating.

A gentleman named Claude, from Sydney contacted me to complement me on my "intriguing profile", bemoaning the fact that I live on the Gold Coast. He invited me to dinner during one of his frequent business trips to Queensland, which I politely declined. An ensuing online chat proved interesting, confirming his view of the dismally disproportionate ratio of female to male daters online that is contributing to the proliferation of tactics utilised by many men. The following entry is demoralising and sure to provoke despondency. When I indicated my interest in a guy from interstate, Claude's advice provided food for thought and serious re-evaluation of my endeavours online.

> *Fair enough, I accept that but I think the biggest problem is not enough good men in Queensland. All sites are the same, and most men on this site are married and looking for extra fling … I'm glad you know and I'm sure some men from here have told you they will come to Queensland just to see you… The reality is there are at least 3 women to one man in Australia and that could be a problem for some good women like you to find a decent man. Don't be shocked, many women on this site are after a one night stand or a fling only.*

Claude was, in fact, seriously overstating the over-representation of women to men, according to (2016) ABS Data[26] on this issue but I was concerned. How can we know what the real situation is when there are so few statistics that can be verified? More research on these thorny issues is certainly warranted. Morale low, I responded that I was not shocked; just terribly saddened and disappointed. Even knowing about the tactics, sometimes when you are longing to find that special someone, you can throw caution to the wind and believe what you want to believe. If that makes me, like so many of my girlfriends, susceptible, this undesirable

---

[26] Australian Bureau of Statistics (2016). http://www.abs.gov.au/ausstats/abs@.nsf/mf/3235.0

personality trait is hard to shake. If you are not promiscuous, it presents a problem for some of the gamesters and the statistics only place women like us further behind the eight ball. You do not want to play, you are out! I, for one, choose to stick to my principles. My self-respect is more important.

Messaging and miscommunications

Watch out for predictive texts on your smart phone – they can lead to some embarrassing and hilarious episodes.

A text message that I was sending to a new contact to start the phone chats nearly made a complete hypocrite out of me. Instead of my intended, "Just touching base with you... etc." the script stopped me in my tracks, "Just toying with you..." Phew! Rescued that one in time!

How about this text message that I sent to Katarina, thank God! Not hard to guess I was texting without my glasses. She had a physically demanding week and was knackered, and I was checking up on her. "Hi Hon, Ate guy still standing? Miss you..." "What the... Qué?" came the response. The message was meant to say, "Are you still standing? Miss you..." Heavens! We could not stop laughing about that literary *faux pas*.

When I mixed the names of the children of two guys, I was fortunate that they were equipped with a healthy sense of humour, or else they were putting it on. What a slip up, unspeakably embarrassing when I mixed the tentatively confessed histories of the men I dated, confusing the names and details of their children. "No. No. That must have been one of your other Blokes!" Oops! My response, "So sorry. I do not date Blokes." Their patience is not infinite... I recounted the episodes of my mix-up with the names of different guys to a man I was chatting with, named Derek and his response was interesting,

> *Your kids must have anticipated that you would be out on many a date if you are mixing up the information between the guys you have dated ... I had it stuck in my mind that you were in Brisbane as the coast has always been an intellectual vacuum... I took one of your subjects you did as an elective at uni and I'm sure we'd get along as we seem to have a bit in common, don't you think?... I sell car parts. Do you have a Holden ?? Drop over if you are around this way... Derek*

Derek, whose tertiary education in one area was similar to mine, assumed that we would get on and after suggesting that he meet me in my suburb for coffee, he became the second of only two guys to call off a coffee date one morning without a valid reason. Interesting! I was delighted by this because he had insinuated certain things that I found offensive and I myself was contemplating cancelling coffee. I minded my manners and had not cancelled; the universal code of ethics, "Do onto others…" made me conscious of the fact that I never wanted to be stood up by a guy.

I almost got myself into trouble when meeting a local guy for a drink one night. I texted him to ask him to meet me outside but without my glasses, the person I sent the text to was Marcelo, Alessandra's partner. My date had the same name as my daughter's ex-partner. Thank God Marcelo saw the funny side. We get on famously.

On the march again!

At that juncture, *Sisyphus* came back to haunt me once more; I felt condemned to push that boulder up a mountain and then to watch it roll down and having to start again. Greek mythology often provided perfect metaphors for my sentiments.

So much for the site that I had joined, supposedly engineered for like-minded individuals. The lengthy rigmarole to join new sites was a definite deterrent and fortunately casting the net wider, the third site had allowed me to view profiles that extended across Australia. I perceived this as useful in the end, best to cover all bases. I should be able to find someone. Hmm… Many guys had reiterated that I was the best lady they had found online, satisfying their requirements. Good line! Flattery. Then again, I was not that easily duped. They assured me that my sincerity and integrity shone through and my morals and code of ethics enticed them to get to know and trust me. I managed to turn their heads, but the need to shut down their profiles to woo only me after one date worried me still. Both sexes had members unwilling to take this dating game at a measured pace.

15

Love at a distance makes for a long journey

Gerry, from the West had said, "Distance is only a small hurdle to be with the one you want!"

After disastrous efforts to locate men on the Coast with whom I could find an instant connection that was not plagued with extraneous issues, I focused intently on profiles from further afield. Why cast the net so widely? My mind kept toying with the idea of a possible move interstate but seriously, I still could not contemplate abandoning a dream career of more than two decades at this stage of life. So why go deep-sea fishing? Could this effectively be an exercise in self-sabotage after all? Why dismiss the notion that someone matching my exaggerated expectations of the quintessentially perfect guy might actually be in my own neighbourhood?

Not possible; distinct lack of culture here. This is a holiday destination and the dating sites for the region most commonly boast masculine profiles where the inspired pursuits, par excellence, all revolve around *boatin'*, *campin'*, *fishin'*, like the infamous advertisement on national Australian television – notorious for its little ditty that rhymes with an expletive. Although many males from the South had moved to the Coast, they often did so because they embraced this lifestyle – clearly at loggerheads with mine. Why do I keep searching further afield if distance is a deal-breaker? That question continued to plague me, but I would not cease and desist...

Time was a-ticking and I was getting nowhere fast. I had never imagined it would be so difficult to find someone in this State. Hard to make changes when I was undeniably quite inflexible. I was not playing games and I had no intention of prolonging this exercise longer than necessary.

The Southerners

The guys from Melbourne, the sophisticated town I love and know so well, and Sydney, are in stark contrast with those who originate from the Gold Coast; especially as many endorse the self-professed title of proud *Bogans*. I am not disparaging these guys as they are honest and down to earth, but they are just not my type. I have a type I like! I confess I am attracted to the Alpha males, usually with a smidgen of *Bad Boy* characterising them. Okay! I keep reminding myself of the adage, "Be careful of what you wish for," because the universe does not disappoint. Need to be more precise... Sometimes, it is the reserved, deep thinkers who measure their words and take a while to plant the first kiss on my lips. Those in between, the *SNAGs (Sensitive New Age Guys)* are great guys but the *Metrosexuals* are not really my type. This is my nature. I make no apology for it.

It has become evident that, despite the stars aligning, sometimes, distance will put paid to a potential relationship. A few guys from Brisbane had offered friendship instead because of the distance. I really appreciated their offer but the road to friendship and love is paved with good intentions that do not always materialise; not to mention plagued by incessant traffic and roadworks!

Gorgeous 50-year-old Leo from Melbourne had one of the most inviting profiles I had come across on my dating journey, but I am happy to say he was a realist and not into games. A lucky Lady must have snapped him up as his profile lasted but a week. He confessed to being as discerning as I am. He responded to my innocuous compliment on his profile, as you do sometimes, bemoaning the fact that we lived so far away. Story of my life! Exchanges such as these are harmless when both parties wish each other well. Honest guys such as Leo and Mr B. (below) recognise the folly of becoming involved in long distance relationships interstate when there is no pragmatic or logistical way of seeing it to fruition. I really admire them. A rare find.

I began to understand that if I really believed that my special someone was interstate, I needed to examine my criteria selection sheet to see just how many boxes my suitor actually ticked.

"Swow down, Speed Demon!" – became my new catch cry, from the mouth of a gorgeous little three-year-old Babe, Marcelo's nephew. Well, he was referring to my lead foot, driving! But it works for internet dating too. In fact, it is just as pertinent to the suitors who were in a mad rush to have the package signed, sealed and delivered.

Mr B.

From all accounts, Mr B. met most of my requirements, except one – he did not live on the Coast. He was a Match! I contacted him, and he responded immediately. I had the good fortune to be going to Melbourne shortly and he was keen to meet me. Mr B. was a 57-year-old, 6'2 gorgeous guy, with scintillating blue eyes; a little reserved but with a quirky sense of Australian humour. He was a financial expert who had realised his creative ambitions and was doing exactly what he loved in the next stage of his career. Seemed like a great match for me.

But physical distance drove a wedge into my mind. I was forced to examine this issue in more depth. Could I be happy, really happy, with a long-distance relationship? Was I simply deluding myself? Commuting to work from Melbourne was not an attractive proposition.

My communications with him did little to help the fogginess of my mind. The more we communicated, the more our chemistry and animal magnetism emerged. And the mutually anticipated first coffee date was brilliant. Mr B. travelled many kilometres to meet me during my short time in Melbourne. He took me to a classy French Café for coffee and cake. My daughter, Angelina, who was picking me up to go to lunch after coffee, was running 30 minutes late. Mr B. kissed me goodbye and headed in the opposite carpark to my designated meeting place. 20 minutes later, I noticed him walking around my car park, still looking for his car. I could not help grinning. Not likely to miss him in a car park! I liked to think that I had had that effect on him.

Two days later, he came to pick me up for another surprise date. I am not fond of surprises. I am a Virgo. I need to plan, be organised, dressed appropriately – I had prepared for all contingencies in my suitcase on this trip. Melbourne was the perfect opportunity to dine in classy restaurants where a dress code existed. My wardrobe was going out of date on the Coast with a dearth of suitable places to wear my European winter gear. So, I pondered… What if I did not like what Mr B. suggested?

As it turned out, this second date proved hilarious too because he managed to get lost even with his GPS. Mr B. finally arrived an hour late, his best laid plans to impress me with a cultural evening thwarted by peak hour traffic, and an unscheduled scenic tour of the area because of road works. We missed the Spanish movie but the evening at his favorite Spanish restaurant met all my expectations. I really appreciated being driven all the way back to my friend's place after dinner. He had insisted. That was certainly impressive. Mr B. ticked 90% of my boxes; he was a Gentleman, a kind soul, intelligent, witty, generous, compassionate and respectful. And I made a fool of myself gazing into his magnetic blue eyes over dinner. I really need to curb this embarrassing habit.

Moved by the success of the first dates, I was happy to see him again on my next visit. The problem of distance was disappearing into the distance. Three weeks before a second trip to Melbourne, I was busy coordinating my stay to include visits to the homes of my daughter, Angelina and her husband, Mark; my sister, my friends, as well as Mr B. He was cooking me dinner and introducing me to his beloved puppies. He thought nothing of clocking up the kilometres to pick me up from my daughter's home this time, insisting it was a pleasure.

Trying to maximise my time, I tried to organise this trip to fit everyone in, hoping to see one of the musicals. Mr B. wrote back, "OMG! You ARE an organiser!"

I interpreted this as criticism and a flaw of character. Was I controlling? I apologised and suggested he arrange the date – "Don't be sorry. It's a Joke Joyce. Relax Max! We'll work something out." I was still uncomfortable and left everything up to him, vowing to tame my 'Planner' gene. But I hate it when guys prefer to "wing it", to "fly by the seat of their pants." No fond memories of such experiences in Europe…

Perhaps I should not have worried. A week later, Mr B. asked me to "please organise our date." I felt frustrated and pleased that I could organise it.

Mr B. was charming again. And I learned a little bit more about liking myself the way that I am. His kindness and patience were limitless. He convinced me – for a moment at least - that I am "perfect" the way I am.

He may not have been the "One," but Mr B. helped me to redefine what I had been searching for all this time. His belief in me helped me believe in myself a little more and this was a welcome change.

Mr B. intrigued me. He not only helped me understand myself, he seemed to understand me. He convinced me to wear "almost" no make-up, telling me I looked so much younger and more beautiful without it. Others had said the same thing, many even, but Mr B. won me over. Well, only a little bit won over, because makeup is my armour.

Transformation

Mr B. is a remarkable Gentleman and a friend, primarily, because of his actions merely reinforcing the hollowness of the words of so many. With Mr B., there was no pretence. We knew we would become great friends from the start, choosing not to complicate our lives with anything more grandiose.

I thought that going for the good-looking guys, I would always end up disappointed, but I have learned that with perseverance, there is just that small chance that a genuine, amazing guy is really looking for love and is legitimately on the site, not married, or involved with anyone else. The distance was still a problem. I did not intend to move interstate, and neither did Mr B. Our commitments were too onerous. So, friendship was the logical outcome of our encounters. No need to worry about the negative connotations of being *Friend Zoned*. This was a term the Millennials liked to flaunt. With our generation, we made some sincere friends that could potentially last the distance. With Mr B. there was no ruse. He was the real McCoy. Whilst circumstances can change, we are unlikely to live close enough to one another to move forward. But, who can say? One day, perhaps...

Louise, with whom I was staying, really likes Mr B. She scolds me for my low self-esteem. She works tirelessly, through meditations and counselling to recalibrate my bruised psyche to help me recognise the woman I am within, beneath the veneer. By now, it should be obvious that this veneer, my make-up, is a leitmotif that is going to haunt me for my entire existence.

Louise wonders why I keep coming back for more of the tough love she dishes out. Maybe I can see I need it. On my last visit, I was momentarily shocked when I met up with her and her husband. She said, "I need a drink when I know you're coming." She was obviously joking, yet it stopped me in my tracks… Australian humour still has that effect on me.

Nevertheless, I need to try to reduce the mask I hide behind. Mr B. was the good cop, Louise was the bad cop. So, I applied myself to the task of reducing the length of time it took to apply my makeup. I managed to reduce it to just 45 minutes while staying with them in Melbourne. Very proud of myself.

Divided by distance, the pull of propinquity

Tom, the One that got away

I never imagined that the guy who fulfilled the exacting list of expectations on my checklist would win the first prize of *Heartbreaker* in my chronicles. Of course, I fell for him, unapologetically. Well, I survived to tell the tale! This lesson will serve us, the Ladies, well. We must preserve our heart.

I was pleasantly surprised when an eligible and attractive male from South Australia, contacted me. Although I understood only too well the challenges of a long-distance relationship, Tom, at 63 had some true potential in my view when he sent me a note,

> *I like how you express yourself and feel like we share the same core values. You sound genuine, intuitive and appear to have an open mind... 3 very attractive attributes. So I'd be very interested to meet you at some stage in the near future should you be interested in exploring any possibilities.*

Tom resembled the irresistible protagonist from my favourite Italian romance novel and uncannily like Sean Connery as James Bond. He was tall, dark and handsome (Check), 6'3, buff, athletic and sincere (Check); he embodied the male attributes, morals and values that I cherished. Well, he lacked the blue eyes and lived interstate. Well, he also had a home on the Gold Coast – blue eyes? I can let some things go.

I was a little cautious of course. Tom claimed to spend part of the year in a suburb of the Gold Coast whilst his main abode was in a desirable up-market suburb in Adelaide. I found all this a little mysterious, but he helpfully decided to give me his phone number, email and website details, business and home addresses. He seemed keen and his credentials were legitimate. He even gave me his address to view his beautiful home online.

Tom was, in some ways, the exception that proved the rule. He also owned a place on the Gold Coast. He had family in South Australia and Queensland and spent considerable time here, or so he said. Distance can be conquered with airplanes – and overlapping commitments in one physical location.

I tantalised myself with thoughts of a meeting in the near future and he said he was looking forward to meeting me - SOON, on the Coast.

Tom revealed he was passing the reins of the business to a younger brother who was more knowledgeable, internet savvy and talented in marketing and promotion than he was. Phasing in his semi-retirement was a brilliant exit strategy. It was time for him to relax, travel more and enjoy the fruits of his labour.

It was wonderful. I thought that perhaps this could actually work. In anticipation of an interesting encounter with Tom, I awaited further communication.

After two weeks, I accepted I had been *Benched, Ghosted*, or once again *Breadcrumbed*.

The communication had dried up completely and I was smarting at having been duped.

Perhaps I was simply impatient. Soon for me means soon. I do not like to wait. But, distance means time. And time can be ambiguous. Does no response mean not yet or not at all? The other clues told me. His profile disappeared, and our messages remained on the site, taunting me and reminding me what a fool I had been. It does get easier, but I was smitten, and so it hurt.

My ego would not let me leave things unfinished, although they had not really begun. I really needed to know how I had erred. So, I sent some last words to wish Tom well, saying it was clear to me that he had moved on and that it was Okay! Tom responded. He told me he was lying low, limiting communication with me. His ex was apparently stalking him. After a considerable number of months, she could not let go of Tom and her compulsive behaviour was making him anxious. I had heard this from other guys online. They said many women were obsessive when their relationship broke down while the guys moved happily on to the next woman. Consequently, Tom was nervous around "women" until she calmed down. In the meantime, she was watching him and making his life hell. He was heading to the Gold Coast in a month or so and said that he was keen to meet me.

I was not sure whether to believe him, but there was nothing more to do or say. Nonetheless, a later message renewed my hope,

Good morning Gorgeous Girl. Was just thinking of you last night. Will see you very soon... I can't wait to get up there ... will try this week but let you know for sure. Psycho all gone thank goodness!

Sounded promising. However, I was certainly not pinning my hopes on this potentially fictitious future meeting. Nor was I going to just let go. I might just get lucky and this might be the "One." Finally, my Mr Right.

But, still I wondered, and impulsive as always, I texted Tom to ask him, "Are you real?" I was tired of the games being played on these dating sites. His response both teased and reassured me.

I know, Coco. It's a pain for me also and I'm too old to be playing games ... but what do we do? It's normal, I suppose whether you are online or not... I'm at the gym. Get back to you in more detail shortly...X Hey, hang in there. You're smart and beautiful so the universe will look out for us ... XX Tom

Tom's soothing words restored my faith in human nature and calmed me down for the afternoon. He even suggested (in a later message) that I write a book replete with the experiences, traps, and saucy adventures based on guys he knew who had been online, just to spice it up and sell a few million copies... But such accounts are not part of my narrative.

Tom turned up on the Gold Coast, as promised. He texted me immediately to organise our first rendezvous. All the signs pointed to a favourable encounter, but I nevertheless asked Tom to provide me with more photos before our coffee date and to remind me how tall he was. I felt I was at a disadvantage, much information on the phone but nothing online because he had pulled his profile. He confirmed he was 6'3 and told me to look for the hottest guy in the café. I replied, "So, I am looking for James Bond then?"

Tom replied simply with a photo of Sean Connery in a classic James Bond pose at the Casino in Monaco. My response surprised him, "Sorry, I have met Sean Connery in Europe. You will have to do better than that." Roger Moore appeared instantaneously, "Sorry, he is no longer with us."

This little exchange was an exciting precursor to the cheeky banter that defined our first meeting. The initial mirth and the quick, intellectual repartee held a great deal of potential, and the date and three more that followed over four successive days delivered on the promise.

Could he be the "One"? The dates increased in intensity and the anticipation of passion and excitement filled the air. From my estimation, we had chemistry; we were compatible on most fronts and there was substance beneath the first layer.

The one problem was distance. Could one online confidant have been right after all, cautioning me not to entertain a long-distance relationship?

After having met four times including dinner with his daughter on the Coast, I assumed that this suitor was legitimate. He was returning the following week to see me, to move the relationship forward. Tom had already made plans to have his boat brought up to the Coast. For all intents and purposes, this guy was moving in the right direction, and I was delighted at the prospect even if there were challenges we needed to face.

But plans go awry. How do you make the Universe laugh? Talk about your plans. Tom did not come back as promised. I also discovered that his communication skills with technological devices were appalling. I felt he needed to engage in a modicum of communication even if he disliked the phone. "Out of sight, out of mind, perhaps?" But I did not want to buy into that. Perhaps I should have saved myself a lot of heartache; let things lie and forget about him.

He simply disappeared on me, but I still had his details. I examined the signs and admitted that Tom was not perfect; I certainly was not. But, I saw nothing that pointed to the biggest deception of simply disappearing on me. Was I such a bad judge of character after all? Doubts and uncertainty plagued me for days, interrupting my already alarmingly disastrous sleeping patterns. I was on the familiar downward trajectory of my roller-coaster ride; I was feeling crushed and disillusioned.

I wrestled with whether to try and communicate with him. My BFFs and daughters counselled against it. Louise texted me,

> *Don't send him stupid messages saying it's all over before*
> *it even begins! This is the typical Aussie male, remember!*
> *When extenuating circumstances arise, they are not good at*

multitasking! Why would Tom, in a text message, completely out of context tell you, "BTW, I don't snore!"? He is into you, don't be silly! You know he has business and family matters to attend to! Don't contact him, you hear?

Whilst I heeded their advice, I was still chafing at the poor communication skills of this successful businessman who spent his time on the phone, who could operate his business from anywhere and still complete a full day's work; I thought we had a real connection, a great deal in common; and, of course, I had actually contemplated spending the rest of my life with him. I had worked it all out.

Well done Coco, but what about Tom? Smart little Virgo! You think? We could divide our time interstate and on the Coast. That would be the perfect solution, or so I told myself. Tom had told me he was going away for two weeks, but communication is available in most places. What a fool! Alessandra and Katarina interpreted the silence and the brief, unemotional text messages over the preceding week, and while he was away, as a lack of interest and that sadly, he was simply not into me. I had even taken him to my office and introduced him to some colleagues. Katarina was convinced that he was intimidated by my accomplishments because his educational level was not equal to mine. I disagreed. This was beginning to really irritate me because I had never presumed to be other than the equal of the guys I had considered as potential partners.

Ego-driven jerk reaction once again? Surely, not Tom? I could not believe this. I was still giving him the benefit of the doubt. Was I really such an air head? I must have conjured up this fictitious romance because it now appeared one-sided. Red-faced, the post-mortem continued as I dissected each and every episode of our dates trying to decipher where I had erred.

With a sinking heart, I finally realised that Katarina and Alessandra were right. They had rescued me. I had been too needy, "Ready! Aim! Fire!" as Katarina put it; guys and gals do not move at the same pace. The writing was on the wall. Even with Tom's promises to come to the Coast around the time of my birthday; if he did there was no contact. My roller-coaster picked up speed, heading to a certain crash this time. I had evidently been delusional. I chose to emotionally detach myself and called Tom to end the charade. I interrupted his meeting and was cut off, a brief text telling me that he would call afterwards. But no call.

I finally sent Tom a dignified text message wishing him the best. He did not have the decency to respond. Why did I contact him after I had been warned not to? Why did I allow myself to be upset by his non-response? I needed closure. I guess I still hoped – against all evidence – that there was a chance.

I was incensed that he had not responded to my dismissal, yet, what was there for him to say? The truth of the matter was that I still hoped that he would feel bad and contact me again and I may even have deluded myself in believing his excuses. In all honesty, I was pushing him to respond, to feel bad, to apologise and grovel, all of which would ultimately make me feel better – empty eventually; but I was so desperate to make this work. Yet, I was powerless to do so without compromising my dignity. That stubborn streak of mine. I was adamant that I would never contact him again.

Tom's message never came! This left me wondering why I was bothering to search for love. Love was not supposed to hurt. I realised that this was too soon; yet even infatuation was painful. Did I really want to put myself through that again?

I am not entirely equipped to handle the troubling emotional issues of the guys I am dating. With distance and time, I recall that Tom had some pressing challenges to handle interstate. I was not quite sure how to proceed. I had totally fallen for Tom, but he was never coming back. I had let my guard down for the second time on this journey. I had already designed my wedding dress in my head. I felt jilted; yet I had technically closed the door on the potential relationship.

Post Script

A few months later, as I had not succeeded in getting Tom out of my mind, I could not help myself. My roller-coaster ride had come to a stop after seven months online. I just had to send him a note to wish him well for Christmas. I was shocked to learn that he had been gravely ill since our last communication and he was recovering very slowly. I was immediately contrite, even felt guilty at having acted so precipitously with my message; yet I defended myself for having ended the promising relationship, saying,

"With no communication Tom, I had no choice. I did not have a crystal ball…" Surely anyone, family, nurse, friend could have dropped me a quick line, or not… What if he had been in a coma? I did not pry. I simply did not know the circumstances of his illness.

Communication in any relationship, far or near, is vital, without which there is no longevity. Both sexes need to be aware of their role in this issue. Past experiences and this current online dating journey have reinforced this issue for me. Whilst I am not generally "needy" in a relationship, I do appreciate some contact from a partner. There is no need for lengthy exchanges; just acknowledgement that a message has been received, and a little more if a response is required. It really helps to avoid misunderstandings and upsets.

Beware of the spiral of despair

Suffering from days of insomnia and fatigue, I realised that I could make rash decisions to give it all away if a nascent relationship, particularly long distance, began to waver; start from scratch with someone new if I did not get the promised phone call from the one I was attracted to. My mind played tricks on me, threatening to push me into a spiral of despair because I began to doubt myself and my potential partner. I became despondent, stress and anxiety invading my thoughts; something that emerged simply because of the inaccessibility of the one I wanted to be with. I seriously debated the virtues of living apart that would afford us the independence to live the way we were doing, juxtaposed with the disadvantages caused by the tyranny of distance. I had to consider whether to proceed, or to give it all away?

My daughters often told me, "Stop over-analysing Mum! It will drive you mad!" They had assumed the pastoral care of their mother in this dating game; the role reversal befitting a generation that understood the dating world better than me. The emotional and spiritual support they generously offered soothed my troubled soul.

When these thoughts enveloped me, the next morning, I had little energy and ultimately, as the expected message arrived, it would restore my faith in human nature and in the man I had fallen for. Or not. All was forgiven and off I went on my roller-coaster on its uphill trajectory that was taking me out of the doldrums once again. The invitation to join the *The*

Happy Divorcées' Club kept mocking me along this journey as I reserved hope for the proposed relationship. Was this really all worth it? My BFFs were telling me, "NO WAY!"

It takes an inordinately long time for two people to really get to know each other. Are we patient enough to wait for that ultimate commitment? Easy enough for daters of both sexes who just want to have fun dating; hooking up with multiple partners and laughing at life; until when, though? It is easy to see why these lucky women of the *Exclusive Club* are so content in their safe little haven without sleep deprivation and submergence into misery.

So once again, I consulted my *Mirror, Mirror on the wall…* and I made the solemn promise to myself that I would never again allow my self-esteem to be decimated. Not until the next time that I make the same promise. Coco, you are such a twit!

The little pep talk in front of my Mirror was most helpful in arriving at a sensible decision.

I believe this introspection helped to reduce my stress. Thank God, I succumbed to a massage and it did me a world of good. I recalibrated my sleep patterns. I am leaving the quest to find my Soulmate to the universe. I am a firm believer that, if I make the right decisions, the universe will conspire to make it all happen. I could not envisage giving up hope. My friend Joseph understood how much I was hurting. His message was simple, "Say goodbye to where you have been and tell your heart to beat again."

I intend to include *my happy ever after* in my chronicle. Like one of my favourite classic protagonists, Scarlett O'Hara always used to say in *Gone with the Wind*, "After all… tomorrow is another day." Uncanny how my European High School friends, from Germany and Hungary had perceived me as Scarlett O'Hara. I had taken umbrage at that but in retrospect, perhaps I modelled my feistiness and sassy temperament on this famous protagonist.

Get back on the horse again!

It is very gratifying to confirm a positive effect of the dynamic changes to my identity as I progress along this journey. Whilst I may go through soul-destroying moments when a guy I finally set my heart on turns out to be the "One" that got away, I vowed that I would no longer allow these events to decimate my renewed self-esteem. Whether the act is deliberate or involuntary, whether I inadvertently build a rosier picture of the potential relationship or not, if a guy uses avoidance tactics such as *Slow Fade* or *Ghosting*, it is bound to affect me just the same.

I have learned an invaluable lesson; not to wallow in self-pity. I bounce back, and I am on the road again. It is incredible how beneficial being on dating sites can be when you need to fortify your soul after rejection, perceived or real, when you need to rebuild your self-respect. His loss. Freedom. Move on! I am absolutely amazed that I have succeeded in doing this. I managed to change my mindset. Get back on that horse. I will catch another fish that is more deserving of me, even if it takes a little time…

Another vital lesson I learned was to keep my heart and soul iron clad until I observed definitive signs that the guy was fully committed to the developing relationship. If he promised to come back to see me, he needed to keep his promise. No lame excuses! This is the most soul-destroying part of this journey. Just when I thought I had found the "One," he ripped the carpet from under my feet.

This may not be a deliberate act of wonton trickery, especially after having spent quality time together, but it certainly demonstrated an immense lack of respect for me, for the special moments we had shared and the destruction of my hopes and dreams. It certainly showed that the guy in question was not as into me as I had imagined. Funny how we can construe images that are completely fabricated on our hopes and dreams. When the amazing encounter with Tom turned out to be a figment of my imagination, it was the one occasion I did not want to listen to Katarina when she saw the writing on the wall; but deep down inside, I knew that she was right when she advised me to "Cut him loose Honey!"

Is it worth the increased stress that a union of this kind is likely to generate? Not all parties are willing or able to relocate instantaneously when they fall in love. Two of my girlfriends are ecstatic that such is their story. I wonder how many distance relationships have such a happy ending? These difficult relationships go beyond superficial likes and dislikes, idiosyncrasies and personal interests. The crux of the issue is to determine whether it is actually feasible for one party to make the move, not instantly of course, but realistically within a few months or a year.

Reflection

Thanks to Mr B. I learned to pick myself up and restore my balance.

I am in control this time, no more "My way or the highway!" Not from any man. I need to watch out for the first signs of a controlling man. He will only show his true colours when the chase is over. Post mortems are useful, if a little late, to discover what a fool I have been. My best friend, Luke had warned me to watch out for signs of this masculine trait and I had to confess that there were two minor incidents where Tom had flexed his control muscles. I had, of course, dismissed them.

What surprised me and brought a whole lot of laughter to my world was Luke's suggestion. "Honey, have you thought of becoming Gay? Life might be a lot easier for you…" He always knew how to provide relief for a painful situation. "Darling, I will never jump that fence. Not happening!"

And the wheel turns. If my escapades on internet dating sites have dissuaded anyone from ever venturing into this unconventional way of finding love, then, take heed! Take a page from my book. Read and learn! Let me do the hard yards and save the heartache, sleepless nights and constant disappointments.

When I understood that with the pain, there were rewards at the end of the journey, I knew I could then jump on board my roller-coaster once more. I wish someone had prepared me for my journey.

I reiterate… It is worthwhile, if only to reach a state of self-acceptance and serenity. I am aiming to be happy in myself and hope that at that point, my light will shine through. I never said it was easy.

16

What does age have to do with it?

Age is tricky. I do not want to reveal my age, and I do not believe that a Lady ought to, but the websites require me to enter my age. My reasons are legitimate. Online safety and finding guys closer to my age remain the main objectives.

I have mostly chosen to fib a little, to tell a white lie. I have been told I do not look or act my age. And I certainly do not feel my age. And anyway, I would love to date a man a little younger than myself for no other reason than I think I deserve it. Unless of course, a guy who is older than me looks ten years younger and is also young at heart; and has looked after himself. Tom was 63 but looked 50 and he was a Larrikin.

I do not want to be knocked back by someone who has created some artificial criterion based on age. Maybe I could be his perfect match if he had not been so foolish as to set such a low age cut off.

So, yes, I tell a fib, but it is an honourable fib. I always reveal my true age in the first chat on the phone or face-to-face during our first date. For that matter, it really does not bother me if a guy I date also fibs about his age if he tells me the truth on our first date. What is good for the goose is good for the gander. Fair is fair. However, this is the only fib, large or small that I will tolerate in this dating game. There is really no point in concealing our age beyond this point or hoping we will never have to confess the truth. The guilt and fear of being ridiculed when found out would consume me if I were to prolong the agony. It would do immeasurable damage.

It is refreshing to meet guys online and on dates who realise that age is just a number, within limits of course. Always fearing that they will abuse me for concealing my age, most of the guys in their 50s and 60s are Gentlemen and do not see this as a deal breaker. It is not that easy to post a witty comment such as, "I have given the age I look. It is rude to ask a Lady her age." No lie. Just aplomb and dignity. I must keep reminding myself that protecting my identity online is of paramount importance. Age is an important recurring leitmotif in this chronicle. Both sides find revealing of age awkward and moreover, both sexes would rather date someone younger than they are – most of us do not feel our age. Should I feel guilty for not being completely honest online if I provide current photos instead? At the very least, everyone should provide one or the other. In my experience, there is very rarely a current photograph of a guy I have dated.

Age-related issues are intricately tied to one's culture. Whilst in some cultures, it is not unusual for ladies to proudly defy their age because they look much younger than their images, in others, if issues based on ageism in social and professional contexts are significant, it stands to reason that total disclosure about age and other personal information should be at their discretion. It is in fact discriminatory today, in some western cultures for employers to demand the age of those applying for work. In the context of internet dating, I believe that we should reveal our veritable age only when we are ready and only to those we plan to meet. Alternatively, we can simply provide recent photos.

Realistically, it would be immature to believe that individuals could get away with lying about age in a relationship. International travel and passports would identify the truth instantly and the subterfuge is bound to cause a massive argument. Fibbing about my age is actually very stressful, believe it or not, because there is always the chance that the younger guy will reject me on that basis, even if I look younger than him. I can relax when I get the green light that age is just a number. It is, therefore, imperative that I raise the issue immediately. Saves a great deal of time!

Peripheral information is also reserved for the first meeting as it pays not to reveal too much detail online, but it seems that non-disclosure is still a huge issue on these dating sites and on first dates. People have become so cynical and trust issues have risen exponentially. Fibbing slightly about my age may be regarded as poor judgment by the opposite sex, but some egregious lies from some males have spelt instant disaster for the relationship.

For all intents and purposes, I already wear my heart on my sleeve, volunteering too much information because, if I demand honesty and integrity of character, reciprocating is called for. Whilst it has been suggested to me by a male friend to suppress the level of my education until I get to know the guy well, I feel it is an affront to consider dumbing down and lying about my tertiary qualifications and international experience in Europe, just to catch the prize. What kind of satisfaction would that generate anyway?

Andrew - the director

Gorgeous blue-eyed Andrew was from Melbourne. Very promising. Our eyes met across the room as the instantly recognisable 6'1, debonair, man-about-town walked down the stairs to meet me at the exclusive establishment where a major function was to take place the next day. Was I in the movies? I was already having fun, dressed for the part, as we managed to raise a few eyebrows at this first meeting. Sparks began to fly and chemistry was in the air. God, I love romance!

Andrew's misleading profile produced an exciting weekend full of promise and intrigue as our first meeting established mutual attraction. I would not have responded had he not engineered his profile to suggest that he was looking for property on the Gold Coast to facilitate his frequent visits. Sounded plausible, so I forged ahead, cautiously.

The intense coffee date was followed by exciting stolen moments at the Industry Awards Ceremony where fraternising with the guests was strictly forbidden, even if I was not part of the entourage. When I admitted to my little white lie regarding my veritable age, the collective ruse became clear, the practice common with both sexes, "Listen My Dear, don't apologise! I tell a fib too. I'm 64!" A discrepancy of 11 years was bold, but Andrew carried it off in style, looking convincingly the age he had declared online, 53!

What transpired that weekend was memorable and I still have fond memories of the entire event. Little had I known that I was auditioning for a part in a romantic comedic piece, akin to a scene from a popular *Sit-Com*. I had unwittingly fallen into Andrew's trap and swiftly became a trophy date but enjoyed the ride nonetheless. The subterfuge continued until Andrew decided to seek me out amongst the guests. He strategically avoided me in the crowd and then to my complete surprise, he sauntered toward me to chat, photos duly taken of the two of us for the record. I decided to ignore the inquisitive glares from the ladies when Andrew brought me to his official table after the formalities had finished.

By that stage, it was clear that I posed no threat to the organisation. At least the sophisticated replica of an Hollywood actor had poise and charm, cutting an amazingly attractive figure on a fascinating date. I enjoyed the game thoroughly and with only a soupçon of embarrassment, I congratulated myself on my performance as I had played my role admirably in that scene from our movie. Okay! I was not a contender for an Oscar, nor was I going to get the man for that matter, but I had a ball, dressed to the hilt for a change on the Gold Coast and there was no harm done. Andrew promised to see me again the following month during a business trip to the Coast but that did not eventuate; nor had I expected him to follow through.

This quirky little interlude had a very positive effect on my identity. I instantly felt more self-assured. Wow! I managed to attract the attention of a real charmer, a smooth-talking Director who showed interest in me. I certainly had no more qualms about not revealing my actual age. Having subsequently learned of Andrews's reputation from credible sources, I was amused and relieved that there had been little time for him to orchestrate intense romantic moments. Andrew was honest at least in his admission that he did not want to leave me heartbroken when he went home after the weekend. I was in no danger of that and neither was he.

Do we really fall in love that quickly? In lust? Or are we simply infatuated and playing the game? But then again, I had not met Tom by then…

The expected text from Melbourne only took five days to manifest, after Andrew's lame attempts at feigning that he was missing me. It was laughable. We had only just met on consecutive, superficial dates over one weekend. Really, too much drama for me! Andrew finally worked up the courage to apologise that he could not, in all fairness, continue to correspond with me because he had met a lady in Melbourne with whom he could envisage a future. I laughed and wished him well, sanctioning his choice of a woman from his own State. His profile had been duly modified to suit his designs after which it swiftly disappeared from the site, no doubt ready to resurface somewhere else. Oh, the games people play!

Abused on several occasions for not posting my real age online, I vowed to continue to defy my age, on a mission to present to the world as glamourous a portrait as I could configure, as youthful as possible without recourse to plastic surgery. Problems with self-esteem? Confirmed! After this episode, I felt I was entitled to do so.

The damaging criticisms imbued on my psyche from previous relationships were evidently much harder to erase than first thought. I feistily defended myself because it seemed our motivations, regarding age, were the same.

Up to the guy to terminate the chat if he so chooses and we move on. No harm done.

The Dreaded Menopause

Female panellists on Australian television shows such as The Drum[27] extol the virtues of women reaching this stage of their life cycle, because they can celebrate their liberation from menstrual cycles, perceived evidently as a big "win" finally. I hear some moan and others sigh in unison. They no longer sweat the small stuff, but they do tend to focus more on their mortality, their own and those close to them. Cognitive decline is no picnic but women take measures to deal with the problems. Biomechanical issues become a challenge that they cannot ignore because acceptance is tough and ageing precipitates a lot of crises in physical and psychological health. These are, on the other hand, not so distinct from the male perspective. What is difficult to swallow is the growing disparity between the sexes, especially where income is concerned. This is an issue that does not seem to gain positive traction in society, even if female disadvantage is being

---

[27] The Drum, June 8, 2017 *abc.net.au/thedrum* (The Drum)

reduced somewhat. The fact remains that deep-seated ageism exists in our society, a challenge increasingly harder to manage.[28]

We, Ladies need to become aware that men find it difficult to cope and relate to their partners during the transitional phase of menopause that can span more than a decade for some with feisty hormones. This is where pent up emotions surface with a vengeance and women let loose without a care in the world. It is little wonder that so many break-ups occur at this stage as women suffering from night sweats and hot flushes need to be treated *delicately*; respected and pampered, molly-coddled; and guys need to be prepared to hear some home truths.

I recall putting up a brilliant, colourful cartoon image of the *SEVEN DWARFS OF MENOPAUSE - Itchy, Bitchy, Sweaty, Bloaty, Sleepy, Forgetful & Psycho* on the fridge during the 18 months that I breezed through menopause. Suzanne Somers[29] has cleverly refashioned the names of the innocent Dwarfs in one of her books on this subject. Phew! I am one of the lucky ones, though I dare say, those in my household did not get the Memo, and did not get off with impunity because of my erratic mood swings. Try blaming a partner for his indiscretions when he is going through the less easily detectable signs of the Male midlife crisis. At best, we have a fight on our hands and at worst, it will be World War III. That could generally spell the end of a relationship.

Depending on the climate in which they live, there is no denying that even the privileged cohort of women in the *Divorcées' Club* (menopause does not discriminate) may feel the heat and the cold a little more when sleeping alone. If the dreaded M word has not yet ceased to plague them, they might go through the nightly ritual of *Solo Strip Poker*. This game starts off with several layers of clothing because it is freezing; then the heat overwhelms you and the ceiling fan comes on and the windows get thrown wide open. One by one, the garments are discarded, dressing gown, bed socks, PJ bottoms, PJ top, until you are left with only your birthday suit.

---

[28] The Drum, June 8, 2017 *abc.net.au/thedrum* (The Drum) Susan Ryan FMR age and disability commissioner).

[29] Somers. S. 2013.The Seven Dwarfs of Menopause. Neen. http://www.neenpelvichealth.com/blog/the-seven-dwarfs-of-menopause/

Then you get cold again and the reverse process begins. You are restless. Just accept it Guys!

For those who have contemplated a union with a new man, it is unthinkable to have a partner cuddle you because of the excessive heat he generates! "Sorry Babe! I love you, but please, mooove your butt! No spooning" There is no win, win situation here.

Menopause sucks! A little hard if you are attempting to negotiate a new relationship with a genuinely *hot* guy you have become fond of. Remember, you probably need to check if he can deliver on the *lurve and affection* before allowing him to court you. A little delicate I would think. Watch out for the cry of indignation. The carrot you dangled over his head, promising him nights of wild passion can come at a price if you are menopausal; you might be intent on securing the love of your life but if you end up bathed in perspiration from hot flushes, Heaven help you! And the poor befuddled guy next to you. "You kidding? What did I do wrong? Really can't figure you women out!"

If you guys are reading this, I may be doing us, the Ladies, a disservice here. Sorry Ladies! There are remedies for such symptoms. Trust me, there is no need to endure these episodes alone. No need to be a Martyr. Help is at hand. *HRT – Hormone Replacement Therapies* are no longer considered as dangerous as they were decades ago, thanks to medical advances that have engineered a much safer alternative, or, so the Medics tell us today. There are benefits but there are risks. I think it is about finding what works best for the individual after consultation with your doctor. On the other hand, Natural products, exercise, a glass of wine, cakes and chocolates work wonders too. I should know.

The Male change of life? "No way" they say.

At the same time, guys like to reject the notion that the male of the species also goes through the change of life. It does not equate to the Female version, medically speaking, but it is effectively a mid-life crisis; all about testosterone, shrinkage. Does funny things to them. It is not uncommon for guys to go through unpredictable mood swings, just like their partners, and sometimes they go to their caves to brood or back to their planet, Mars, in self-denial that they might just be suffering from body image depression; particularly if they have been diagnosed with prostate issues or low sperm count; or, if they have experienced erectile dysfunction, testicular cancer or a myriad of other ailments that can assail the male Boomers.

Men rarely admit to the disturbing emotions they deal with, especially with their partners. "Talk to your mates!" we tell them. "No way! Men do not have Besties. We do not talk about our issues. We like to argue and fight. Emotions are for women." They claim that this period is a fabrication of women's minds. Some of the guys in the 50+ age brackets of this narrative are easy to detect on dating sites. They are the ones who have no qualms about alluding to their sexual prowess, distinguishing themselves from the masses; they are also known to use allegories, "You know what I mean? Wink, wink, say no more! Plumbing in perfect working order. Ready, willing and able." Okay, Guys! We get the message loud and clear. Cannot be easy to discuss these issues with a new lover. Have you thought of the little blue pill? At least you have a quick solution for erectile dysfunction, should you require it. You can also improve your libido!

Society is inclined to refer to male mid-life crises (because some guys clearly experience extended or several crises) as a period when guys buy a sports car, take on a young lover or conquer high mountains with no experience. That will reinforce to all and sundry that they are strong and virile. This societal interpretation seems much more acceptable. How can men contest the existence of a crisis when they witness their mirror images in films such as *Grumpy Old Men?* They are frequently dubbed *Cranky Pants,* yet they live in denial. This exposé might provide a little insight into what women can expect on this venture into internet dating. It pays to be well equipped to handle the fall out. If women are ready to spend the rest of their life with *Mr Cranky Pants*, then, online dating will be a breeze. I am seriously threatening to abandon this cyber voyage as we speak…

Talking to myself helps, "Come on Coco, you can do it! Perhaps a Cub is what you need? Embrace the inner Cougar in you, Coco! You have been called this for years. Time to own it!"

In case you are not convinced of the value of a lifetime membership in that Elite Club of clubs, one of my BFFs, Jessica, states categorically that she has no intention of going down the path of dating again because her last efforts have converted her into a cynic. She can no longer tolerate the growing number of guys, irrespective of age, in their thirties, forties or fifties, who simply cannot cope with rejection (after two or three dates sometimes); they exhibit pathetic behaviour that puts a Prima Donna to shame, or worse, they metamorphose into Sociopaths. Not one word of a lie. Quite a revelation but one must wonder. This dating game is certainly provoking dramatic shifts in thought processes with ensuing bizarre behaviours that contrast sharply with the dating scene of old.

Well, well! The *Divorcée's Club* might be the life for my BFFs, but I have a strong mettle; I am not deterred by reported unsuccessful escapades and horror stories of internet dating, including my own. Luckily, menopause was a transient phase that I relegated to the past. Thank God for that! Not sure whether I would have contemplated throwing myself into the crazy dating world, were I still besieged by the debilitating effects of this life transition. I have happily discarded the seven peculiar identities associated with those days. Weighing up the unfettered life of my Divorcée BFFs against the challenges of internet dating, there was no turning back. In for a penny, in for a pound.

Defying Ageism

Ageism is a perennial problem in our Western societies. There are women who wish they could belong to the privileged Ladies' Club but cannot. Lamentably, the other side of the coin is not so rosy. The hardships that single middle-aged women undergo are making headlines in societies that proclaim their first world status. The situation is proving challenging for government policy makers as we witness an increasing number of women who find themselves alone for a myriad of reasons and completely destitute. There are many factors that contribute to this deplorable state of affairs in Australia, where *The Glass Ceiling* is increasingly being attributed as the root of the problem.

Debates on disparity between the sexes in the work force feature regularly on multimedia platforms. Whilst it is natural and desirable for women with a maternal instinct to take extended leave for child bearing and rearing, choosing part time work over fulltime, no one can deny they are at a disadvantage financially; this automatically curtails their ability to participate in the work force and there is little to no income to fill the coffers of their retirement funds. They work just as hard as their husbands, and some even harder if they are engaged in child care and part time work, but they are rarely remunerated commensurately with the number of hours they devote to family support and assorted occupations, even if employed on a full-time basis.

Accordingly, if they return to their profession, their superannuation is significantly reduced whilst their male counterparts enjoy healthy retirement packages; that is, if, their funds are not depleted by acrimonious divorce settlements. This is one reason why a large group of women now constitute the "new impoverished demographic" as they enter the next stage of their life cycle; not unlike the elderly who are beginning to wonder why science has prolonged their lives only to see them live in poverty and misery. It is not surprising that many women from these groups accept relationships that others may find unsatisfactory, insalubrious, abusive or devoid of affection, simply because two incomes, two pensions might just mean survival or an ostensibly dignified existence.

Is this too high a price to pay? Some women simply have no choice and often, this is the reason they remain in loveless marriages, even if they are subject to the cycle of abuse defined as the *Battered Wife Syndrome*. A couple of guys I dated recounted stories about widows who ended up cohabiting with a partner, devoid of emotional investment. They described the situation as fraught with guilty emotions if either had lost the love of their life. I imagine they would have to weigh up escalating poverty status, with a life where they barely subsisted, before contemplating such relationships. Who knows how widespread this may be? It seems like a plausible solution. Could these potential scenarios help explain the increased rate of women engaging in hookups online hoping to snare a rich man? Not easy to condone if that is the case, but it could provide perspective.

Many women in their fifties or sixties have suffered a lifetime of sexism and gender discrimination, belonging to the *gender* or *pink-collar ghetto*. Espousing vocations of teaching and nursing in many cases, their lower incomes are often considered as augmenting their partner's salary, a view often erroneously endorsed by men; and should they separate or divorce, this is the demographic that is increasingly facing poverty and homelessness.[30] If they can extricate themselves from this deplorable state,

---

[30] The Drum, June 6, 2017 *abc.net.au/thedrum*

they can subscribe to the *Happy Divorcées' Club* or, like me, they can succumb to the temptation of joining the growing number of women who try their hand at online dating.

How can a generation of men and women consider themselves equipped to deal with the dating scene of this new millennium? The majority have been ensconced in long-term relationships since the era when monogamy and marriage were supposed to last a lifetime. In their twenties or early thirties, the struggle to meet the 'right' person did not appear to be such an issue. Times have changed. Today, monogamy is often misconstrued, increasingly by both sexes, as 'just another variety of wood', a notion germane to individuals who surf dating sites for 'easy' encounters. The reality is, those searching for their Soulmate, genuinely hopeful of attracting the right partner, are faced with disappointment and dismay when their endeavours go horribly wrong.

As the search takes daters from one site to another to seek satisfaction elsewhere, a dual effect manifests. The huge discrepancy in the legitimacy, effectiveness and success of different dating sites promising to satisfy the diversity of needs of the public is highly contingent on cost and reputation. The more selective, costly sites claim to guarantee anonymity and noteworthy results, if one is easily fooled that is, because no site can vouch for the veracity of the profiles submitted. Whilst the free sites promise instant hookups, one can hardly expect quality, moral conduct and integrity from the subscribers; on the other hand, the dearth of measures to control the search criteria creates a site devoid of filters. This is where the two-way street comes into effect. I have found myself either kept busy fending off unwanted advances from repeat offenders or in a warped way, received a boost to my self-esteem as I view the number of hits my profile obtained.

This ego-trip is short lived however. Double-edged sword unfortunately; Buyer beware! It is ultimately up to the individual to determine just how much he or she can afford and endure.

Age and the dating game

Age-related issues are responsible for an interesting behavioural paradigm in the world of dating today. I have found the need to move on to the next level as soon as possible far too common. In my case, of course the one with whom I believed I was most suited and had the best connection was the one that got away. So contradictory! He had to be the one I wanted who was not as into me! *C'est la vie!* "We crave that which we cannot attain and disrespect that which we cannot escape."[31] This maxim is apt in the context of internet dating and responsible for a great deal of pain. These sentiments forced me to be brutally honest with myself.

There is on the other hand, a cynical perspective on the issue based on the nefarious practices commonly found on dating sites. I realise that if I am *Benched* or *Ghosted,* and if the "other" relationship does not work out, second best is simply not acceptable. It is ultimately up to me and only me, to decipher which version is more conceivable. I must keep in mind that the odds are against us, individuals who adhere to our principles and hope, against hope, that when the right person becomes tired of playing games, he or she will come knocking on our door once more. A rude shock probably awaits them though. We are worth so much more than this. If a guy who hurt me preferred to play the field, I know instinctively, that this guy would have no part in my life. Not at this age.

The issue I must factor into the equation is that this stance could see perennial loneliness established in my life. The reality is though, when dating guys over 60, sometimes affections are not always requited. Is it hard to find a match because certain affective pursuits are no longer as important for one or the other? Individuals move at a different pace anyhow. If we cannot make a promising relationship work synergistically, there is little point in pursuing it. This might explain, to some extent, why both genders are hell bent on catching that younger partner? Before giving up, I must bear in mind that I could be throwing away the chance of finding someone genuine, for want of trying to adjust to each other's disparate lifestyles, whims and idiosyncrasies. The longer we remain on our own, the harder it becomes to readjust.

Throughout this journey, I remained acutely aware of the potential to break the hearts of the guys I was dating, disappoint them. My objective was not to lead them on. Delicate issue. It was not easy to say goodbye to "genuinely nice guys." This induced me to terminate friendships with

---

[31] Dobson, J. In Woodward, O. 2014. Orrin Woodward on Life and leadership. http://orrinwoodwardblog.com/category/leadershippersonal-development/page/4/

males who could have become my significant "other", simply because of their rush to formalise the relationship. They removed or hid their profiles online, claiming, "Surely you can hide your profile for a month to discover if you have found the One." No pressure! The stress and anxiety this created, obliged to decide too soon whom I wished to date seriously, made my journey traumatic.

Women on the rebound

Gerard, (Chapter 5), the friendly Mad Professor and intellectual businessman I met from Brisbane provides some interesting insights for this chronicle. He argues many of the males have given up after dismal results in their efforts with online dating because in their experience, a huge number of women are on the rebound. Their baggage is not stowed away; instead, it is precariously balanced as they attempt to soothe their broken hearts and vaporised dreams, and no doubt bemoan their decimated bank balances. Gerard recounts that after engineering a quick fix, one woman insisted that he stay the night on their first date, and against his better judgment, he acquiesced. How often have we heard, or experienced the effects of too much alcohol on the sexual performance of some guys over a certain age? However, even when some have imbibed too much, many still cannot resist a woman who has initiated sex.

Gerard was very candid with me, explaining he was, like most guys, impetuous; their egos delicate, in tandem with their increasing vulnerabilities. He confessed they were powerless to turn the woman down. If their virility was in question, chances are they would not say no. He said male mammals were not wired to reject the mating call of the female of the species.

Hmm... I wonder if in the wild, the experiences match those of the Homo Sapiens. The ego plays such a huge part in the formation of a new relationship; both sexes hope there will be longevity in the proposed union but there are no guarantees. One cannot ignore the importance of primal attraction, chemistry and pheromones, but, forget compatibility and it is often doomed to fail. Big ask! Not at all easy to find everything you are hoping for in one individual. The need to compromise is of paramount importance.

Gerard continued his account of that embarrassing night.

Self-justification helped a lot; and Gerard explained that what transpired, was in fact common. The woman, after spending the entire time talking about her ex, was unapologetic for monopolising the conversation and she ruthlessly ended her date when he was unable to deliver; he was taking too long. She swiftly terminated the encounter but not before being sated. No explanation! The woman just left.

I really felt for Gerard. He was a lovely guy. Some people may be used to this contemptible behaviour but for those of us entering the 50+ dating scene, it pays to be ready for such anomalies. They are becoming too real and this cannot be good for the guys who are hoping to make a fresh start. For this reason, Gerard believes these guys do not find the practice of internet dating amusing or addictive; just hard and disappointing and they ultimately make little effort to present their profile in an attractive light. "What's the point?" they ask. If the expectations of the women are so high, they are destined to fail, so they give up. What an eye opener. Pretty depressing.

Expectations constitute a massive consideration in internet dating. Despite the verbal and non-verbal cues that are sometimes imperceptible, but exchanged nonetheless via various channels, there is a degree of excitement and anticipation that the first meeting will meet those actual or perceived opportunities. The disenchantment that ensues is palpable if one or the other has built up such an exquisite vision of the prospect for their first meeting. If they have embellished the attributes of the suitor, and it does not eventuate, watch out! This is generally unpleasant, but it can be quite comical when individuals have inadequate filters and they cannot hold their tongue. Let's face it. If they feel they have been deceived, comments such as the following are not uncommon, "Well, you are nothing like your photos. When were they taken, ten years ago?"

Female Sharks

Internet dating attracts all types of individuals. Just like the male denizens that constitute *Liquorice all Sorts,* some female amateurs, who, under the guise of a pseudonym, readily confess to an insatiable appetite for lust, are guaranteed innumerable encounters, free meals and frequent saucy escapades online… and off. Anecdotally, a growing number of this female demographic, now visibly encompassing daters ranging from 18 to 40 years of age, operates on the premise proclaimed in *Beyoncé's* song, "If you liked it, then you should have put a ring on it" in the face of an increasing number of male Commitment Phobes. Just like their male counterparts, why would they need to commit with so much candy to tempt them?

Alternatively, it is a free-for-all. This attitude, from what I have been told by Gerard and other guys, absolves them of their increasing promiscuity. Are women now actively rivalling guys in their online exploits? Some admit to this unashamedly on multimedia platforms. Free drinks and meals however, appear to be largely contingent on the age factor from all accounts, more likely a generational privilege, chivalry high on the agenda of the more mature guys. The younger set prefer to *go Dutch,* halving the bills, if the social foreplay holds little promise of a second date and more specifically, sexual intercourse. How 'free' is debatable, as many women ostensibly want more, and some get much more than they bargained for.

Whilst there is a growing number of female daters who are on a mission to match the males in tallying up the number of hookups they can accrue on dating sites, this is their choice. Each to her own. Some on the other hand, are intent on mischief, scamming and deceit and these female members fit neatly within the realms of the *Dark Web.*

Jonathan, with whom I enjoyed a coffee date, referred to a vicious cycle that categorises women on the rebound. This feature is becoming established on the dating scene. It seems these women remain intransigent in their quest to make males pay for the indignities they have allegedly suffered. He also suggested they continue to search for instant sexual gratification whilst some never quite give up hope to find love. Are they motivated by revenge or desperation, intent on filling the void that grows ever larger? Or, when they discover that the man is not what they had hoped for, is it easier for them to give up, opt for sex and retreat to the sanctity of their solitary life? So many scenarios exist, all open to interpretation, but, with so many stories circulating, one could be forgiven for thinking that where there is smoke, there is fire.

Do the men give up when they discover the unrealistic expectations of the women, ceasing in their attempts to attract a genuine partner? All they want to do, as I have heard so many times, is to get off this "ZOO!" Yet their photos remain permanently draped on the cyber walls of internet dating. If I paint a tragic picture, I believe this to be true. Some of the profiles I have read are heart-wrenching at times and despite current trends, it pays not to tar everyone with the same brush. We must be prudent; but also recognise that there are some sincere and unaffected individuals out there who deserve respect. The trick is to work out which ones.

Mr B. from Melbourne recounted episodes where various women proved to be as ruthless as many of the males online. Some of the women he communicated with briefly, callously ended all contact when they discovered that his self-employment status was less than satisfactory, ascertaining this only after the first or second message or first date. Becoming immediately aware of the deceitful tactics they employed shortly after joining the dating site, Mr B. revealed only his immediate occupation that suggested his irregular income could define him as a pauper. He remained prudent in not disclosing his eclectic professional background and residential area for obvious reasons.

This is an effective strategy if one wishes to expose the artifice many individuals, male and female are currently engaged in.

Even after a pleasant evening out, Mr B., who is a gentleman with impeccably old-fashioned values, spared no expense as he treated all Ladies with respect. One scheming woman systematically cut short the encounter with no explanation. Mr B. is under no illusion as to why and is certainly not fazed by the common ruse. He suggests that this transparency in the tactics of many women is becoming commonplace. The shrewd male will hopefully discover quite quickly if he is being duped or not, one would hope. He withdrew his profile shortly after meeting me and our friendship is solid despite living on opposite ends of the country. He is too busy to go back online.

The guys wooing me are keen to separate me from the manipulative behaviour of many women on dating sites (plural because they are everywhere and apparently unstoppable). It is very noble that they feel it their duty to warn me, particularly if my interests lie interstate. This issue is multifaceted. I wonder whether the allegedly atrocious behaviour of the women could also be attributed to their treatment at the hands of the players online? Not inconceivable… If so, I can only hope they are not bent on revenge, attempting to combat the unfair advantage the males are said to enjoy.

The apparent ease with which men succeed to bed so many women is attributed to the desire of many women to give them what they want. Who really knows how prevalent this view is? Some guys have intimated that the women in their fifties are fast mimicking their younger counterparts because they feel so much more vulnerable. They are petrified that life is passing them by. They need to snare a rich man and failing that, any man, if he can minimise the loneliness and despondency they feel for their future. Because of their vulnerabilities, post-divorce or separation, these women appear to have no time to play the dating game, to establish friendships first because time is-a-ticking. To snag their men, they jump into bed on the first date to test the waters, so to speak. If he cannot provide what they seek, they move on. Next! So on, and so forth.

We hear so often that the malaise of society is but a reflection of that society. I feel that this behaviour is an indictment of the deterioration we are witnessing in the values of our western societies but whatever viewpoint we may adopt, the need to be on our guard is of paramount importance. These women may feel justified in their actions, but it is up to individuals to act according to the dictates of their conscience, without casting aspersions on those who do not espouse our moral conduct. This is not a gender issue. The only actions we should judge are our own.

The wily Josie

Daniel, (Chapter 3) from Brisbane, with whom I also formed a beautiful friendship, had spent a short time on one site when he found a woman from the Gold Coast. He warmed to her quite quickly, admitting retrospectively that she had used her wiles to lure him. When he arrived at the rendezvous, he was assailed by Josie, no other way of describing it, as soon as he closed his car door. She had been lying in wait for him, not exactly sure of the kind of car he drove but the car park was not full on this beautiful Saturday in Spring. Almost knocked down by Josie's amorous embrace, Daniel first thought he had a live wire and she would settle down soon. Not a chance! Josie not only kissed a man she had never seen before but proceeded to "jump him." 6'2 Daniel is endowed with a muscular, athletic physique but the shocking behaviour of this woman had him at a disadvantage for a few minutes, as she ravaged him with her kisses and her hands that were travelling where they had no place to go. How easy is it for a man to tear himself away from such a sexual embrace? Well, Daniel had the presence of mind to stop Josie in her tracks as people started to stare in shock and awe at the unfolding scene.

He suggested they move inside, find a table on the terrace of the canal frontage restaurant. He sat her down and headed to the bar, recomposing himself as best he could, reliving the bizarre behaviour of this woman he had just met. Waiting to order at the bar, a guy next to Daniel struck up a conversation, banal enough to begin with, but quickly revelatory. After the perfunctory bar chats that Australian males engage in, this man launched into a tirade about his wife, the woman Daniel had met in the car park. He spent 15 minutes telling Daniel about the revenge tactic orchestrated by Josie because of his indiscretion. Indiscretion? Daniel exploded, having been turned into a pawn in their sick game. It went a little like this,

> *I don't suppose you realise I'm the husband of the woman who was jumping your bones in the carpark.*

> *What the hell? You must be joking?*

> *No. I suppose I deserve it because I cheated on my wife. But this is a revenge attack. I could not have imagined this. Josie knew that I was here, and she put on a show just for me.*

This admission of guilt was enough for Daniel to empathise with the poor Bloke who was most contrite for having cheated on his wife, and it was obvious he wanted forgiveness and was doing everything in his power to win her back. Daniel shook his hand and marched to the table where Josie waited, unaware that he had been chatting with her husband. He promptly put the glass of Chardonnay on the table and told her in no uncertain terms,

> *You're sick! I don't know what you're on but before you act like such a slut again, in a carpark no less, I suggest you go and see a shrink. Delete your profile online and stop your revenge attacks! Go back to your husband!*

Daniel explained that sometimes, "you seem to warm to a possible match, but you have a reality check and go cold on it. Well that's my experience!" No wonder this episode induced him to shut down his profile quickly when he went back online. Just like he had done the evening I first noticed his postage stamp photograph. Wow! It takes all sorts. I have heard of other disgusting behavioural habits of some women online and it does not augur well for the women of the Gold Coast if this image is being disseminated nationally.

Beware of female Gold Diggers

My account is my experience with males, but the females – according to my male suitors and friends – are increasingly turning into Gold Diggers. It is not unreasonable to suggest that if women are left destitute after divorce or separation, this ruse could simply be a survival mechanism. This situation is deplorable and despite the circumstances in which the women find themselves, their motives are hard to condone. I wonder if they have any dignity left to speak of.

It occurred to me that many men are not searching for "true love" but for good enough. It may well be that a pretty woman who wants his money is quite acceptable, but from the perspective of my suitors, I can vouch for the fact this is not their objective on dating sites. One of my male friends suggests that despite men being perceived as commitment-phobic (which they probably are before attachment), men tend to be much more "content" in relationships than women post-attachment. The majority of relationship breakups are initiated by women.[32] And many men are apparently unaware of how unhappy she is and find themselves left asking "What happened?" In my experience, some guys have selective hearing when their partners recommend a visit to a counsellor because things are not working; she is unhappy; she believes they need to work out a solution. When the pleas fall on deaf ears, they are floored when the woman decides it is over. The section on reasons couples cheat supports this argument to some extent (Chapter 13).

It appears on the other hand, the males have an inexhaustible supply of women when it comes to the Smorgasbord portrayed on trusted dating Apps, ostensibly 'legitimate' relationship sites. Once they progress to an

---

[32] McClintock, E. A. https://www.psychologytoday.com/blog/it-s-man-s-and-woman
-s-world/201412/why-breakups-are-actually-tougher-men

actual date, many guys are disillusioned by the façade the women present in their profiles, just as I have been with many males. On one site, without engaging in *Catfishing*, one can superficially view all profiles, male and female. To assess the veracity of the unforgiving views about many women, I had a cursory look at the titles page with images portrayed. I was not interested in delving further.

I must admit there is a marked difference in the approach, language and presentation of the female profiles based only on their introductory image and headlines. The photos are attractive and the poses generally well-considered. Many women appear to be articulate and witty. Most declare they are on a mission to find love. They are stylish, well made-up and appear genuine in their quest to find love. How can one really tell, on the other hand what is behind these profiles? We are all individuals and what we wish to portray will be misconstrued by some people, whether we are male or female; whether we like it or not. Who can account for these dichotomous outcomes? It is simply human nature.

My investigations suggest that many women are highly disgruntled with the online experience because they believe there is serious inequity in the dating game when it comes to desirable partners. This is despite claims to the contrary from the male perspective, that there are more men available. Some women, from the thirties and forties age groups and beyond, bitterly protest the antics of many males online, and this provokes their mission for revenge. They embark on a search for love or hookups online, claiming unreservedly that the gene pool of men is depleted and dismal, worse in some States than others. The vitriolic comment, based on the dwindling number of guys worthy of dating, is apparently the result of men's first choice for the younger, attractive females, because they claim, guys are spoilt for choice with a bevy of beauties on the Smorgasbord menu.

The derogatory comment targets the Gold Coast in particular, but curiously, so many locals originate from the southern States. Theoretically, the good guys should be here too. The problem is that the Coast is so transient that newcomers of both sexes do not tend to stay for long. These are harsh words that reverberate on social media sites and echo sentiments expressed in popular Hollywood films. This judgmental perception of the males online could well be the result of broken relationships, financial ruin or simply an addiction to *Chick Flicks* that echo their own disastrous relationships with unfaithful partners. They fail to realise that toxic relationships, disastrous relationships are painful for both men and women. They are not necessarily the norm. Realistically, it is not easy to determine which sex actually has it tougher. Revenge is sweet; it is the name of the game for this cohort of women for whom denigrating men is a favourite pastime.

The mine/mind fields of internet dating

The cobbled road less travelled, as one negotiates the mine fields of internet dating, or should I say, "mind fields", entails a dynamic process of construction and readjustment of one's identity in the search for the significant "Other." Ultimately this road is likely to be paved with broken promises, deceit, bruised egos and shattered dreams. If we are successful, we may find the 'One'. Some sites will try to convince us that this is a certainty, posting real or fictitious photos of 'happy couples' that have found each other thanks to their clever use of algorithms. The antics employed by many dating sites are transparent to most but unfortunately the susceptible continue to fall prey to the hype that is promulgated by social media.

I realise that if I do not become a total sceptic, I may, at best become blasé, but I could end up displaying signs of ruthlessness, discarding profiles because they do not meet my requirements; I may become so fastidious that every little negative aspect turns into a monumental NO! NEXT! Can I realistically afford to wait for the "One", aged 50+? COMPROMISE is what is needed to achieve a balance between reality and the exhaustive list of attributes that I hope my perfect match will embody. Must I accept the individuals who show promise, despite their shortcomings? The reality is that even when I feel I am getting close to securing the type of relationship I have been searching for, I may end up sabotaging my chances of settling down with this person because of the need to make a total readjustment to our lives. And so, I persevere, despite the challenges. What do I have to lose? Except my sanity and sleepless nights.

The Menopausal status is likely to affect many of the women who are reticent to jump into online dating. If they are Post-Menopausal, they should, theoretically, have a little more patience. The debilitating effects of this transitional phase have an enormous influence on every facet of our lives. It appears that, of late, an increasing number of male and female daters are simply giving up. They have lost their zest for life, become apathetic towards everything. Some may prefer the old-fashioned ways of dating and the communicative tools of old, but they simply need to get with the program if they wish to keep dating. Progress waits for no one!

Dealing with Emotional Baggage

The world of internet dating still intrigues me. Though I question so many things, I am firmly embroiled in this virtual dating scene. Individuals on internet sites automatically assume different behavioural patterns because they are essentially free to create and recreate their cyber identities at whim. There is no one to censure them unless disqualified by disgruntled individuals who report them; they are free to lie, to embellish their images, and enhance their personality to attract the best possible partner; they can play havoc with the sentiments of unsuspecting targets.

Internet dating is proving to be an effective strategy in dealing with emotional baggage. Seeking love, sex, companionship online even if one is on the rebound seems increasingly popular. It represents a quick fix, and for some, it may just prove to be.

Some daters have one aim; to get off the dating site. Age continues to be significant; clearly more pertinent for the fifties and sixties age groups, whose members appear to weigh up their characteristic circumspection in forming new relationships with the intoxication they feel as a result of ostensible interest from younger users. They still believe they can have it all. I still believe I can have it all… More fool me!

My experience online has revealed that the brief length of time many guys remain in a relationship with a prospect found online induces me to believe that perhaps after a long period of time trapped in a loveless union, some are keen to make up for lost time, aware of the debilitating and soul-destroying effects of ageing on all of us. Whereas, in the days of old, when couples experienced difficulties, they rarely threatened their partner with separation or divorce; for so many reasons, today, the speed with which relationships are ending is a worrying sign of the times. Curiously, this is in spite of the allegedly increasing number of couples engaged in illicit affairs because, with the allure of internet dating, they can have the best of both worlds.

This is a disposable society. No one is indispensable, not in affective domains and certainly no longer in our fields of work. Couples are less inclined to seek help to sort out their psychological or emotional issues; it is too easy to structure an online profile to obtain exactly what they are searching for. However, if they discover that the dating game is fraught with unsatisfactory liaisons, is it too late to go back to what they had? The new trend is taking firm hold. Some individuals string one encounter after another, many obtaining exactly what they seek to achieve. Until, that is, they approach 65 or 70 years of age and realise that perhaps, just perhaps, one of the individuals they dated and released far too quickly, might just have been the "One" with whom they could spend their twilight years. This may sound a little pessimistic, but I suspect quite a few individuals engaged in online dating are currently crying over spilt milk as I write these words.

The ego is delicate. Whilst many members of the older generation recognise the customary tactics of younger Gold Diggers searching for a Sugar Daddy, or Mummy for that matter, women who are tired of immature males are generally lumped in the same basket – increasingly being accused of seeking a rich man. The strange outcome that I have discovered over these last few months is that whilst the wealthy, older set ultimately rejects the younger players as suitable partners when approached, they are happy to indulge in romantic and or sexual interludes with them to reduce the loneliness of this journey. They simply return to the search when it ends or continue to search concurrently with the existing relationship until they find someone else. Such is the playground of internet dating.

So, what of the youngsters whose mentality of instant gratification is fast being mimicked by some mature-aged daters? The younger set females are increasingly aware of their biological clocks ticking away whilst they fulfil career objectives and participate in new online playgrounds. For the younger males, there is an abundance of profiles to indulge their wildest fantasies. Some find the notion of chasing a *Cougar* exciting, hoping to add a few more strategies to their sexual repertoire. They may experiment for a while and this is likely to be therapeutic for the women until they are left high and dry.

I need to remain circumspect. I have heard too many tales of woe. The thirty-something males will ultimately choose young women with whom they want to spend the rest of their lives, children high on their procreative agenda. Time to settle down... Yet, when are they ever going to get the opportunity to investigate such enticing opportunities? Well, if this dating scene is anything to go by, looks like there will be a plethora of profiles of all ages on which to focus. After the games some daters play, many males are increasingly equipped to deal with everything a woman wants. Mel Gibson's role in the movie, *What a Woman Wants* comes to mind. What power. What magnetism. Imagine having the tools to attract the woman of your dreams after the expertise acquired from willing mature sexual female instructors online?

Whilst many of us are searching frantically for a new, meaningful relationship before time runs out, the games are set to continue. Such trying times!

I have learned a thing or two on this journey. "Dating" was not the same in my youth - a strict European upbringing signified a tight rein on the girls in my family. In my youth, I did not feel the pressure to marry early. It was normal in those days. I suspect the ease of moving from one profile to another, selecting the most appealing characteristics in a partner and discarding those we find lacklustre, implies there is a risk of losing them if we are embroiled in the beginnings of an unsatisfactory relationship; the risk of losing the "One" if we take too long to decide is what in fact creates the resolve. Our haste affords the current love interest fewer chances of succeeding and we move on, often leaving individuals waiting on the sidelines until we make up our minds. Are we all inadvertently guilty of this behaviour in this dating game? Tough one! I am examining my conscience.

ENDINGS

17

"50 ways to leave your lover"

My relationship endings have always been painful. But here I am engaging in dating and I already know that many of them will end by going nowhere. I feel like a glutton for punishment. To find the "Relationship", I must endure many endings.

Paul Simon sang of 50 ways to leave your lover, "Slip out the back Jack, make a new plan Stan, just set yourself free."[33] I have never found it that easy, but I have found that there are classes of endings:

- letting them down gently
- stalling
- let's just stay friends
- end contact politely
- the *Band-Aid Solution* - thank you, but no - the cleanest, most honest, but hardest of all!
- and the types that make it harder for the endings
- the persistent types - who make it harder still, but just to make it more complicated, sometimes their persistence pays off. Certainly, I feel a certain frisson of pleasure at being pursued, especially if

---

[33] Simon, Paul. 1975. https://www.azlyrics.com/lyrics/paulsimon/50waystoleave yourlover.html

there is some chemistry, even if not quite enough. And maybe I was wrong, maybe I should try again.

-   the "Gen(uine) whys" - but "why?" they ask repeatedly

It has taken me a long time to learn that when someone asks me, "why are you ending the relationship", they are not looking for the reason why, for there is no reason why that is sufficient. They are asking why to continue engaging with me. And as painful as it may be, I feel that the best approach is to answer, "I am sorry, it will not work" and not go any further.

It is difficult to ease the pain of those who cry out for attention online. Anonymity is sometimes a wonderful tool. I wonder how many female daters simply ignore their messages, or worse, abuse these individuals for having deigned approach them? I have heard many stories where callous women have decimated the character of guys who had the nerve to contact them, dismissing them with vitriolic language just to discourage them once and for all. I am not a social worker, but I believe that a curt response with a word of encouragement can in some measure assuage the pain I can intuit in some guys who confess to having had no luck in online dating. Some guys have told me they have been online for years because they cannot stop searching. They are despondent but not totally; there is still a small chance that they will find some companionship, if nothing else. Are many women in the same boat? It is up to the more discerning guys to test the waters in that department. I have incorporated selected entries in this chapter that touched a chord along my journey.

If there is no chemistry, there is no point in pursuing the lead only to let someone down. If I can make their day by responding and wishing them luck, it may enhance their self-esteem but there is a fine line between needlessly encouraging them and building their self-worth. I have felt the pain of so many guys online who are accustomed to no response at all. For this reason, I persevere, time-consuming surely, but I try to respond to all advances curtly. I am happy to report the nice guys I have dated have also engaged in this task. Some lonely individuals persist in contacting me however, over four months to be exact, and it becomes tedious and tragicomical at the same time in the end.

"Keep an open mind…"

Alex was 51, tall, attractive and self-assured; he was forthright and knew exactly what he wanted from a relationship. Having recently purchased property on the Coast, he travelled frequently between States. The initial contact seemed intriguing and I chose to ignore the allusions to his "kinky" nature that I discovered was amusing and weird, but seriously not a problem. He had a quirky personality and he was a really nice guy. I set him straight from the start, saying that I had no intention of going out without underwear! I was not into his games. He was happy with friendship to begin with.

What transpired at the second date had me worried as Alex's conversations switched a little too frequently to a favourite subject, the *Fifty Shades of Grey* trilogy. A modicum of panic set in as I reflected on the bizarre and inquisitive nature of our earlier chats and soon it escalated.

"I want you to keep an open mind" he had said to me on the phone during the week. You may get the gist of where further comments were leading but I did not. He had left me bemused and slightly offended as he had kissed me good night at my car after the first date and I wondered what I was doing wrong for the previous comment to be reiterated several times. I had always believed I had an open mind. I was seriously worried by then, yet I was curious. We all know what happened to the cat …

As Alex voiced his opinions and summarised the plot (or lack thereof) of the infamous trilogy that I had not read or seen, my anxiety intensified, in tandem with the apprehension the previous discussions had generated - 'peculiar", intrusive questions becoming weirder. I was by then most uncomfortable. The guy had me running after only two dinners.

I was not keen to investigate what the "open mind" entailed but I had a rude awakening the following week, ending contact because I no longer wished to pursue this lead. The film premiere of the *Fifty Shades of Grey* aired on television that week and I decided that I needed an "education." Katarina had texted me and we both began to watch it. Within 15 minutes, our text messages appeared simultaneously. Christian Grey had pronounced the notorious line, "I want you to keep an open mind" to Anastasia Steele. "What the…? Did you see that? I think I have dodged a bullet." "OMG!" Katarina had written, "I think you dodged a bullet, Darling. What a relief you nipped that one in the bud." Our phone discussion continued late into the night. As you do with your BFFs.

Jack – a retirement offer

Believe it or not, one gentleman, Jack, aged 66 tried to entice me on his boat at sunset the day we met for drinks on our first date. I was bemused by his audacity and self-confidence and marvelled at the absurdity of the suggestion as I declined firmly, on each consecutive date. He did not give up easily, but I am not quite that impudent.

I surmised from the analysis of male behaviours that guys in their sixties on dating sites had agendas that differed dramatically from mine in many cases. Jack was a cheeky Larrikin who enjoyed dual citizenship. When I read his profile, I was sure he had a sense of humour based on the following line, "I'm just over 6', with most of my hair and teeth." I had to give him credit for knowing that for some Ladies, this was important, particularly at his age. His first message contained significant information about the shenanigans on dating sites and I was keen to discover the nefarious practices from a veteran user.

> *Well - when I read your profile (yep didn't just peer closely at the pics) I got the sense that English might be your second language - but reading your email I can see you're far too literate for your own good haha. Cute and savvy should be a winning combination but in an odd quirk of fate you might find it kinda works against you on here! Better change the subject, much safer.. Hmm - it does pay to be a bit cynical on here - too many pics are 10 years old and 10 kgs light. But nothing beats chatting on the phone and the first 5 seconds of a coffee date - Please don't sound like Kath or Kim !!* [2002 Australian Sitcom].

The boys and their toys! I had begun to enjoy my roller-coaster ride by that stage.

Jack kept me in fits of laughter during four dinner dates, four, because I did not know how to let him go without hurting him. I really liked him, but the stars simply did not align. Jack offered me a brilliant future, early retirement and the opportunity to pursue a wide range of choice activities focused on leisure, especially for extensive travels in Europe (in First or Business Class), skiing and cruising. I reiterated on each occasion, that I was a career woman and retirement was not a consideration any time soon. We were definitely on different wave lengths.

> *I want to take you to my favourite wine region. I have great plans for us, but I can tell you now, I am not taking a FRIEND, Babe! I do no need another friend! Get my drift? Shame about that road trip in the BMW from Rome to Ireland that I had in mind for us...*

Jack's words occasionally come back to haunt me when tedious administrative duties at work provoke thoughts of early retirement. They are however, only transitory. I do nonetheless, dream of a life where I can indulge in a little recreation; unencumbered by realistic concerns in the real world.

After several dates with suitors in whom I saw no potential, I decided to take the pressure off by adjusting the search criteria to exclude guys over 62, vowing to learn from my mistakes. I had not encouraged Jack, nor promised him more than friendship, yet he had persisted with text messages, had been expansive in his flattery, phone calls, static and hilarious animated *Emojis* embellishing every text message. He checked twice to see if I had had enough of the games online, asking if I was ready to take up his offer. He was a joker, never really taking anything seriously and he delighted in deflecting intellectual discussions to more entertaining topics. Had he not been a kind family man and honourable guy, I would have distanced myself a lot earlier. I was learning. I was clearly not prepared for this journey at that stage...

Though it was not stipulated that I too should shut down my profiles, Jack and Marcus, (Chapter 6) in their sixties, whom I credit for invaluable lessons in dating, had nonetheless been quite transparent when they made me feel guilty because I had no intention of obliging them. I refused to shut down my profiles, instead choosing the option, "Taking a break" offered to us. To exacerbate matters, Jack's best friend had gone on the same dating site and had been rejected by me online. This behaviour infuriated me because of the subterfuge, Jack confessing to his friend's tactic and thinking it was hilarious. I learned quite early to automatically reject any profile without photos.

Whilst ostensibly a path to true love, the online dating journey proved to be a lot of fun in the beginning, full of thrills even if the destination was not achieved.

Am I not good looking enough...?

Charles had contacted me a few months into my journey and his frantic work schedule kept him away from Brisbane a little more than he cared for. I could see after the first date that there was no longevity for a proposed relationship. I had difficulty in letting him down. It was never easy. He was a very nice guy, good looking and honourable, but we had little in common.

After a painful text from Charles, "If you truly believe I am not good looking enough, funny enough, smart enough, sustain conversation enough, let's move on now," my response was woeful. "We can only do [the promised] lunch if there is no pressure. I am confused right now and do not know what I really want. I feel that I have waited too long before throwing myself into this dating world. I am really sorry."

When Charles responded, "Thank you for being honest... All the best!" Why did I not leave it alone? Had to have the last word. Idiot! Lunch was back on, but somehow, Charles' last message inadvertently made the task of walking away easier.

"Always love to have lunch with an attractive lady. Your shout right? Lol."

Laugh out loud? Are you kidding? I was livid. I did not need to be reminded that I was paying for lunch. That was just not on. Yet, Charles continued the texting game even with my curt, innocuous replies that did not deter him from asking for more photos. I wanted to give up, but a promise was a promise. Whilst I continued to date guys who were geographically distant, I had to be careful because they were not interested in being *Friend zoned*. In the end, Charles decided to walk away, seeing the futility in just meeting for a lunch that would lead nowhere.

Steve - Age is no problem!

"Age is just a number, Coco." Music to my ears!

52-year-old Steve was gorgeous, with green eyes and a great physique; 5' 10, he stood proudly in a crowd. I agreed to have coffee with him. The introverted individuals I met found it far easier to express their deeply-personal sentiments in writing, rather than face the possibility of ridicule and ultimate rejection in face-to-face interactions. Rejection is hard and both sexes online tried to put their best face forward to avoid heartache and disappointment. Steve and I had established in our first communication that we had a few points of reference in common, but we were not exactly on the same page in our sentiments.

Wishing to brighten my day, Steve texted me, "I just wanted to give you a compliment to brighten your day. "Very few ladies I have met (offline) look as good as their pictures, you were an exception in that, you were actually better. Have a great day ☺." He was most complimentary and his posts generally entertaining, quite incongruous with his introverted nature that I later discovered during social interactions.

Steve's message following our coffee date revealed that he was smitten, "Thank you for the most wonderful first date. Looking forward to seeing you again. I want my heart back! Don't want to alarm you!"

He, in fact, did just that! I was willing, however, to see if we could move on from this date but I was conscious of not prolonging a situation that would not evolve into a fulfilling relationship. Whilst I really liked Steve, the animal magnetism was not there, and the second date confirmed my suspicions. His subsequent text was a worry, "I'm captivated by your presence and your beauty. I enjoy your company and look forward to our next date." It all seemed a little contrived to me but I knew that this was not his intent. He was sincere.

Steve's photos were recent and his information legitimate. Refreshing, unlike most of outdated male profile photos that irritated me by that stage. He was a little too reserved in my opinion, in sharp contrast with my ebullient and spontaneous nature, but the 51-year-old Melbourne export to the Gold Coast soon showed his true colours. He was a deep thinker who weighed up a situation before volunteering opinions on a huge variety of issues. Like me, he had found it hard to fit into the mould of the stereotypical definition of the locals, but he succeeded finally; and like most guys I had come across, Steve had adopted the laid-back lifestyle and did not miss Melbourne.

Steve was proud of his achievements and was focused on self-improvement. He had an inquisitive mind and an excellent memory. A little unnerving, actually. Arriving at our first coffee date, he had ordered my coffee that was always a little challenging for the baristas – the coffee you have when you are not having a coffee. Very impressive but a little disquieting when someone could remember "everything" I said. This self-employed businessman was also an intellectual; he recounted a funny encounter with a Spanish lady in whom he had taken a fancy. Trying to say something witty in a foreign language is admirable but often gets lost in translation because literal translations from Google are ineffective. Steve sent her a message saying, in Spanish, *Gustaria ser un chocolate?* The closest interpretation of what he asked her was whether she wanted to BE a chocolate? Instead of, *¿Te gustaría (un) chocolate?* (Would you like a chocolate?) I found it charming that he had attempted to woo her in her native tongue and he appreciated this.

Alarm bells went off when Steve admitted it was time to move to a new place, where he could not yet say. Take note, Coco! That intrigued me because he had contacted me with a view to forming a relationship and I had told him that relocating was impossible for me at that stage, career and family making the situation non-negotiable. He was definitely not into games, so why was he contemplating a move? This was a no brainer. Why would I want a broken heart? Steve's business projects were surely going to take him interstate. Was he willing to change his plans just to placate me? The effects would not be comforting. What satisfaction would he get from sacrificing his plans of a better future elsewhere? Was he hoping I would dissuade him from leaving to follow his dreams? The questions buzzed around in my brain.

Steve's eclectic talents would stand him in good stead wherever he went and he was sure to be successful in his ventures but he was clearly not happy here. I had found his profile attractive because, whilst he enjoyed the sun, the surf and the sea, his prowess as an international skier and his travels made him interesting and open-minded. It was uplifting to spend time with guys such as Steve and I took the time to decide whether there was a chance for a real spark to develop between us. I kept in mind, however, the fact that he was keen to move, when, was the question…

I was only too keenly aware of my impetuous nature, my zeal to forego due diligence before stepping into a relationship; I could end up in tears. If chemistry and pheromones had not been released, it would take more than travel and similar international interests to ensure that a relationship would last. Compatibility and communication were crucial; as were other subtle issues that naturally emerge when couples get together. In my haste to avoid pregnant pauses that I found embarrassing, I talked a little more than usual.

On our third date, to which I reluctantly agreed because I was intent on avoiding disappointment and pain for both of us, Steve and I discussed the other online contacts we still had. We both conceded there was no harm in continuing to chat if we were giving our connection a fair go. Neither of us wanted to make hasty decisions. Steve promptly revealed an erroneous perception that he had formed of me, reluctantly sharing his initial thoughts, "When I first saw your profile online, I was concerned that you could be involved in a relationship and that what you wanted was an affair."

I was bewildered and found this disquieting. This was insulting, given the frank conversations we had already had. This was tantamount to the despicable behaviour that had prompted me to write this chronicle - the *raison d'être* of this publication. I was hugely concerned that if the image I was inadvertently projecting to the dating world was so flawed, that I would immediately be misjudged as a player, immoral and calculating. This was not the first time that suitors had been incredulous that I should be seeking love online. The problem they confessed was that they could not comprehend how a woman like me could possibly be on dating sites. While flattering, this inaccurate assessment of my identity was becoming tiresome and upsetting. I was deeply hurt by Steve's assumptions.

Steve was so mortified by my vehement reaction that he almost disappeared beneath the table in the popular restaurant where the owner happened to know us both. He was clearly contrite, apologising profusely. In retrospect, the disconcerting incident two weeks prior to that may have given him that impression. It was probably my own fault for having mixed the names of suitors and their children, including Steve's.

Steve had found my confusion hilarious, but I was ashamed. I really needed to improve my game. We could both see the writing on the wall and I admitted that I could not see the connection flourishing. Friendship was all I could offer him. He insisted that he was happy with that, knowing there was nothing more, but he was not giving up. I agreed to see him again, still wary of possibly hurting him. "I'm a big boy, I can look after myself, Coco."

I felt sure that Steve would stay on the coast if we were to end up together, but by that stage I had decided that I could not fabricate the magic ingredients needed to move the relationship forward. We maintained contact, but, as was par for the course, this tacit strategy allowed both parties to save face. We did not meet up again and I do not know whether Steve left the coast after all. He was one of the nicest guys I had met online.

I felt privileged to meet several attractive guys in their early fifties who were sincere in their approach and for whom age was truly irrelevant. That was most encouraging. I was petrified of being rejected based on age, but I was fortunate that this was not a gender issue where dating was concerned.

The rewards of internet dating

The nefarious, ugly side of online dating is indisputable. It can be despair inducing and dangerous for those who are unprepared to face the challenges. When we learn to navigate our own personal roller-coaster ride, we shall hopefully emerge on the other side unbroken and a lot wiser. And, with a deeper understanding of who we are.

The other side of the coin of internet dating is, nonetheless, worthy of investigating for its positive transformations of identity and the potential of a committed and loving relationship. The progressive methods of dating in the 21st Century afford the intrepid *Internaute* - French for 'Internet surfer', a fascinating opportunity for self-reflection and resultant personal growth. Whatever else happens on this journey, no one can take this away from me.

The stuff of Fairy tales is not so farfetched after all. My friend, Sophie has found her Soulmate after a few years online.

Pretty Woman re-enacted

50-year-old Sophie is beautiful inside and out. This kind and caring Lady is passionate about her profession and generous to a fault with her customers. She had been engaged in online dating for six years when she met her real-life Prince Charming, a perfect match; and algorithms had nothing to do with it as they ironically met OFFLINE! The sensitive, respectful and most generous man she has ever known showers her with exquisite gifts weekly to celebrate their anniversary, diamonds included. Timing was perfect, and the universe set all wheels in motion.

After a brief encounter following a lead online, Sophie turned down the suitor because of a lack of chemistry and compatibility. She recommended a specialist for a medical issue that concerned this Gentleman and, a couple of weeks later he played Cupid, organising a date between Sophie and his friend Phillip who had left the dating site. They connected offline and serendipity intervened as unexpected circumstances created the perfect backdrop for these two. Sparks began to fly, and their romance blossomed instantly. Within three weeks, they were a couple, living in Phillip's residence on the hill. Phillip has welcomed her youngest child into his home and when his grandchildren come to stay, it is literally one big happy family. Luckily, they both embrace the Gold Coast lifestyle, including the outdoor activities that Gold Coasters revel in. This couple in their fifties is living the dream, making plans to travel, work and play, setting the scene for the rest of their lives. Sophie has no intention of abandoning her career. I cannot stop smiling when I witness the transformation in Sophie's life.

The most surprising thing of all was Phillip's generous consideration for the dating site from which he had just unsubscribed, incredibly, the source of the publication on the infamous online tactics. Phillip logged back in just to tell them their heart-warming story, as both were former members of this website, and the agency had the gall to charge him a registration fee.

Sophie's fairy-tale conclusion is all I need to inspire my happy ending.

Self-preservation is imperative on this journey.

As I carried out a perfunctory search on two dating sites to check the final details for this chronicle, I remained circumspect, first and foremost. I had stopped communicating with the contacts.

When I reflect on the dates I have been on, I realise that I am the one who has terminated all budding relationships except for Michael (Chapter 2); an issue in itself! Why is the six-million-dollar question.

When Michael and I bumped into each other at a function, months after our brief encounter, he was mortified that he had let me go. For me, it was simply too late to go back there once more. It is certainly a balm for my self-esteem that I have not been "dumped" and my conscience is clear because I have gone to great pains to maintain companionship with some of the guys who can accept friendship. A few have acquiesced. If companionship were all I wanted, that would be easy! Those who have engaged in any form of dating, on or offline, will understand that, sometimes it only takes a small incident, a silly comment, weird behaviour etc. to bring a promising encounter to an abrupt end. Tough to explain to those who are not privy to the whole picture.

My thoughts turn to the last stages of my journey online and specifically on the birthday of my beloved Godmother. I believe that she, like my father and grandmother are always close by, watching me, laughing at my stupid antics and smiling and clapping when I get things right. What can I say, I am very spiritual, "I believe in Angels and Fairies." On that day, unexpectedly hearing these words from the beautiful French actress and singer, Jeanne Moreau, who had just passed away, my spirituality was reinforced.

When I look back on the trajectory of my life and career, I can attest to the power of Positive Psychology that has played a large part in the outcomes. It always will.

I learned to appreciate the Coco reflected in the eyes of the Gentlemen I have dated, and I am satisfied with my endeavours to redefine my identity. How uncanny that my *Mirror, Mirror on the wall...* should finally be in sync with their perceptions of me.

We clearly originate from different planets, in my opinion; the more I interact with these guys, the more I realise that our viewpoints are polar opposites. Yet, we seek to please the other, to find the missing link that cements a relationship. How complex we are.

One thing has been resolved however. I have endorsed the synchronised image of the new Coco, and integrated it as part of my emotional intelligence, my physiological and behavioural identity. I am at the end of this cyberspace journey and I do not know what the future holds for me. I am no longer concerned. I am attempting to live in the moment, to be grateful for what each day brings. Let tomorrow take care of itself. *Carpe diem!*

I know that my relationship with Mr Right will be based on mutual respect, love, affection, tenderness and honesty. Why should I accept anything less? I have learned to be a bit more patient, a bit, I said, and I know that the universe will reward me for it. I have learned an enormous amount in the seven-month journey of internet dating and I have reached my destination, a little bruised, but still intact.

I had a moment of serious doubt when one of my close male friends suggested I had placed myself in an invidious position because I had not accepted any of the Beaux I had dated. He perceived me as atypical compared to the kinds of women who were engaged in online dating. He evidently knew me well as opposed to the readers of my chronicle. He was concerned that some women might resent me or envy my capacity to attract so many (seemingly eligible guys), where they may have struggled in their personal quest. That is their prerogative. You know the score, "You can please some people some of the time…" Yet, his words provoked a sense of disquiet in me; but I remain resolute because of my integrity. I know who I am, where I have come from and where I am going. And, only I know why these potential relationships went no further. My decisions to end them were neither arbitrary nor capricious. I have shared as much as I am prepared to share. Read between the lines and make up your own minds!

Self-preservation remains imperative in the online dating scene, even more so now, at this stage of my life. I seem to be doing things backwards. I should have "dated" in my youth, like most young people. It is what it is. I do not live in the past. This is dating in the age of Millennials and we, the Boomers, need to get with the program or bail out. I know what I prefer to do.

I will only let go of my heart strings very, very SLOWLY. Thoughts of beginning a new relationship after close to four years hits me instantly. Reality sets in. Mine was evidently not a fairy tale journey. Two people with different hopes and dreams, and vastly different agendas, in addition to individual professional pressures could spell disaster.

On the brighter side, if anyone needs encouragement to jump on the roller-coaster ride of internet dating, bear in mind that you might not find your Soulmate online, but the process will be mind-blowing, and you will certainly gain self-understanding and self-respect. Romance Gurus are now concurring that most of us will eventually find love online. Sophie and Phillip's story, as well as Alessandra and Marcelo's are living proof of this. Now, that is positive psychology! However, whilst we enjoy the journey, it is imperative to stay alert.

As I was categorically warned by a suitor, "If you are cute and savvy, you will survive online dating!" If I can provide a measure of hope for fellow internet daters of both sexes who value truth and integrity and are single-minded about searching for love online, I will have achieved my objectives. I know that for some guys out there, we are not alone in this quest. I intended to end this journey with a heartwarming tale of a success in a venture that has been the most challenging of my life. And I have. We are not a pathetic bunch, just romantics who believe that we can remain true to ourselves and others. In real life, I discovered that I must make my own happy ending.

Finding myself first is definitely a precursor to finding my Soulmate.

A line from a romantic comedy, *No Strings Attached* made me smile because it made so much sense. The one we fall in love with is not necessarily the one we had our eye on; and it most certainly never happens the we imagined it. Pure logic! Except to a romantic, perhaps?

Should anyone ever feel as lonely as many of us on this cyber journey have felt, the lyrics of Martin Garrick's hit song, *Scared to be lonely,* are thought-provoking. We get the gist quite quickly, "Is the only reason you're holding me tonight 'cause we're scared to be lonely?"[34]

No need to be afraid. I acknowledge that I must be true to myself, first and foremost. My motto guided me along my journey and I remain true to myself.

Mieux vaut être seul(e) que mal accompagné(e) - It is better to be alone than badly accompanied! My time will come. I just need to take a leap of faith and never lose hope.

---

[34] Garrix, M. (Lyrics/Lyric Video). ft Lipa,D. Youtube "Scared to Be Lonely" https://www.bing.com/videos/search?q=Msartin+Garrick+Scared+to+be+lonely+lyrics&view=detail&mid=35A960033648A094593135A960033648A0945931&FORM=VIRE

18

The Dénouement

Deliberations

So, how did I get here? My roller-coaster has come to a halt. This journey is, I believe, over. Until it begins again. And again!

I look into my *Mirror, Mirror on the wall*... Have I found "The One?" My mirror is being cryptic...

Paradoxically, after having deliberated long and hard on ways to find my Soulmate, I have stopped wondering how loveable I am, based on the outcomes of past relationships. I have finally realised that I must like myself as I am, unconditionally, before expecting anyone else to like me and fall in love with me. Challenging, but I am getting there. If I do not like myself, how can I expect anyone else to like or love me unconditionally? The "One" is not beyond me, that intangible figure of perfection that ticks most of my boxes. It begins with me, liking and accepting myself. I am unique, yet, as hedonistic as I may appear to be, with all my faults and idiosyncrasies, I have learned to accept it all.

If love is ephemeral, it stands to reason that "Other Ones" may come and go in my life journey. I accept that now. We meet, we fall in love, we live happily ever after, or, we separate. Whilst it takes two to Tango, the only "constant" in this equation is me. Coco! Like it or lump it, I have no choice but to accept that conundrum. The freedom to choose is wonderful;

we can choose the one we want from an incredibly colourful palette, from that Smorgasbord with its quirky personalities that online dating offers us, or find him offline, but ultimately, as wonderful as he may appear to be, in so many ways, None can meet the exacting standards that I set for myself. I am the only one responsible for my mirror image. My yardstick is for myself, not for others. When I finally accept myself as I am, then I am ready to accept Mr Right. Who may say for how long?

When I stop worrying about how others see me, and REALLY examine myself, I am at my most vulnerable, open and honest. I am really quite a contradiction in terms, invincible and vulnerable at the same time… And my Mr Right? Does he exist? I am convinced that he does, but, for me and no one else. He does not belong to a fairy tale world where Cinderella finds her Prince Charming. He is real because our hearts and souls will recognise each other and the more we discover about each other, the more we can accept that we are Right for each other. Our journey may take time, but this is a mere drop in the ocean of time.

Mr Right will not be perfect, and neither am I, but he will be right for me, simply because I am ready to accept him as he is, imperfections and all. He will be in my life at the right time and in the right place, for however long that may be. Love offers no guarantees for the future.

I have no control over anyone else, and it is Okay. I can face this now.

My voyage of self-discovery is a work in progress. It is dynamic, like my identity, and will be until my dying day.

Just when I thought that the "One" that got away was the only one…

Have I met the one?

One day, I received a call from my best male friend Luke. We had not caught up for a while; but sometimes we communicate telepathically. Same star sign! I jokingly feigned not to know him, "I do not have this number on my phone. Who is this?" Luke's laughter resounded in my ears as he responded joyfully, "You sound amazing. So happy. I bet there is a man in your life. Come on! I need to meet him. I have to approve first." Luke was very proud of my recovery and praised me for having transformed my life. He kept abreast of the developments of my online dating journey, counselling me when necessary. Both male and female perspectives have been crucial in this venture. My contentedness was apparently visible to everyone I knew, and this put a smile on my face every time.

Francis, the Captain

The irony of my meeting with Francis is sweet. After my internet dating journey, when my roller-coaster had come to a stop, I met him in my favourite trendy bar on the coast, where Katarina and I had met for a drink.

The 6'2 Gentle Giant from Brisbane cut an amazing figure as he walked into the crowded bar, his healthy head of salt and pepper hair, stylishly cut, giving him the allure of the distinguished Gentleman I had requested of the universe. His impeccable dress sense was unmistakably European, and I could not avert my gaze... even if I had been taught not to stare... Check, Check, Check... I had come to believe that I may have been too discerning in my quest to find the man of my dreams but this encounter proved contrary. There he was, right before my eyes.

Francis walked over to our table, and the most magical green eyes I had ever seen pierced through mine, sending shivers down my spine. This unpretentious, shy 56-year-old was hoping to borrow the spare chair, but Katarina was not letting him go. My *Wing-Lady*, confirmed adherent of the *Happy Divorcées' Club* is endowed with a wacky sense of humour and not interested in another relationship. Francis hesitated but an instant before accepting her invitation to join us. He was quickly smitten, as was I. He confessed in a text message that night, "I really enjoyed your company. I must admit you simply blew me out of the water when I initially laid eyes on you! I was just a little lost for words." Wow! I had to pinch myself. The thrill of the chase... not me chasing this time! Well, not really... Lady Luck by my side. This was real.

The chemistry and pheromones kicked in immediately and the intellectual sparring that evening was magical. We were on fire! My fairy tale ending was taking shape... I did not want to jinx this.

Francis is a man of integrity, smart, romantic, affectionate, patient, and empathetic, and I actually get his quirky sense of humour. He is not well-travelled, but he is ready for new adventures, keen to discover the world through my eyes. He is diametrically opposed to me in many ways. This is the second Beau who is not a Type A personality, so different in temperament and physique but there is no denying that opposites really do attract; but is this enough? I plan to leave this to the universe.

We share many things in common, clearly, but we also have a lot to learn from each other; Francis retired early and his laid-back lifestyle, personality and interests are almost the complete antithesis of mine, especially regarding my intercultural pursuits. I am gregarious and love to socialise with friends. He is not a recluse but prefers quiet little restaurants or entertaining his family and close friends at home. I enjoy travel, fine dining and the buzz of the entertainment world; the arts; music, theatre, ballet, dancing and intercultural travel.

I wondered if that could pose a problem because Francis has never indulged in these cultural pursuits. He has been outside of Australia only briefly, two weeks in an Asian country. He does not have the wanderlust gene, except the desire to be on the water with his beloved puppy.

Fast forward three days later...

The universe was clearly mocking me, intent on bringing me down a peg or two. A fish out of water on the Gold Coast, I had been adamant that I would not end up with a guy who embraced all things *Campin' Boatin' Fishin'* as these activities were polar opposites to my favourite pastimes - including equestrian events, polo, horse racing... Then, in walked the Captain from Brisbane and his gorgeous Labrador named Lucy, and both adored all manner of water sports and adventures, sailing, jet skiing, fishing. Okay, I could see myself casting a fishing line from his boat with a glass of Champagne in hand; but, hell would freeze over before I contemplated Glamping anywhere on this planet in other than Ireland or New Zealand, where snakes were not a feature of the landscape. Okay! Not in summer anyhow!

After the indecisions about long-distance relationships, here I was, faced with the perfect opportunity to compromise on my exacting search criteria in my quest for my Soulmate. I was not prepared to lose this man sent to me from the heavens. And he was a celestial match, our earth signs, Taurus and Virgo matching hand in glove. Francis was the first Taurean I had ever dated. But, was this enough? After the tumultuous journey, I had reached my destination. Was this the final one? Who could say? The universe had the habit of taking things out of my hands anyhow.

The forgetful Captain

Francis drove down to the coast to meet me at the designated Italian restaurant for our first dinner date ready to impress me; flowers finally wilting in the back of his sports car, "I am so sorry! I forgot your flowers on the back seat!" He never showed up empty handed from that first date, the fragrance of beautiful flowers providing a heady sensation in my home. An evening full of mirth and banter held much promise for consecutive dates. Distance was non-existent for Francis, a mere bagatelle. He made frequent trips down to the coast just to take Lucy for a run on the beach. So, now, he was intent on wooing his Lady. The Captain's forgetfulness made me laugh. On a visit to my home, Lucy had to make do with what I could find for her on one occasion because Francis had forgotten her dinner… His best friend never left his side. "Must love dogs!" and I did.

I revelled in the sincere efforts Francis made to win me over. His old-fashioned charm and impeccable manners serving as balm for my wounded soul after promising encounters had left me disconsolate. Francis was no sycophant. I found it refreshing when he complimented me, and it did not occur to me to doubt his integrity. I was pleasantly surprised when my charming Australian beau confirmed that my efforts to remodel my physiological identity had succeeded. I felt as though he had put me under a microscope. Had to admit, I was quite chuffed. I did not enjoy being placed on a pedestal though, my professional accolades and accomplishments prominent in his mind. He was genuine and went to great lengths to prove to me he was in for the long haul.

Francis has an unassuming character and is totally unaware of his boyish charm. He quit the rat race to indulge in his favourite pursuits, all manner of activities with his beloved dog, his best mates and his toys. He is fit and strong and quite competitive at sports. He beats me at my favourite sport, mocking me the more I react to his dominance in the game; he has not played for years but he continues to whip my butt! I am delighted to have found such a good player. Francis has earned his rewards and he encourages me to decompress and chill instead of pursuing life at my frantic pace; to spend more time with him on the water. He has just sold his yacht and is negotiating the purchase of his new cruiser. I am giving this due consideration, but it is a tough ask for a workaholic…

The second date was memorable. Lucy was adorable but none too pleased when Francis chose the sports car instead of her "second home." She knew the rules. Francis opened the door of the Ute and she knew she was coming. The sports car was out of bounds. I hoped she would not hate me... As Francis headed to my home for the first time, with Lucy in tow, I wondered if he was lost as Francis had just spoken to me. 10 minutes later, he drove in, embarrassed, telling me that he had just paid a visit to his "Mistress" but she was not home – the Lady down the road, one block away. Nosy neighbours peered over the balcony wondering what the Ute with a brown Labrador was doing in the Old Girl's drive way. She was in her eighties. Quite a bit of excitement for the quiet neighbourhood... He had set a few hearts aflutter.

Best friends go everywhere together, do they not? Francis let Lucy jump out and she flew past him to greet me politely for the first time at the door. Stopped in her tracks by Francis' stern warning that she was not allowed in the house, Lucy made an about-turn and raced to one corner of my garden and unceremoniously did her business to mark her territory. Shock and horror for Francis, the cheeky boyish look on his face a sight to behold. The hose came out and Francis cleaned up. Lucy rummaged around my garden, engrossed in her reconnaissance mission to make sure there were no interlopers and then she relaxed. She was in charge!

Welcome Lucy! She continuously sets the scene for the humour that defines our spirited discussions.

As if this were not enough for Miss Lucy, the next visit was almost a re-enactment of her first. Had she forgiven the Captain for leaving her behind for yet another date at a swish restaurant on the coast? On this occasion, the second time at my home, Lucy was delighted to see me. No sulking! This time, she raced past Francis and headed around the periphery of my fence and, yes, once more, made her mark on the outer boundaries of my property. Lucy was in her element! Or should I say, the Captain was, literally putting his foot into it! Francis took a while longer to clean up this time. Say no more...

Becoming acquainted with Lucy was a significant step of this new relationship. We headed down the coast with her for a walk and play on the beach and lunch at the surf club, laughing all the way. The outing was crowned by a beautiful sunset on the rocks as we watched the dolphins. On our way to the beach I had to walk barefoot over the twigs and stones on the track because I refuse to wear thong sandals. As I had emphatically turned down Francis' offer to purchase a pair for me, my "Oohs" and "Ouches" along the stony path met with little sympathy from my Prince Charming, "Harden up Princess!" I had it coming! I deserved that! As Francis leaned over to kiss me at the romantic spot on the rocks, the possessive Miss Lucy, on a short leash because Francis had forgotten the regular one, immediately stuck her head right between us, splitting us apart. She was having none of that. A little decorum please!

Francis set out to woo me fervently, in hot pursuit of this Damsel who was not exactly in distress. Okay! Gardening-challenged for sure, this chore anathema to me. I love my *Birds of Paradise* but they are a task to prune and maintain. Why fight it? Francis loves gardening; he had come from Brisbane one day shortly after we met, to tend to my garden whilst I was at work; Lucy at his side as he toiled in the hot sun whilst I worked in my air-conditioned office. Wow! Garden transformed! Some much-needed TLC at last! For me and my garden. Francis even sent me pictures of the progress reports, the weeds piling up; so much so, that most of the day's clippings headed up to Brisbane in the back with Lucy. My bins were full. Miss Lucy not impressed, once more. I was, however, forgiven as Lucy I got on very well.

The "One"

I believe I have found the "One." The prospect of spending quality time with Francis on board his new craft fills me with anticipation. My sea sickness tablets are already packed. What is a Lady to do when the Captain sends this text four weeks after meeting me, "Would you like to run away with me and live happily ever after Gorgeous?" My sassy quip, "Are we ready to sail away into the sunset, Captain?" was intended to slow the process down a tad, a gentle reminder to enjoy the journey...

And, the cosmic joke is we met OFFLINE! Things do not come easily for me; never have. He lives in Brisbane, which is why I hesitated, second guessed myself and then I realised that I would regret it if I did not give this relationship a go.

Real life fairy tales differ substantially from their original counterparts. "Steady on Prince Charming, hold your steed and put away your mighty sword!"

On the other hand, Sophie's love story demonstrates they do exist... So, maybe I will have mine after all...

I had gone on and on, ad nauseam about distance, and I was clearly holding out hope for an online connection; I needed to see the fruits of my labour - and then the universe sent me the man who checked many of my boxes. Yet, the challenges are real, the least of which that Francis is not a local, despite his protests. There are times when we need to just chill, canoodling and holding hands, debriefing on the days' activities, as we watch a movie. Cannot replace the texts that the Captain sends daily, "Missing you..."

Still, the distance seemed a bridge too far...

We decided to put all our energies into making this relationship work, in spite of the distance and the glaring differences in our life styles and personalities. Francis is a gorgeous man, inside and out, one of the kindest, most respectful and romantic men I have met.

Well, at least we live in the same State. The paradox is that the transitional process of establishing a new relationship is working well, precisely because of the distance. We each have our well-established routines, but focus on ways to spend time together; and hopefully little by little the twain will meet... Who could ask for more? I am trying hard not to overthink the issue...

The respect Francis shows me is second to none; he fully appreciates the exigent schedules imposed by my career but also the efforts I make to organise quality time for us to spend together as we try to build a relationship.

This is the stuff true love is made of, not because it is perfect, far from it, but because it has the potential to survive all the challenges. Neither of us is perfect but we are on the same page. There are however, no guarantees.

The "One." Elusive? Illusive? Have I found him?

My fairy tale romance is a work in progress. Perhaps Francis is Mr. Right... but maybe he is the one who will lead me to the "One." Who knows? The most important lesson I have learned is that there is no "Forever." I accept with open arms the man who has come into my life and hope the relationship will last the distance. For how long? Who knows? That is not important. For now, I have found what I have been yearning for...

And the chimera continues...

Debriefing The *Happy Divorcées' Club*

What a journey! Time to debrief the members of the *Happy Divorcées' Club*.

"Ready or not, Ladies, please listen!"

You suggested to me recently that the reason I was suffering from physical and mental fatigue was my complete obsession with online dating and telling my story.

Oh dear! That sounds about right.

You warned me that the persistent and intense delving into the workings of my psyche could be dangerous, that apparently, I could end up ill. Well, I listened.

I could not continue to put my mind through such philosophical and psychological meanderings, intense mental gymnastics, without it threatening my health. I heeded this advice and tried to create more balance in my life and work, even if there was always another project on the drawing board. I had to force myself to avert my gaze from the computer screens that were damaging my eyesight.

Well, the good news is, I made it!

The way forward

It is time for a final assessment of the impact that my online encounters have had on my identity following the arduous yet exhilarating roller-coaster ride of internet dating. I have employed useful strategies along the way to make sure I learned from my mistakes. The finer points of my physiological make-over – my transformation in subtle ways that have created a more acceptable image of who I am, at least from my perception, are not visible to everyone. I am self-assured, enjoying the confidence I feel as I step out of my shell, for once accepting that others are not looking at me to judge me. I have learned to construe positive images from all encounters, taking them at face value, unless blatantly obvious that the intent is malicious.

The image reflected from my mirror corresponds, for the first time in my life, more closely with the image that is projected from the eyes of those I meet, especially the great guys on this internet dating journey. These images are consistent but by no means static. I owe it to them for their contribution in the remodelling of my identity, the new liberated me! I am finally comfortable in my skin; I feel good and I am enjoying life. It is a heady sensation to finally let go of the self-consciousness that has defined my entire existence. My self-compassion and self-acceptance are key to this new vision of me.

From a Virgo's perspective, acknowledging that no one is perfect and particularly accepting the fact that we are all ageing, continues to be challenging, however. I am not yet ready to surrender to the ageing hormones, but I am paying more attention to my body, being gentler on myself, even if I do push myself to my limits in my sporting activities, particularly as I play sport with males. It is all about balance.

The internet dating venture I began a few months ago seems distant now. I stopped checking messages long ago. The thrill I experienced when messages were delivered to my mailbox was real and invigorating but now the journey is over. I was not in this for the long-haul, and I accepted the fact that it would take time. I had a few false alarms. If I find myself one day back on this road, I am confident that the ride will no longer be vertiginous. I have learned to navigate the tracks now. I can hop on and off as I please and enjoy the journey. The beauty of it is, I believe I will not need to...

It will also take time to heal the hurt I have felt at the hands of the trolls and other monsters. But I am getting there, I like to think – even realising that trolls and monsters are humans. There are more important things in life to worry about and the power of perspective has proved to be an amazing adjunct in the dynamic process of integrating changes to my identity. I only need to compare my trials and tribulations with the plight of the Refugees to snap out of it. I have become more self-aware, less dependent on the opinions of "others" where intrinsic features of my personality and emotional wellbeing are concerned. That is a definite plus.

My self-esteem has been reinstated. In future, I refuse to empower anyone to decimate my self-worth. But, I am cognizant of my role in having triggered this behaviour in past relationships. I do not intend to facilitate a power play with a male who takes merciless pleasure in pressing my buttons for his sheer amusement. I respect myself. I still show myself as a super-confident woman, but I am aware that is something of a façade. It can be scratched, but under the patina, there is a super-confident woman. I vow not to be laid low again. I daresay I will be challenged, but I feel encouraged because I have been through hill and dale, I know I can get here again.

I have recovered the gregarious, cheeky nature of the little child I was when I arrived in Australia. I had lost my way through extenuating circumstances that were outside of my control. I am now home. I know what I want in my life. I had found it easier to define what I did not want, but now the qualities I seek in a partner are clearly imprinted in my mind.

I have learned about compromise; about the effects I have on guys when I act like a Princess: my penchant for the good life, the brand names, the makeup, the perfumes, the fashion I enjoy; the exciting venues I like to frequent.

I find it curious that after consulting my *Mirror, Mirror on the Wall...* with meticulous regularity, it occurs to me that there is really no looking glass that tells us the future. The clairvoyants often get it wrong too... I have realised that reflections are in the now. I have a hard time accepting the present, that is a fact (the creeping age lines, the propensity to put on weight and the determination to win that battle; the daily challenges that individuals who are set in their ways must face...), let alone the future that promises more of the same!

I am still the eternal optimist. My glass is always half-full. But will it evaporate away? Or perhaps rain will fill the glass? And more importantly, is the water fresh or stale? Only the tasting will tell us. I must have agency to learn. Inaction teaches me nothing. Life lessons were not meant to be a breeze and the teacher is a tough master. I stumble and I fall, and I pick myself up again. *C'est la vie!* Forever learning!

Ultimately, for the future, there is only hope. I will not allow despondency to envelop me. And hope, or optimism, is probably even more important than love. Francis and I represent two people who share a hope for a happy future; we are probably destined to greater success than two people who love one another madly, truly in this moment. Life is so transient and in this world of instantaneous connections, fuelled by social media, at least in the 50+ age groups, as we face our mortality, we are learning to live for today instead of living in the past or making long term plans. Yet there must be hope in my life…

My online journey was somewhat fraught with danger and hopelessness; but I became aware of the pitfalls of internet dating, and I learned to negotiate the road less travelled.

I needed to snap out of my fantasies and concentrate on the 'now'.

A long-lasting relationship for Francis and me will be based on past lessons and experiences and the dynamics of our independence will be negotiated bit by bit.

Mindfulness is critical. At this moment in time, I am happy, I am content, and this Princess has a good chance of living happily ever after… At least, that is the plan… Destiny has a way of surprising us, mere mortals.

The empowering anthem designed for one of my favourite perfumes, *"Sì"*, by *Giorgio Armani* [35] eloquently sums up my journey. This is just a snippet. I said,

"Sì ai sogni. Sì alla seduzione. Sì alle emozioni. Sì all'amore. Sì a un nuovo inizio. Sì a noi due. SI A ME STESSA! Yes to dreams. Yes to seduction. Yes to emotions. Yes to love. Yes to a new beginning. Yes to the two of us. YES, TO MYSELF!

I certainly owe it to myself to be true to myself, to say, *Sì* **(Yes).** These profound sentiments, uttered in their entirety, are more beautiful and evocative in Italian. I often reflect on the words conjured in this commercial. Clever *Georgio Armani!*

"Well done, you!" comes the chorus of approval from my BFFs. "At long last!"

I am proud that I have had the courage to throw myself wholeheartedly into internet dating to find love. I have achieved my objectives as the journey has proved therapeutic and cathartic. This adventure has effectively been a panacea to my loneliness. Francis, and my amazing new friends are testament to this. I am satisfied that I have remained discerning. I am not high maintenance; I simply know what I want, and I am respected for my strength and determination.

My self-confidence and inner light are now shining like a beacon.

THE END (For now…)

---

[35] *Sì* by Giorgio Armani. The BHD Tv. 2013. https://www.youtube.com/watch?v=dY1oYzWmpFo

ABOUT THE AUTHOR

Dr Marie-Claire Patron has been at Bond University, Australia for 27 years. She is Assistant Professor in Intercultural Communication and Head of French and Spanish Language. She has taught, interpreted and translated in Australia and Europe, including eight years in Spain for business, law, banking and the building industry. Her current research areas are (auto) ethnography, narrative and the internationalisation of students. She holds qualifications in Languages and Linguistics (BA, Monash University, Victoria; Graduate Dip Ed, Rusden, Victoria; MA (LOTE), Bond University, Queensland; PhD in International Studies, University of South Australia). Coco through the looking glass is Marie-Claire's sixth book.

Printed in the United States
By Bookmasters